MW00463367

Mediterranean Israeli Music

Amy Horowitz

Mediterranean Israeli Music

and the Politics of the Aesthetic

WAYNE STATE UNIVERSITY PRESS DETROIT

14 13 12 11 10 5 4 3 2 1

Library of Congress Cataloging-in-Publication Data

Horowitz, Amy.
Mediterranean Israeli music and the politics of the aesthetic / Amy Horowitz.
p. cm. — (Raphael Patai series in Jewish folklore and anthropology)
Includes bibliographical references and index.
ISBN 978-0-8143-3465-2 (pbk. : alk. paper)
1. Music—Israel—History and criticism. 2. Music—Mediterranean Region—History and criticism. 3. Music—Political aspects--Israel. 4. Music—Political aspects—Mediterranean Region. 5. Music—Religious aspects—Judaism. 6. Music—Religious aspects—Islam. I. Title.
ML345.I8H67 2010
780.95694'09047—dc22

2009037071

Publication of this book was made possible through the generosity of the Bertha M. and Hyman Herman Endowed Memorial Fund.

Designed by Maya Rhodes
Typeset by Alpha Design & Composition
Composed in Adobe Garamond Pro and Middleton

Contents

List of Illustrations *vii*
Preface *ix*
Style Note *xvii*

1. Cultural Boundaries and Disputed Territories 1
2. Relocation and the Emergence of Ethnicities 33
3. The Mediterranean Israeli Music Phenomenon 59
4. Sounding Right: Zohar Argov 85
5. The Posthumous Consecration of Zohar Argov 105
6. Transgressing Boundaries: Zehava Ben 129
7. Disputing Territories 155

Notes *177*
Song Lyrics *197*
Works Cited *221*
Select Discography *231*
Videography *233*
Index *235*
CD Liner Notes *243*

List of Illustrations

Posters in marketplace booth, Tel Aviv Central Bus Station, 1991 *13*

Newspaper headline countering derogatory labels, *Yedi'ot America*, 1990 *16*

Cassette booth in the Ramle marketplace, 1993 *19*

Cassette cover, Avner Gadassi, *Menagen ṿe-Shar,* 1978 *21*

CD cover of Egyptian cassette booth, 1990 *24*

Girls with Boom box, at *Mimouna* in Jerusalem, 1993 *24*

Mizraḥi singer with gold cassette necklace, *Mediterranean Song* songbook cover, 1987 *26*

Immigration to Israel 1948–99, Israel Ministry of Foreign Affairs, 2002 *37*

Kurdish ensemble Sheva Aḥayot, 1993 *39*

LP cover, *ha-Shir ha-Erets Yisre'eli* (Song of the Land of Israel), 1958 *43*

Kurdish zorna player at Jerusalem *Mimouna* festival, 1993 *48*

Cassette cover featuring song lyrics by Natan Alterman and Avihu Medina, 1983 *51*

CD cover, Nissim Saroussi, Jerusalem, 1979 *52*

Two *asli* cassette covers, Zion Golan and Moshe Gi'at, 1982, *64*

Cassette cover, Daḳlon, *Ḳol ḳore li ba-midbar,* 1990 *68*

Cassette cover, Haim Moshe, *Ahavat Ḥayai*, 1982 *70*

Haim Moshe, "Not Ashkenazifying," *Yedi'ot Aḥaronot,* 1986 *71*

Margalit Tsan'ani performs at a wedding, Tel Aviv, 1992 *73*

Cassette cover, Margalit Tsan'ani, *Menta*, 1988 *74*

Avihu Medina, "There is No Such Thing as *Mizraḥi* Music," *Ma'ariv*, 1990 *80*

Cassette cover, Zohar Argov, *Elinor*, 1980 *91*

Cassette cover, Zohar Argov, *Hayu zemanim,* 1982 *93*

Cassette cover, Zohar Argov, *Nakhon le-hayom*, 1982 *95*

Mural depicting Yemenite *aliyah*, Kerem ha-Temanim, Tel Aviv, 1993 *102*

Zohar Argov and Avihu Medina, 1986 *103*
CD cover, Adam Ray, 1994 *107*
Playwright Shemuel Hasfari, Beit Lessin Theatre, 1992 *112*
Mizraḥi musicians, Tsefat, 1992 *133*
Zohar Argov's mother and sister, Zehava Ben concert, Jerusalem, 1993 *136*
Zehava Ben performs at anti-drug concert, 1993 *137*
Audience with Hebrew and Arabic anti-drug posters at concert, Jerusalem, 1993 *138*
Cassette cover, Zehava Ben and Zeev Revach, *Ṭipat mazal* sound track, 1992 *141*
Amal Markus performs at "Women Go for Peace" conference, Jerusalem, 1990 *145*
Women in Black vigil, Jerusalem, 1990 *146*
Cassette Cover, CD graphic portraying Zehava Ben in Egypt, 1995 *148*
Zehava Ben and Muslim recitation cassettes displayed together in East Jerusalem, 1993 *149*
Israeli soldier wearing Moroccan fez, 1993 *151*
Avihu Medina, "the ghetto is not dead," *Yedi'ot Aḥaronot*, 1986 *158*
Yitzhak Mordekhai and Itzik Kala at *Saharana*, Ashkelon, 1992 *168*
Cassette cover, Samir Shukry, *Rona Shely* *170*
Israeli soldier with Zehava Ben's *Ṭipat Mazal* cover affixed to weapon, Jerusalem, 1993 *174*

Preface

Mediterranean Israeli Music and the Politics of the Aesthetic is an ethnographic study of the emergence of a pan-ethnic style of music in Israel between the mid-1970s and mid-1990s. This two-decade period encompasses the coming of age of the Middle Eastern and North African creators of the grassroots music network in the 1970s and the sea change in the music's reception by mainstream Israeli society in the 1990s. The book interfolds three organizational structures. One, it shifts from one voice to multiple voices, fanning out from the ethnographer's univocal account of her immersion in the Mizraḥi community to the multivocality of the community members, their music, and the musicians who play it, focusing on three preeminent musicians. Two, the book positions the ethnographic present of the text with respect to three pasts: the mass migration of Jews from North Africa and the Middle East to Israel in the 1940s and 1950s, the experience of these immigrants as an emerging pan-ethnic community in Israel in the 1970s, and the effect of new recording technologies on opening markets for disenfranchised music makers. Three, the book sets folklore within the frameworks of nationalism, ethnicity, ethnomusicology, Jewish studies, Israel studies, Middle Eastern studies, and politics, contributing to a larger conversation about appropriation, inheritance, and the politics of the aesthetic.

My challenge was to provide a deep account of the historical background and political context of the story without eclipsing the music and music makers who are at its center. I focus on three of the most significant of these, Avihu Medina, Zohar Argov, and Zehava Ben, who are among those responsible for amalgamating, reimagining, and interrelating multiple musical traditions into the new sound that coalesced into a recognizable Mizraḥi style and moved this new musical formation from the Mizraḥi neighborhoods to the national arena. The new musical form resisted and empowered new ethnic and identity formations in the contested cultural spaces and traditions of late-twentieth-century Israel.

I begin the book with my first accidental encounter with the music in the mid-1980s. In chapter 1, I introduce my methods and perspectives as well as the fundamental concept of Mizraḥi-ness as contested and relational. Mediterranean Israeli music's emergence and growth during the 1970s was, in part, due to the invention of the cassette recorder and four-way cassette duplicating machine. This local cassette network was part of a larger global phenomenon in which disenfranchised ethnic groups claimed their voices despite rejection by mainstream institutions. I conclude the chapter by proposing the concept of dueling nativities and appropriate appropriations as a way to trouble the prevailing concepts of indigeneity, appropriation, and inheritance.

In contrast to the personal lens that introduces chapter 1, chapter 2 opens from the perspective of an Iraqi Kurdish family in Jerusalem, including their complex and ongoing relationships with their Kurdish and Israeli homelands. This chapter outlines the conditions that contributed to a pan-ethnic Mizraḥi community of communities in Israel. Drawing on the many excellent histories of Israeli ethnicity, I provide the necessary (brief) background to understand the mutual relations of music and ethnicity in the emergence of Mediterranean Israeli music in the 1970s through the 1990s.

Chapter 3 gives voice to Avihu Medina, a significant architect and performer of the genre. Mediterranean Israeli music is a contested and relational genre. Drawing on Medina's understanding of the complexity of the music at a moment when it cohered as a pan-ethnic genre, this chapter observes some of the performers throughout the 1970s, 1980s, and 1990s to demonstrate the impossibility of pinning down a constantly emergent style that nonetheless became recognizable. This chapter explores the significant role that Medina played and continues to play as a performer, composer, and organizer whose thoughtful self-reflections have become part of the history of the genre.

Chapter 4 turns to the performance of Zohar Argov, the Yemenite singer who caught the attention of a national audience. Argov's compelling voice was instrumental in resituating Mediterranean Israeli music from restricted play in Mizraḥi neighborhoods to increased air time and national attention in the 1980s. This exploration of Argov's musical style and repertoire considers how this particular singer at this particular time catalyzed a breakthrough that only came to fruition after his death.

Chapter 5 presents a convergence of Mizraḥi neighborhood memories of Argov with new discoveries of him by mainstream European Israelis. These groups of audiences and critics posthumously transformed Argov from neighborhood singer to national legend. Through a close reading of an avant-garde play about Argov and analysis of interviews with family and friends that formed the basis for it, this chapter charts the emergence of Argov as a tragic hero.

Chapter 6 highlights Zehava Ben, a singer who achieved notoriety in the 1990s and who successfully appropriated a variety of sounds, including the renowned Egyptian Muslim singer Um Kulthum. Ben is a Moroccan Israeli Jewish woman who refused to subsume any of these multiple identities. She was a symbol of border crossings in the context of the fragile peace process emerging in the early 1990s. This chapter further develops my argument about the complex relationship between inheritance and appropriation.

In the final chapter, I bring into focus the intersections, overlaps, and divergences between the story of Mediterranean Israeli music and the story of Israeli social struggles. My book ends in the mid-1990s at a point of political and musical transformation. Today when Mediterranean Israeli music is heard everyday on the radio, it is important to reflect on this history and also to understand that increased radio play has not solved the ethnic struggle.

This project has been a work in progress for more than twenty-five years. As with any long-term relationship, it is difficult to separate out my singular insights from the creative marks left by other contributors to the work. My debts of acknowledgment, like the contours of the music genre that fill the pages of this book, are a web of interconnected, overlapping, often multiply situated people whose collective influences cannot easily be categorized, temporalized, or quantified. In fact, like the coproduction of music itself, I see the composition of this book as an orchestration of multiple influences, motives, and voices, for which I have endeavored to write the score. What follows is a joyous charting of many connections that sustained and informed my understanding of this study from its inception as a doctoral dissertation completed in 1994 to its reconfiguration in the form of lectures, book chapters, journal articles, and presentations from 2000 to 2005, and finally to its current book form. To those who have died before the book was completed, I offer libation: Uzi Ḥiṭman, Ornan Yekutieli, Al Friedman, June Jordan, Herschel Bernardi, Ralph Rinzler, Gershon Shaked, Saleh Houja, Zalie Miller, Galit Sa'adya Ofir, Shafik Salmon, and Jo Amar of blessed memory.

My deepest gratitude goes to the musicians, composers, and organizers in the Mediterranean Israeli music network. Their openness to sharing their knowledge made this book possible. Haim Moshe's comments about Michael Jackson and Stevie Wonder's "Yemenite" vocal style triggered my curiosity about Mizraḥi music. Avihu Medina served as my main teacher, constantly challenging me to look beneath the surfaces. Margalit Tsan'ani, Itzik Kala, and Zehava Ben invited me along on various performance occasions, and Meir and Asher Reuveni, Avigdor Ben-Mosh, David Azoulay,

Yehuda Kessar, Yehuda Cohen, Shafik Salmon, and Yosef Ben Yisrael helped me comprehend the work behind the scenes to build the music network.

I thank my doctoral committee at the University of Pennsylvania's Department of Folklore and Folklife: Dan Ben-Amos served as mentor and advisor. Bernice Johnson Reagon's early reading of each chapter provided critical feedback from a scholar who is also a protest singer. Yael Zerubavel inspired a deeper wrestling with the complexities of Israeli society. Roger Abrahams raised the issue of the marketplace, which is at the heart of this project. During my master's degree studies at New York University, Kay Shelemay invited me to participate in a project on Syrian Jewish music in Brooklyn. My fieldwork for that project raised questions that would become central to this book.

Richard Allen, Brian Spooner, and Mary Martin at Penn's Middle East Studies Center supported my study of Hebrew through a Foreign Language Area Studies Grant. The Graduate School of Arts and Sciences provided me a Melton Fellowship. The Lady David Foundation provided me a grant to spend a year in Israel in 1993.

During my fieldwork, I benefited from the support of Israeli colleagues and friends Tamar Katriel, Edwin Seroussi, Pamela Kidron, Jeff Halper, Freddie Rokem, Ruth Freed, Dalia Houja, Steve Kaplan, Irit Guggenheim, Ziv Yonaton, and Motti Regev. Galit Hasan-Rokem and Amnon Shiloah read and commented on several chapters of my dissertation.

Israeli artists, community leaders, cultural workers, and music industry friends Shelly Elkayam, Shlomo Bar, Meir Paz, Shimon Parnas, Yoel Rekem, Ranan Dinur, Tayseer Elias, Dani Yadin, Dalia Lutwak, Dovis Miller, Esty and Shlomi Namdar, and Anat Stern provided support at early stages of my research. Jeff Yas, Etai Rosenbluth, Yifat Susskind, Shira Katz, Daniel Wool, Daniel Kramer, Jessie Bonn, Gil Freund, Karen Azoulay, and Carol Ann Bernheim assisted me during the dissertation preparation phase.

In Jerusalem, Freddie and Galit Hasan-Rokem, Tsion and Leah Namdar, David and Irit Guggenheim, and Esther Veedel opened their homes to me. I am grateful to the families of Saleh and Majda Houja and Arline and Zalie Miller with whom I stayed for extended periods of time.

I appreciate the generous support and insight of my Palestinian friends and colleagues. The inter-Jewish Israeli issues at the heart of this book unfold within the context of the Palestinian-Israeli conflict, and I wish to thank Kamiliya Jubran (my *'ūd* teacher), Said Murad, Jack Persekian, Francois Abu Salem, Vera Tamari, Iman Oun, Suad Amiry, Salim Tamari, Randa Sha'ath, Nahida Dejani, Albert and Madeleine Aghzarian, and Nazmi el Jube.

Friends from my youth who introduced me to the complexities of Israeli culture, Vera Yanovtschinsky, Gideon Levy, and Yaron Elhanani, continued to inform my thinking throughout the decades I worked on this project.

Ysaye Barnwell, Toshi Reagon, Ginny Berson, Virginia Giordano, Kathy Glimn, Sharon Farmer, Michelle Lanchester, Urvashi Vaid, Pete and Toshi Seeger, Susan Allee, Penny Rosenwasser, Steve Rathe, Alice Walker, and most especially Holly Near, Madeleine Remez, and Bernice Johnson Reagon, artists and activist organizers in the people's and women's progressive cultural arts movements, reached out to me as I straddled academia and grassroots community activism in the early period of this research.

While I was doing fieldwork for my dissertation in Israel, I was offered two irresistible challenges that occupied the next six years of my intellectual life. One was to head a research project on the Israeli and Palestinian cultural traditions of contemporary Jerusalem; the other was to serve as assistant and acting director of Smithsonian Folkways Recordings. These intense engagements took me away from the Mediterranean Israeli music project for the next years. My work with the many courageous researchers, community leaders, and artists on the Jerusalem Project deepened my understanding of the complexities of this study and my tenure at Smithsonian Folkways Recordings provided a practical understanding of the recording industry. Thanks to James Early, Peter Seitel, Galit Hasan-Rokem, Suad Amiry, Tamar Alexander, David Shoenbach, Vera Tamari, and Salim Tamari of the Jerusalem Project.

The Herbert D. Katz Center for Advanced Judaic Studies at the University of Pennsylvania gave me the Maurice Amado Foundation Fellowship that permitted me to return my attention to this project in 2000. Discussions with Carol Zemel, Mark Kligman, Gideon Efrat, Gershon Shaked, David Ruderman, and Ety Lassman helped me expand my initial project. I am especially grateful to Barbara Kirshenblatt-Gimblett and Jonathan Karp for creating *The Art of Being Jewish in Modern Times* that so beautifully reflects the power of the year we spent together. Ted Swedenburg and Rebecca Stein invited me to participate in a conference panel and edited volume, *Palestine, Israel, and the Politics of Popular Culture*.

In 2001 Amy Shuman asked me to participate in a symposium at the Ohio State University. Richard Ned Lebow, then director of the Mershon Center for International Security Studies, offered me a visiting fellowship, and the next director, Richard Herrmann, offered me an ongoing position as research associate. I found an engaged intellectual home at Mershon, the Center for Folklore Studies, the Middle East Studies Center, the Melton Center for Jewish Studies, the Institute for Collaborative Research and Public Humanities, and the Departments of International Studies, Comparative Studies, and English, where I have enjoyed working with Alam Payind, Tamar Rudavsky, Dorry Noyes, Matt Goldish, Tony Mughan, David Horn, Valerie Lee, Jackie Royster, John Mueller, Steve Cecchetti, Margaret Mills, Sabra Webber, Adena Tanenbaum, Nina Berman, Michael Swartz, Jan Radzynski, Daniel Frank, David Stein, John Roberts, Pat Mullen, Joseph Zeidan, Chris Zacher, Rick Livingston, and Ed Adelson.

My ongoing dialogue across disciplines with political science friends Don Sylvan and Amanda Metskas resulted in several presentations at the International Society of Political Psychology meetings and a related project exploring the relationship between Israeli music listening patterns and political affiliations. Scott Sprague and Paul Kotheimer of Humanities Information Systems offered ongoing technical assistance. Ali Bakr Hassan, Arabic and Islamic studies librarian at Ohio State, generously provided assistance with Arabic translation. Yossi Galron Goldschlager, Judaic studies librarian at Ohio State, offered crucial assistance in intensive transliteration work, and in the course of this work I also benefited from his memories of his youth in Ramle.

Eric Schramm, Maya Rhodes, Carrie Downes Teefey, and especially Dan Ben-Amos and Kathryn Wildfong from Wayne State University Press saw this book through publication.

This book has been enriched by conversations about Mizraḥi culture, politics, and music with Galit Dardashti, Ella Shohat, Ruth Tsoffar, Ammiel Alcalay, Oren Yiftachel, and Uri Ram. Eva Broman shared her copious knowledge and passion for Mizraḥi renditions of Greek and Turkish repertoire. Peter Seitel generously read every word of this book. Amanda Metskas provided invaluable editorial assistance and Katharine Young served as editor and engaged intellectual co-conspirator. Barbara Kirshenblatt-Gimblett and Edwin Seroussi's ongoing support and crucial ideas enriched and challenged my thinking over the years.

While I was doing fieldwork for my dissertation in Israel in the 1990s, Reuven Namdar served not only as my research assistant but also as an emotional and intellectual lifeline. His support has continued throughout the long haul.

I am blessed with family and friends Arnie Polinger, David and Devorah Zaslow, Suzanna Walters, Deborah Kapchan, Jean Diamond, Steve Shirrell, Alyson Meyers, Holly Near, Bernice Johnson Reagon, Adisa Douglas, Toshi Reagon, Andy, Al, Pam, and Sandy Horowitz, Alice Carron, Mauricio and Violaine Fuks, Rosie Krakovitz, Kate Kelliher, Susan and William Walsh, Beth Ellingwood, Julie Saar, Michael Swartz, Suzanne Silver, Susan Couden,

Leslie Yenkin, Jonathan Petuchowski, Eugenia Erlij, and Drew Brody, who created a web of support.

I thank Lino and Evan for their ongoing inspiration and I thank Amy S., who walked every step of the last years of this journey with me and was endlessly engaged with its intellectual underpinnings.

I am grateful to my daughter, Ariel, for sharing her childhood with this work in progress, for being my guru of compassion and creativity, and for the new understandings I have gained about the inner world of young musicians.

I lovingly dedicate this book to my parents, Emanuel and Diane Horowitz.

Style Note

Transliteration

The Library of Congress Romanization rules guide the transliteration throughout the book except in instances where words have entered the English vernacular. The spellings of names that have gained currency in English books, or that have become familiar to English readers, are generally retained. In cases where individuals offer their own English spellings for their names, songs, or other creative products, their transliteration preferences are employed. For example, in the case of singer/songwriter Avihu Medina, Medina rather than Medinah is used. In some cases where foreign language terms have gained currency in vernacular Hebrew, the Hebrew transliteration is used. In all cases, the goal has been to offer maximum readability and consistency.

Identity Markers

Throughout the text, I have specified the ethnic identities of singers, songwriters, journalists, music industry officials, and other significant characters. While at times this practice may appear cumbersome and prejudicial, I believe that a book focused on the asymmetrical conditions of Jewish Israeli ethnic groups necessitates such explicit ascription. Marking ethnicity assists readers who are unfamiliar with the cast of characters discussed in the book.

Cultural Boundaries and Disputed Territories

> The final paradox of the search for purity is that it is an attempt to force experience into logical categories of non-contradiction. Those who make the attempt find themselves led into contradiction. Hypocrisy is the new contradiction that arises out of the "act of purification itself."
>
> —Mary Douglas, *Purity and Danger*

Embarkation: Accidental Research in the Central Bus Station

It is August of 1984, and I am searching for the Bar Ilan bus. Equipped with Sony audiotapes and Canon lenses, I have been conducting interviews in various cities with practitioners of alternative Israeli and Palestinian performance traditions.[1] In the course of this project, I have passed through the Tel Aviv Central Bus Station several times, but it is only on this occasion that I become an accidental ethnographer and the station something other than a transit point between interviews. On this day, I am drawn to one of the cassette stalls pumping out a pulsating Mediterranean beat.

At the entrance to the stall, a young Georgian merchant shouts out a sales pitch through a microphone above the distorted treble tones of an amplified cassette. It is difficult to distinguish his voice, advertising one free leather belt for each purchase of three cassettes, from the low-end feedback of the cassette itself. Transfixed, I watch him conduct his transactions. No matter what else they buy, his customers consistently select one particular cassette. From its pale yellow cover, a lean man stares out at me with hungry eyes. When the young merchant notices my interest, he points to the overhead speaker and tries to shout above the cassette's Yemenite vocal melisma[2] surrounded by Greek bazouki, flamenco horns, and Western beats.

I go in and purchase the tape and only then remember to ask for directions to the Bar Ilan bus. Coming out of the booth with me, the man points ahead. "There, you see that big red building over there—the one under construction? Head that way and take your second right."

As I turn to go I ask him, "What is that big red building?"

"Oh that!" he laughs. "That's the 'new' central bus station! It's been under construction for forty years."

Heading toward the building, I shout back over my shoulder, "Excuse me! And who's this singer?"

"Zohar Argov," he shouts back.

Later that evening I puzzle over why, in all my discussions about alternative Israeli music, no one has mentioned Zohar Argov. When I share the story of my cassette purchase with friends in North Tel Aviv, their reactions take the form of a stream of unexpected ethnic slurs like *Musiḳat ha-taḥanah ha-merkazit* (Central Bus Station music), *Musiḳah shel tshaḥtshaḥim* (cheap music),[3] *Musiḳah sheḥorah* (Black music).[4] Such designations, uttered in disdainful tones conversationally and, as I later learned, in newspaper articles by European Israeli detractors, and not used by the performers or producers themselves, place this hybrid music firmly outside mainstream cultural markets.

I have accidentally located a deep cultural nerve. The nerve center seems to be the Central Bus Station. The next morning I return, not to a transit point between interviews in different cities but to the focal point of a new research project: an emergent homegrown musical hybrid that attracts high pitched enthusiasm and revulsion along the fault lines of Israel's ethnic divide.

Musical Routes

The cassette booths in the Central Bus Station were part of a vital underground music distribution network created by the children of North African and Middle Eastern immigrants to Israel. They composed these songs out of the disparate musical elements that coexisted, collided, and at times contended for authority in transit camps, development towns, and poor neighborhoods beginning in the 1950s and 1960s. In these unstable, mutating, improvisatory spaces, previously distant and distinct styles of Moroccan, Egyptian, Iraqi, Kurdish, Yemenite, and other North African and Middle Eastern music styles mingled in unexpected but not uneasy proximity.

The musics emerging out of the dislocation and relocation of North African and Middle Eastern Jewish communities were not simply products of disorientation; they were themselves disorienting. These musics crashed into each other, creating relentless waves of accidental, incidental, and intentional sonic proliferations. Liturgical music smashed into popular forms, becoming tarnished and gathering vitality. Popular musics from Baghdad, Beirut, Aleppo, San'a', and Tehran jostled each other, making themselves louder, overwhelming competitors. Traditional musics, amped up, careened through the carnival of sounds and fused with liturgical forms, producing echoes, emotions, travesties.

The new immigrants and their children eagerly created a dialogue between their Middle Eastern and North African musical forms and the already established popular songs of Israel. The latter canon, which emerged first in the 1880s in the diaspora and then developed further in Palestine, was a composite of Eastern European folk music, mainly non-Jewish, reupholstered with new romantic nationalistic Hebrew lyrics. Its minor scales were not entirely remote from North African and Middle Eastern modal music.

As Middle Eastern and North African immigrant musicians made music out of their encounter, they began to forge a counter sound track to the established repertoire, whose European Israeli creators in turn appropriated select elements of the new hybrid music while roundly rejecting the musical form itself. But the historical moment was irreversible. The music and its makers were caught in a maelstrom whipped up by the fierceness and vitality of the surprising Middle Eastern/North African Israeli sound track at its center. Throughout this book, I use the term *sound track* instead of *canon* to refer to this new musical formation to emphasize both its auditory rather than classificatory status and its mutability as it moves through space and time.

In the cramped quarters of the new Israeli nation, dozens of local musics were freed from their former communal contexts and set loose in one of the most surprising sonic laboratories of the twentieth century. This convergence of over eighty musical genres and styles in a relatively short time offered itself as the space in which the first generation of native Israelis could locate themselves, influence emerging cultural formations, and insist on the vitality that nourished them. It was the vitality created by unexpected sonic proximities that ultimately defeated efforts to dismiss the new songs as foreign incursions. This rough-edged musical corpus was an act of defiance against exclusion, and an act of hope in the face of rejection.

The new popular style created by Middle Eastern and North African musicians rearranged musical forces. They joined Mediterranean, Arabic, Slavic, and even Indian tunes with Western rock beats, Greek bazouka harmonies, and melismatic Yemenite vocalizations. The musical styles, instruments, and rhythms that these rearrangements comprised showed evidence of both generic patterns and idiosyncratic contours. The formal center of the sound weave was most often the voice, which carried the traditional melisma, as well as the regional color and timbre of the particular singer. Around the centrality of the vocal line, the composer freely spun the synthesized sounds that emulated *'ūd*, *qānūn*, and *darabukka*,[5] as well as violin, electric guitar, piano, and even rock 'n' roll trap sets.

The architects of the modern Jewish national homeland strove for coherent artistic categories in the interest of unifying a protean mass of human beings under the aegis of a romanticized nationalist ideology. The ideal was to combine ingathered diasporic Jewish communities into a homogenous whole. But by the 1970s the subaltern voices from North Africa and the Middle East created a crazy quilt of juxtaposed and contradictory ethnic borderlands. Radio editors and programmers, record company executives, and official promoters rejected their subversive music.

At the same time, neighborhood networks of cassette producers, grassroots distributors, club owners, and wedding-hall promoters validated and sustained the new music. The cassettes forced themselves into the music industry from the outside in and the bottom up. By the 1990s, this musical movement helped to reset the parameters not only of contemporary Israeli music, but of Israeli national identity.

The new pan-ethnic music that took shape between the 1970s and 1990s is the subject of this book. The period is roughly defined as extending from the end of the Yom Kippur War until the assassination of Prime Minister Yitzhak Rabin, which brought to an end a hopeful and idealistic phase of the Israeli-Palestinian peace negotiations. During this period, external events such as attacks by Hezbollah, the Lebanon War of 1981, and the first anti-radar Scud missiles during the 1991 Gulf War pressured Israel from without. At the same time, ethnic, religious, and class cleavages within Israel shifted the political landscape, consolidating North African and Middle Eastern coalitions that had ousted the Labor Party from power in 1977. This new music arose from a rapidly changing society. After 1995, external pressures on Israel pushed its internal struggles underground. The buses, the bus stop, the bus station, the marketplace—the heartland of so-called cassette music—became dangerous territories. Explosions punctuated their envelopes of sound; corpses and burnt out buses populated the memory spaces of the marketplace; nobody lingered among temptations. Buyers swung by to grab necessities in their panicked flights between the safe havens of work and home. Since the period of this study, ending in the mid-1990s, music has been reforming, but that will be a new history. Here, I examine its early formation.

I began conducting the main research for this book in Israel in 1986. I continued through the First Intifada (literally, "shaking off" in Arabic) from December 1987 through September 1993 and on through the Israeli-Palestinian peace process in 1994. Since 1995, I have conducted a number of focused interviews with performers, composers, and impresarios, including Avihu Medina, Zehava Ben, Eli Banai, and Meir Reuveni. Yemenite singer and composer Avihu Medina and I were invited by the Israeli Consulate's Ministry of Education to present ten lecture/performances at American universities in the fall of 1996. We also presented a program on Israeli music and ethnicity at the Israel Studies Conference at Rutgers University in 1997 and at the Ohio State University in 2002.

Terms of Engagement

Mediterranean Israeli music is recognizable to its listeners, creators, and producers, yet for mainstream Israeli critics the music defies classification into recognized genres. This dramatizes my claim that sound boundaries between contemporary musics are disputed territories not only of music but also of scholarship. The seeming mishmash of styles confounds mainstream critics and renders the music illegitimate in their eyes. The cassettes juxtapose and combine European, Middle Eastern, and Mediterranean musical elements into hybrid forms.[6] Is the music liturgical or secular? Eastern or Western? Popular or folk? Contemporary or traditional? These juxtapositions and combinations also appear in the song texts, which transition, without warning, into various styles of Hebrew, punctuated by distinct ethnic markers and a patchwork of other languages.

The media coverage and subsequent scholarship on Mediterranean Israeli music parallels the legitimizing process of this contested music genre itself. Mediterranean Israeli music's cassette debut in the marketplace in 1974 was accompanied by a handful of articles in the daily Hebrew language newspapers that covered the music as either local gossip or as a sidebar to the story of the ethnic revolution then fomenting among Israel's new *Mizraḥim* (Easterners)—the newly consolidated pan-ethnic identity forged among North African and Middle Eastern ethnic groups. In the early 1980s, the Syrian Israeli ethnomusicologist Amnon Shiloah and the European Israeli sociologist Erik Cohen copublished two landmark articles on the musical, social, and political dimensions of Israeli popular music. Shiloah and Cohen identified musical trends that describe immigrant musicians' sudden encounter with a new culture in Israel. These trends are outlined as chronological stages from the 1950s through the 1980s: Israelization, Orientalization, ethnicization, popularization, and academization.[7]

Anthropologist Jeff Halper and ethnomusicologists Edwin Seroussi and Pamela Kidron similarly examined Mizraḥi music to develop ethnographically grounded observations that unveil the "coded" musical meanings for creators and listeners.[8] They distinguish the musical community, or "taste public," according to ethnicity and class identity, arguing that *Musiḳah Mizraḥit* remained marginal not only because of its unaccepted sound, but also because of its association with "low culture."

Motti Regev's work on Israeli rock 'n' roll explores questions of nativities and "foreign" musical influences.[9] Regev elaborates Shiloah's notion of Israelization and, following Pierre Bourdieu, examines "the production of meaning"[10] in the struggle for elite recognition of marginal popular music forms. Regev suggests that *Musiḳat ha-ḳaseṭot* ("cassette music") was considered a poor imitation of rock artistry rather than a native Israeli cultural phenomenon.[11] Regev sees the "coming of rock" as an outside genre's struggle for acceptance as an authentic expression. Although he does not differentiate between *Musiḳat ha-ḳaseṭot* and other marginal popular forms seeking similar legitimization, he notes that the popularity of *Musiḳat ha-ḳaseṭot* was viewed as a threat to "serious" Israeli rock by mainstream music industry producers, critics, and consumers.

By focusing on Israelization and Israeliness, Shiloah, Seroussi, and Regev provide a model for studying music as culturally situated, without wedding it to particular "authentic" or "original" contexts. They provide the groundwork for my exploration of sounds separated from one context and recontextualized in another. I look not only at the people who travel, but also at music that travels where the people do not or cannot. Music seeps across checkpoints through which people cannot pass and makes the cultural destinations themselves disputed territories. This seepage results in dueling and dual claims to authenticity as well as unexpected rhizomatic or weblike networks of affiliation.[12] The question of "whose music is it?" foregrounds the instability of the authentic as a category.

Dialogic Representation

I begin by acknowledging the instabilities of the cultural performances I document as well as the instabilities of my own "ethnographic production." Ethnographers have variously recognized the instability of either the ethnographic object or the ethnographic project. Both are unstable. Moreover, the instability cannot be resolved by either intimacy or distance. Instead, my project tacks between "object distance" and what I call "object intimacy," in an attempt to keep alive the ambiguities, paradoxes, and contradictions that constitute the discourse of cultural representation. I trouble the binaries of subjectivity/objectivity, insider/outsider, and verisimilitude/precision (where verisimilitude is the evocative rendering of situations, the likeness of the real, and precision is their dry catalogue). Specifically, I hold open my own multiple conversations with performers, producers, marketers, pirates, media people, critics (of both aesthetic and political kinds), as well as with fellow academics, included as coparticipants in the conversation rather than as members of a separate discourse. By making multiple voices audible, my project strives not for a single truth but rather for copresence.

The First Dialogue: Scholar and Musician/Activist

When I found myself lost in the Central Bus Station, the cultural nerve that I sensed turned out to be my own. This is easy to acknowledge retrospectively. At the time though, standing amidst the blaring, distorted cassettes, hawking peddlers, and bus fumes, I sensed only vaguely that my unnerved feeling had less to do with accidentally stumbling into a new research project than with a visceral sense of familiarity. This feeling was overshadowed by a simultaneous sense of betrayal. My pristine American notions of Israeliness—crisp and clean looking sabra children[13] dancing in blue and white outfits—was laid bare by this overstimulating scene of disorientation and thunderous decibels. As the languages and smells collided and at the same time found comfortable proximity, my ability to access and embrace the unfolding scene drew upon stories I had fashioned into my own memories of my immigrant grandparents maneuvering through the Lower East Side and then Brooklyn in the early twentieth century.

This was not a conscious knowledge; I did not understand this moment as a product of an inner dialogic relationship, as my own internal awakening. On the contrary, I busily scribbled field notes about others, other languages, other ethnicities, other intranational struggles, long before I looked inward at my own inheritance. It was my embedded legacy that served as the foundation for the resources of observation and empathy that I brought to the field. Tapping into this legacy, albeit instinctively, I conscientiously and consciously attended to the coexistence of rigor and passion—the twin foundations that supported my ability to return again and again to the cacophonies of the Central Bus Station market. This cultural geography was neither alien nor romantic, though it was surprisingly nostalgic for me. It took getting lost in someone else's marketplace to awaken the longing for a place called home amidst the dueling nativities of my own past beginning to come into relief in this unlikely place.

I come from a family of Jewish musicians who immigrated to the United States at the end of the nineteenth century. My maternal great-grandfather, Abraham Miller, was a violinist and teacher who combined Yiddish songs with neighboring Romany repertoires. His daughter, my grandmother, Nettie Miller Silverman, and her nine brothers and sisters carried this Yiddish/Romany mix forward into conversation with the urban jazz traditions in early-twentieth-century New York City. They were community musicians, performing at weddings, bar mitzvahs, and neighborhood parties, and they taught music to augment their living. I only heard about my musical history as stories about the good old days, as I grew up in Washington, D.C., far from Brooklyn, where I imagined music had filled every waking moment of family life.

My own musical experience was in sharp contrast to the family stories. As a child, I sang in a citywide choir, performing songs from thirty countries at official Washington functions, embassies, and the White House. I remember performing with other children from the Young Pioneers at the Soviet Embassy during the Cold War, being told by the choir director to keep my distance from these Communists and at the same time realizing that I, too, was Russian. Around that time, I asked to play a stringed instrument; my mother, perhaps out of her own longing for the sounds of family gatherings, now only memories, brought home a violin. The closest renderings of my inheritance were the biblical cantillations that I learned in preparation for chanting my bat mitzvah Torah portion in a Reform Jewish ceremony and the Israeli folksongs that were part of my experience at Jewish summer camp. My short-lived violin training was in the classical tradition, far from the folk traditions that were my legacy. In high school, I sang classical choral music and madrigals, learned to play the guitar, and composed folksongs. The music of my forebears was absent from my own world.

Curiosity eventually led to my becoming International President of the B'nai Brith Girls in high school in 1969, at which time I was introduced to Israel's official culture (photo ops with Abba Eban and other dignitaries dotted my itinerary in 1970). I returned to Israel in 1973 and witnessed the unraveling of the Israeli social fabric with the Yom Kippur War.

It was in high school that I became active in the anti–Vietnam War movement. By the time I got to college in Ashland, Oregon, my growing commitment to political activism was focused on the music of social change and women's issues. I worked for the emerging "Women's Music Network," a loose consortium of women artists, record and concert producers, and activists who built an alternative to the mainstream industry in the late 1970s. There I met the protest singer Holly Near, became her professional and political manager, and worked with her record company in Los Angeles. In 1977, I founded Roadwork in Washington, D.C., a nonprofit organization that produced Sisterfire, an annual international women's festival for the next five years, and helped dozens of racially and ethnically diverse women's performance groups to further their careers. In particular, as artist representative I worked with Bernice Johnson Reagon, founder and artistic director of the African American women's a cappella ensemble Sweet Honey in the Rock, for the next seventeen years. This unigendered but multiracial, multicultural work tuned my ear (in ways that I can only understand retrospectively) to the new Mediterranean Israeli music emerging at the same time in Israel.

In hindsight, it is not surprising that I gravitated to the study of Mediterranean Israeli music when I began my doctoral studies at the University of Pennsylvania in the late 1980s. By then, Sweet Honey in the Rock was able to fill Carnegie Hall with little effort, and my work was completed. I had never meant to be an artist representative. What had interested me was the activist sensibility required to create a national and international touring system for the group, which allowed them to remain in control of their artistry. Dr. Reagon, herself a Ph.D. from Howard University, suggested I consider the Department of Folklore and Folklife at the University of Pennsylvania. She proposed that I draw upon my years of grassroots cultural work with Sweet Honey and other women artists in designing my scholarly path.

As a discipline, folklore attracted me because it straddled the borderlines between the humanities, social sciences, and the arts and seemed to combine the best of ethnography, oral history, literary criticism, anthropology, and even political science. Housed variously in English, anthropology, and foreign language departments, Folklore's discomfited and self-reflexive posture within the academy and the public sector resonated with my own ambivalence about my grassroots and scholarly commitments and desires. Eventually, I came to believe that these mutually interacting impulses helped me remain true to my material as well as to the academy. It was my work in grassroots women's music that helped me recognize the profoundly revolutionary impulses of Mediterranean Israeli music even though the genre was defined as explicitly apolitical. In retrospect, the move from my work with Dr. Reagon and Sweet Honey in the Rock, Holly Near, and Sisterfire to Mediterranean Israeli music seems an obvious, transparent continuation of the same struggles and questions. But as I began to outline this new research problem, it felt entirely uncharted.

The Second Dialogue: Names and Claims

As an activist, musician, and scholar, and also as a Jew of Ashkenazi descent, I started my research already having struggled with my shifting status as an outsider or insider in various contexts. As a scholar, the first problem I encountered was nomenclature: ethnic designations for Israeli Jews from North Africa and the Middle East are often superimposed from outside and above. As poet/writer/literary scholar Ammiel Alcalay observed:

> Even naming these "natives" accurately is problematic. Are they Asian, African, North African, Middle Eastern, Turko-Iranian, or "Sephardo-Oriental" (to use Katznelson's quaint appellation), Sephardi, Arab, non-Western, Eastern, or even, as they have been pejoratively labeled in official Israeli terminology, "the children of the Oriental ethnic groups"? Every category seems to come at the expense of another, either leaving something out or succumbing to a negative definition that presupposes one group to be the standard of measurement or all groups to be in possession of some common, primordial "essence." As Ilan Halevi notes, "these vaguenesses of vocabulary, reservations and obstructions reflect in reality the shifting character of the barriers themselves, and the fact that the language is not ready for the social reordering that is underway."[14]

Each designation has its own problems. Palestinian literary critic and activist Edward Said has analyzed Orientalism as "a Western style for dominating, restructuring, and having authority over the Orient."[15] While Said does not refer to Jews from Islamic lands in his landmark study *Orientalism,* more recent scholarship has used Said's work to discuss the limitations of the term Oriental Jews.[16]

The term Sephardi (plural: Sephardim) refers to Jews whose ancestors lived in the Iberian Peninsula prior to the expulsion of Jews and Muslims in the late fifteenth century. This identification is often self-ascribed by those who call themselves *Samekh Ṭet,*[17] which foregrounds their European roots and distances them from North African and Middle Eastern Jewish communities among whom they have lived for the last five hundred years.

The term Ashkenazi (plural: Ashkenazim), by contrast, refers to Jews who trace their ancestry to the Rhineland in the Middle Ages, and the Jews who migrated from there. Notwithstanding the problems in creating pan-ethnic categories, it is sacred texts, melodies, and styles that differentiate Sephardi from Ashkenazi communities. There are, of course, exceptions. The Ḥasidim of Eastern Europe adopted elements of the Sephardi liturgy, while the Yemenite liturgy bears some unexpectedly close affinities to Ashkenazi pronunciations.

The term Mizraḥi has expanded to incorporate most non-Ashkenazi ethnic groups in Israel, including Middle Easterners, North Africans, Sephardim, Iranians, and Georgians. While the literal translation is "Eastern," the term is applied to some Israeli Jews from countries to the west of Israel, such as Morocco. Those included in this category sometimes resist the pan-ethnic designation because it is used to mark and therefore exclude non-European Israelis. Such broad categories obscure the diversity of those who emigrated from more than one hundred countries and comprise dozens of ethnic subgroups. For the purpose of this book, I refer to the creators and their audience by their particular self-identified ethnic group, such as Yemenite, Kurdish, and so on, or, when a broader category is relevant, by the term Mizraḥi. I refer to European Israeli Jews as Ashkenazi.

Both Ashkenazi and Mizraḥi designations have taken on new meaning in the context of Israel. Ashkenazi, formerly a specific designation for a particular subgroup of European Jews, has grown to encompass a pan-ethnic designation for European Jewry. The Mizraḥi identity is a wholly Israeli development that emerges from the commingling of diverse Middle Eastern and North African Jews. While there was rich contact among Middle Eastern and North African Jewish communities prior to their arrival in Israel, the new proximity in which they were brought together under one national banner as a disenfranchised minority led to this development. Recently some Mizraḥi scholars, artists, and actvists have embraced the term Arab Jews.

I had assumed that the Israeli ethnic struggle between Ashkenazim and Mizraḥim would be analogous to the American racial struggle between African Americans and European Americans, but this assumption proved culturally, historically, and politically incorrect. The history of American race relations, with its origins in the inhumane transport of African captives into slavery, does not parallel the fraught arrival of Middle Eastern and North African Jews to Israel from the late 1940s through the mid-1950s. Nevertheless, in Israeli society, numerous policies and practices have been harmful to both the Mizraḥi Jewish and Palestinian Arab populations, and Mizraḥi activists have drawn inspiration from African American civil rights struggles in the United States. Some Israeli movements, most notably the one that designated itself the Black Panthers,[18] even attached African American identity markers to their local struggle.

Racial, ethnic, and cultural struggles among Israeli subcultures are specific to their context. In my work I resist unequivocal characterizations of Ashkenazim as oppressors and Mizraḥim as victims and instead reformulate a spectrum of integrative and differentiating ethnic interactions. On the broadest official political level, Ashkenazi policies have created Mizraḥi inequities, while Mizraḥi reactions to Ashkenazi political and economic power range from denial to accusations of deprivation, reflecting a desire to enter the mainstream and the pain of exclusion.

The Third Dialogue: Outsiders and Insiders

Insider status and outsider status offer ethnographers contrasting sets of insights and limitations. Insiders often get richness, intimacy, access, continuity, and historical depth, while outsiders are often able to see the naturalized as constructed, examine assumptions, introduce comparative perspectives, and approach the field with a nonpartisan eye. Indigenous ethnographers[19] or "insiders studying their own cultures offer new angles of vision and depths of understanding. Their accounts are also restricted in unique ways."[20] Backyard ethnography is no more reliable a venue for the "native" scientist than the investigation of far-away cultures is for a foreign one.[21] Ethnographic strategies run the gamut from autobiographies that privilege subjectivities to quantification aimed at achieving a more objective reading. If insiders acknowledge familiarity by novelizing, outsiders acknowledge unfamiliarity by objectivity. Neither is sufficient; both can be enlightening.

My intent here is to clarify the particular terms of my own engagement as an outsider ethnographer with kindred cultural roots. While disclosure per se does not assure the reliability of the method, the ethnographic process rooted in thick descriptions of participant-observation remains the best available method to document cultures on the ground; as Alessandro Portelli argues, documentation on the ground preserves the contradictions and ambiguities that are part of people's lived lives.[22]

Disclosures of the encounter between the foreigner who becomes the "temporary neighbor" and who must rely on "native" colleagues in order to acquire linguistic and contextual skills in order to carry out fieldwork are a staple of ethnographic research. In my project, Reuven Namdar, an Iranian-Israeli writer/poet and sociology student, shared in the research and ethnographic process. Ruby and I attended concerts and club performances together, interviewed singers and producers, conducted library research, discussed songs, and examined song lyrics. We visited production and distribution sites and puzzled over the shifts in meaning in this emerging genre.

Our shared experience in the process of wrestling with encountered meanings, especially cross-culturally, created a weblike, dialogic instrument for studying a similarly weblike and dialogical music form. Among the many

Bob Marley shared space with Prime Ministers Menachem Begin and Yitzhak Shamir, both of the Likud Party, on a wall of this marketplace booth across from the old Tel Aviv Central Bus station in 1991. The juxtaposition of a revolutionary reggae singer and right-of-center Israeli politicians caught Ruby's attention as we stopped for coffee in the pre-dawn hours after a night in Tel Aviv's Mediterranean Israeli music club district. (Photo by author)

affiliations relevant to this project—musical, ethnic, religious, political, age, gender—I also note that shared academic affiliation can (and did) bind Ruby and me in ways that distinguished us from the local community under study. Academics, whether insiders or outsiders, often share a common language and tradition of training that are distinct from the communities under study. In this project, Ruby was both an insider research assistant and a graduate student in sociology. At times, Ruby was able to interpret nuances that I as an outsider researcher did not perceive. Simultaneously, as an outsider researcher, I often registered cultural details that were either not consciously apparent to Ruby or so apparent as to seem inconsequential. In working through the experience together, mutual observation, not only of the performances themselves but of each other, enlivened and deepened our understanding of the unfolding cultural dynamics.

It was often in the early morning hours, driving back to Jerusalem after a full night in Tel Aviv's club district, that Ruby and I pieced together the fragments of understanding that we had gleaned from our parallel interactions with people. Often the same informant would share very different stories with each of us. We discovered that neither the ethnographer nor the local research assistant can provide a global perspective on the field of study; each manifests particular subcultural affiliations and limitations. And community members are ready to disclose very different aspects of their wisdom to someone they perceive as an insider than to someone they perceive as an outsider. The dialogics of gender and sexualities underscored every encounter. In fact, my ability to engage in a relaxed manner in club and concert hall settings was due in large measure to Ruby's presence. The depth of our findings was greater once we acknowledged that Ruby's role as a male local research assistant to a woman outsider was much more than an interpreter of nuances or an object of potential data. Ruby's impact on the project was profound, and in return the project has had an impact on his published works.[23]

As James Clifford notes, "Acute political and epistemological self-consciousness need not lead to ethnographic self-absorption or to the conclusion that it is impossible to know anything certain about other people."[24] On the contrary, our collaborative ethnographic approach created a series of personal and scholarly checks and balances, a system that allowed each of us to draw on our life's experiences as resources of analysis, while also guarding against projecting the research inward.

The Field: Initiation

The new musical phenomenon reached a social peak between 1984 and 1986 without effectively penetrating the national and commercial realm. But the sound tracks had begun to spread beyond poor neighborhoods far enough that radio deejay Shimon Parnas (who later became a music editor and television personality) referred to it as "Israel's little music revolution."[25] It was during this period, as I conducted research for a five-part Pacifica radio series, "Israeli and Palestinian Artists: Creators on Restless Soil," that I stumbled upon the music. This serendipitous encounter resulted in a show entitled "Cassette Singers: The Second Israel Finds a Voice."[26] In the course of my research, I interviewed Jeff Halper, an American-Israeli anthropologist living in the Kurdish/Yemenite Jerusalem neighborhood of Naḥla'ot, where he had begun collecting cassettes in the mid-1980s. His theorizing about the ethnic dimension of this music cued me to the roots of this new formation. I interviewed Yemenite singer Haim Moshe and Iranian cassette company owner and producer Asher Reuveni in the Mizraḥi neighborhood of Shekhunat ha-Tiḳvah, where they spoke of Ashkenazi co-opting of the music while simultaneously avoiding labels that would distinguish the genre from "Israeli music like any Israeli music."[27] Leading Yemenite singer Zohar Argov had already appeared on national television four times.[28] The music carried no name other than (at best) *Musiḳat ḳaseṭot* ("cassette music") or *Musiḳat ha-taḥanah ha-merkazit* (Central Bus Station music); more often, as with my North Tel Aviv friends, it was referred to as the music of *tshaḥtshaḥim.*

Some of the questions that emerged during my initial research included:

- How do practitioners and listeners talk about the conditions out of which the cassette tapes emerge?
- How do they describe and evaluate the history of these neighborhood tapes as they grow into an alternative music network that competes with the mainstream music industry?
- What can the practitioners and listeners teach us about the music itself, about Hebrew texts rubbing shoulders with Arabic, Persian, Turkish, Kurdish, and Greek lyrics and about melodies stitched together from Arabic, Mediterranean, and Western forms?
- Where do they situate a contemporary music genre that can be considered part of the continuum of their traditional repertoire, while drawing from a wide range of popular sounds?
- How do they talk about this refashioning?
- How do we account for this music's rejection by large numbers of European Israelis as well as by some members of Middle Eastern and North African communities?
- Is there a Palestinian or Arab connection to the music?

These questions remained central throughout subsequent fieldwork phases, though some of the problems I identified initially proved to be much more complex than they first appeared.

Preconceptions and Reconceptions

I returned to study the new genre in depth for five months in 1991 and for another three in the winter of 1992. By then, a great deal had changed. Setting boundaries on such a rapidly changing phenomenon became a further problem of research. By this time, singers and cassette company owners had formed a network federation through which they brought charges of

"לא שיר של צ'חצ'חים"

עשרות ישראלים מגיעים מדי שנה לניו יורק, בתקווה לתפוס כאן מקום טוב בשוק הזמר המזרחי. אחוז קטן מהם שורד, מופיע במועדונים, חולם להופיע בחגיגות בר-מצווה ובחתונות, לעשות הרבה כסף

ריקי פן. בארץ קראו לה "זמרת הביטלס". החלום שלה להוציא תקליט רוקנ'רול

שלמה חביב. מנסה להגיע לכמה שיותר אנשים

לוח שידורי "שלום אמריקה"

A headline appearing in a North American newspaper for Israeli emigrants in 1990 labeled the music by what it was not: "Not the Song of *tshaḥtshaḥim*." This derogatory term for Mizraḥi youth on the fringes of society reinforced the prevailing view of the music as inferior. Ironically, the music relied on both Western and Eastern motifs, instrumentation, and arrangements. It was the music makers, singers, impresarios, and audiences who were largely Mizraḥim. The sound was sometimes a synthesis created in conjunction with Ashkenazi arrangers. (Courtesy *Yedi'ot America*) discrimination to the Knesset (Israeli parliament) and tried to redress years in which this genre had been excluded from Israeli radio and television. They had even come up with an official name for the genre, Mediterranean Israeli music. Furthermore, although the vast majority of sales still took place in Israel's outdoor marketplaces, the music was now also available on CDs in many record stores. Perhaps the most significant change occurred in the aftermath of the death of leading Yemenite singer Zohar Argov in November 1987. By the early 1990s Argov's music was transformed into a national legacy that crossed ethnic lines. His life became the subject of a theater production[29] at Tel Aviv's avant-garde Beit Lessin Theater, several major motion pictures, documentaries, and annual memorial concerts.

To document such a broad and rapidly changing musical and social process, I attended and recorded over one hundred performance events in clubs, wedding halls, synagogues, and festival sites during seasonal and life-cycle events, such as bar mitzvah celebrations, weddings, and religious holidays. These events, plus mainstream popular music occasions, took me to Tel Aviv, Jerusalem, Haifa, Be'er Sheva, Arad, Karmiel, Mount Meron, Netivot, Rehovot, Bar Ilan University, Masada, and Eilat, as well as Atlantic City, New York City, Philadelphia, and Rockville, Maryland.

Often the bus trip or unexpected lulls in activity produced the most interesting data. On the way to a popular music festival held in the desert town of Arad in 1992, I was treated to almost a full hour of male Ashkenazi teenagers parodying Mizraḥi vocal style. Then, while sitting by a swimming pool at the Eilat Jazz Festival headquarters, I learned that I had just missed a Yemenite music festival at a nearby hotel, the Teymaniada, and discovered my ignorance of one of the key locations of public notices: Israel's growing network of local papers, called *meḳomonim.*[30]

Finally, taking a day off to hike the back trail of the Ein Gedi oasis, I stopped to talk with an Israeli man who was walking with his son. When I told him about my research interests, he mentioned that he might be able to help. I have to admit that I could not figure out what this blond, blue-eyed, Ashkenazi man might have to offer. I later discovered that he was Uzi Ḥiṭman, an important composer and performer of Mediterranean Israeli music, who died in 2004.

In addition to live performances, I observed a number of studio recording sessions in order to track the actual production process. Yemenite instrumentalist Yehuda Kessar mentioned a guitar that he had built with "quarter tone"[31] frets and shared with me the original home recordings of Zohar Argov that he had brought to the Reuveni brothers in the late 1970s. I sat in on television, radio, and newspaper interviews with Haim Moshe,

Avihu Medina, and Margalit Tsan'ani. I traveled to outdoor marketplaces in Tel Aviv, Jerusalem, Ramle, Be'er Sheva, Haifa, and Beit Shemesh and spent many hours talking with cassette merchants and consumers. It was in the Arab-Jewish market of Ramle that I first discovered that Mediterranean Israeli music had penetrated Palestinian communities. Walking over the pedestrian bridge that divides sections of the market, I headed for an Arab cassette booth. There, I found recitations from the Koran, Egyptian pop stars, and Israeli Yemenite singers occupying the same commercial bins and learned that one of the major markets for pirated cassettes of Israeli singers was Gaza. Later I discovered that this mixed Arab-Jewish town near Tel Aviv was the center if not the birthplace of Israel's alternative rock scene in the late 1960s and 1970s. Some of the Mizraḥi artists I would meet subsequently, Nissim Saroussi among them, had participated in this then-subversive musical challenge to the mainstream. While the mainstream trajectory of these underground musicians (the Churchills, for example, became the backup band for the renowned Israeli pop star Arik Einstein) places it outside my story, the experimentation with Eastern and Western styles and especially with Greek music initiated by musicians like Miki Gabrielov and Haim Romano can be seen as a parallel and intersecting stream. As Gabrielov stated: "We were certainly influenced by . . . Arab music. Naturally this came from Haim and myself. We came from an eastern, call it Asian background, while the rest of the guys in the band were westerners. . . . You have to realize it's not as if we've made calculated decisions as to the use of these sounds, it came from our background. . . . Reaching the eastern sound was not an 'intellectual' process."[32] While visiting Haim Moshe's production office and radio personality Salmon Shafik's studio, I reviewed dozens of fan letters received from Palestinians living in Israel and the West Bank and from Arabs in Jordan, Syria, Lebanon, and Egypt.

This insider data was augmented by taped interviews with mainstream music journalists and singers, record company managers and executives, radio editors, representatives of IUPA (Israeli Union of Performing Artists)[33] and ACUM (Composers, Authors and Publishers Society of Israel),[34] Ashkenazi singers, and skeptics.

The Community: Education

Though no two Jewish Israeli families are alike, most host or attend Friday evening or Saturday afternoon meals. Both secular and observant families surrender in a variety of ways to the rhythms that separate the Sabbath from the mundane work week. During my research in the 1980s and 1990s, I was

Even before the digital age, pirated cassettes of Mediterranean Israeli music were heard in Gaza, Syria, and Ramallah. Here in the Ramle marketplace, Yemenite and Moroccan Israeli vocal *muwwals* and Muslim Egyptian koranic recitation share tenuous retail space. (Photo by author)

the beneficiary of this weekly ritual, receiving invitations to many homes. Besides companionship and relaxation, each visit was a rich source of ethnographic data. I observed and discussed musical tastes and learned about new singers and repertoires. Most secular Israelis watched the same edition of the Friday evening news and music and culture programs. I observed reactions to general social and artistic trends and to specific performances by Mediterranean Israeli musicians.

I spent most of my Sabbaths and holidays at the home of Saleh and Majida Houja in Katamon Vav, a largely Mizraḥi neighborhood in Jerusalem. The family originated in Mosul, Iraq, and Zakho, Kurdistan. At the time of my fieldwork, they had seven children and eight grandchildren scattered between Jerusalem and Philadelphia. Changing attitudes toward Mediterranean Israeli music among Mizraḥim unfolded around their table. Through them, I began to understand why some Mizraḥim rejected their own musical traditions, especially some first-generation Israelis born during the 1950s and 1960s. Some Mizraḥim responded to the impact of assimilationist policies, in which European cultural traditions enjoyed a privileged status, by rejecting their own musical style. Although in many cases the family embraced Middle Eastern, North African, and emerging Mizraḥi styles, this was not universal. Attempts by Mizraḥim to reclaim their musical traditions became especially apparent after 1992, when Mediterranean Israeli music began to receive increased radio broadcast time. In addition, the progress of the Middle East peace process resulted in an increasing number of appearances in Israel by internationally acclaimed North African and Greek performers, providing real-time cultural exchanges between neighboring musicians—encounters that had been precluded by Israel's political isolation during the previous decades.

The Cassette: Documentation

Between 1984 and 1992, I examined some seventy cassettes by many of the best-known Mediterranean Israeli singers, including Zohar Argov, Haim Moshe, Tsiyon Golan, Margalit Tsan'ani, Shimi Tavori, Avner Gadassi, Daḳlon, Samir Shukry, Jo Amar, Ofer Levy, Moshe Gi'at, Zehava Ben, Eli Luzon, Itzik Kala, Avihu Medina, and the band Tselile ha-Kerem. These singers and groups performed during the course of three decades (1970s–1990s). Their repertoires and performance styles provide a wide spectrum of examples of vocal technique, production quality, and East/West musical combinations.

The cassette product is one of the best sources available for analyzing repertoires and musical anatomy. Cover designs volunteer additional graphic

Decoding the aesthetic markers and song lists on Mediterranean Israeli music cassette covers proves crucial to understanding the genre's power within Mizraḥi communities and raises questions regarding its illegitimacy for Ashkenazim. Avner Gadassi's *Menagen ṿe-Shar* (Play and Sing) captures the difficulty in sorting out the cacophony of cultural forces at play in the historical moment under study. Gadassi, seated and playing a *darabukka,* is surrounded by a visual feast of Eastern and Western cultural images. An analysis of cover photos, typeface, graphic design, and song titles serves as data in the project of mapping this emergent music network. (Reuveni Brothers, courtesy Meir Reuveni)

data on artistic aesthetics. At the same time, the extent of data concerning lyricists, composers, arrangers, and singers, as well as descriptions of the individual songs, varies, as does the accuracy of the information. While verifying publishing details at ACUM, I discovered, for instance, that many songs listed as "folk" or "Turkish traditional" (or not listed at all) could be traced to copyrighted creations of foreign composers.[35] While the song credits are not listed on the cassette, at ACUM I discovered that the melody for Argov's groundbreaking song "Elinor" was written by Greek composer Christos Nikolopoulos. The difficulty of adjudicating what counts as breach of copyright attests to the fraught status of musical borrowings in the West. New musical forms arise out of cross-breeding, leakage, tinges, contamination, and outright theft.

Sales figures are equally unverifiable. The merchandising of these cassettes began informally, as neighborhood entrepreneurs sold homemade products. The industry grew, yet advertising and broadcast opportunities were withheld from the cassette producers. Since royalty payments and taxes are based on the number of products sold, cassette company owners have been unwilling to share totals. In an interview on 12 April 1991, Yemenite singer Eli Luzon claimed that his cassette *Ezo medinah* (What a Country) sold over 500,000 copies.[36] In a conversation with me, Meir Reuveni estimated that the combined sales of Zohar Argov cassettes exceeded three million. Moroccan singer Zehava Ben's first cassette, *Ṭipat mazal* (A Drop of Luck), is believed to have sold 80,000 copies in the first few weeks.[37] That same year, journalist Tal Peri reported that Ben's cassettes had sold over 500,000 copies.[38]

Through the examination of cassettes, the cross-examination of live performance events, and the interpretation of interviews with artists, managers, and audiences (some of which I conducted personally, others of which I culled from newspapers), I developed a tentative mechanism for generic classification of musical forms. This system of naming must be viewed as a fluid clustering imposed by an outside ethnographer in order to chart the musical choices through which singers and audiences express and reflect the various aspects of their multivocal identities.

Yet to understand these constantly shifting categories requires both the analysis of song lyrics and the transcription of musical samples. I have analyzed the lyrics of several pieces and compared them to both contemporary popular mainstream Israeli lyrics and to the canonic *ha-Shir ha-Erets Yisre'eli* (The Song of the Land of Israel) repertoire.[39] These comparisons helped me clarify the aesthetics of the genre. I have also transcribed several musical scores in order to specify the identity markers that each instrument and vocal part brings to a given song, and how the song as a whole signifies encoded meanings that reflect the multi-ethnic/cross-cultural experience of the singer and audience.

The Cassette Network in Perspective

Mediterranean Israeli music is a local example of an international revolution in popular musics. The opportunity for Mizraḥi artists to realize musical self-determination was made possible in part by a new technological invention. The invention of the portable cassette recorder by the Phillips Corporation in the early 1970s allowed Mizraḥi entrepreneurs to mass-produce and distribute music excluded by the mainstream Israeli music industry.

The explosion of a worldwide network of local cassette markets in the early 1970s produced an unforeseen convergence of technological invention and sociopolitical revolution.[40] As a technological invention, the cassette provided an affordable and accessible mechanism for musicians and consumers, whose sounds had theretofore been excluded from local commercial recording industries. Community members could compose, combine, dub, and enjoy musics that were neglected by mainstream recording and broadcasting companies. "With a homemade cassette you can get your work heard on international radio and be a citizen of the world."[41]

Policy makers in the cultural domain, intellectuals, and journalists reacted negatively to what they felt to be the trivial musical and textual content of most newly produced cassettes.[42] As a sociopolitical revolution, the cassette subverted the sanctity, purity, and decibel level of public space. Musical styles broadcast at full volume by portable cassette players ("boom boxes" or "ghetto blasters") invaded previously restricted public arenas, infusing the air with uninvited sounds.[43] An Egyptian newspaper headline illustrated the sense of cultural danger and defilement. "This Aural Poison" metaphorized listening as the ingestion of possibly noxious, even lethal material.[44] This expression of discomfort with new technology was rooted in a sense of anxiety over whether the new medium would redefine aesthetic and social boundaries or reinforce preexisting norms.

Previous examples of "new" musical technologies, whether broadsheet, metronome, radio, electric amplification, or record, produced a series of side effects that both invigorated and undermined previously accepted musical ideas and categories. Even as it liberated and decentralized musical production, the cassette concurrently violated, detained, and superseded previous forms by inscribing them on magnetic tape. The technological shift evolved within the structure of the status quo and provoked an insurrection that overturned existing parameters. It was, in Thomas Kuhn's terms,

Top: As David Lodge remarked in the liner notes of *Yalla: Hitlist Egypt*: "Five thousand years of music have in the eyes of many been destroyed in the last five. Culture is under threat: young people are going their own way, making their own music." The cover of this 1990 CD release on the Island Record label signals the international invasion of the cassette, an invention that disrupted mainstream music industries globally. (Courtesy Island Records) *Bottom:* In Jerusalem, three teenage girls show off a boom box during the Passover *Mimouna* celebration. (Photo by author)

an "anomaly," a violation of expectations.[45] For instance, the singularity of Egyptian singer Umm Kulthum's fame during the 1950s was a result, in part, of the airplay she received. Thousands of fans in downtown Cairo stopped all activity when her voice filled the city streets. In that case, the government maintained control of the paradigm by determining the parameters of an acceptable urban sound track.[46]

Dissident cassettes broadcast new voices in the marketplace, challenging Umm Kulthum's singularity. Ali Hemida's electronic Bedouin pop hit, "Lolaaky," shared air time with recitations from the Koran and Rai music from North Africa. The portable and affordable cassette recorder shattered the power base of those who controlled access to expensive recording devices. Indeed, the Egyptian market itself exploded as over four hundred companies distributed thousands of legal and pirated cassettes.[47]

The global proliferation of local music cassettes since the 1970s made naming genres and keeping them discrete a messy business. As geographically distant local musics were broadcast on the radio, local musicians could immediately copy, insert, and create new versions of previously "foreign" styles, and cheaply disseminate these new performances in cassette form.

The cassette technology itself contributed both to preserving and to subverting traditional styles as well as to the proliferating innovative new styles that overlapped, confounded, and defied geographical logic. It is especially important to point out here that the local control of this new technology meant that not only were global musics traveling to new locales but also that local musicians were able to relocalize these soundscapes into their own styles. Instead of a process of globalization, this is better described as relocalization.[48]

The ability to record and rerecord on two tracks made splicing fragments from other tapes or recording directly from radio transmission possible for community musicians who would have lacked the financial resources to hire studio time. By taking control of this flexible and affordable technology, musicians, producers, and arrangers could fuse multiple musical traditions into a single song and juxtapose seemingly distinct styles on a single cassette. Another result was the coexistence of unneighborly cassettes in marketplace booths.

Until the creation of the cassette, Mizraḥi creators were dependant on the Ashkenazi-dominated music industry, which prevented the production of certain mixed genres. With cassettes, Mizraḥim flooded the marketplace not only with the familiar neighborhood songs, but also with new hybrid styles that resituated Andean pipes with Kurdish *zurna*, Flamenco *muwwals* with San Remo flavor, and so on.[49] New cassette technologies not only provided community musicians and entrepreneurs a route around the music industry's exclusionary practices; they also provided a medium on which they could

On the cover of *Mediterranean Song*, a songbook featuring Mediterranean Israeli music repertoire, a nameless, presumably male, Mizraḥi singer sports a gold cassette necklace. Such necklaces were popular throughout the world during the height of the cassette era. Today, numerous online sites feature retro products reinvented out of recycled cassettes or refashioned with the cassette insignia. Cassette wallets, handbags, charms, and dinosaur toys abound. (Reuveni Brothers, courtesy Meir Reuveni)

record and disseminate the new sound mixtures that were now accessible to them despite geographical, political, and social distances.

The irony here is that what constituted "acts of purification" in the Israeli context was a battle between the sanctified hybrid, called The Song of the Land of Israel, and newer styles that did not attempt to mask their hybridity. The hypocrisy here is in the selective nature with which hybrid forms were accepted or rejected. For the most part, until the 1990s, Mizraḥi hybrids, like other non-canonic hybrids around the world, were rejected by the mainstream music industries. Thus the Tel Aviv Central Bus Station, reverberating with the multifarious offerings of Mediterranean Israeli music cassettes, was akin to the cassette marketplaces in Cairo, Teheran, Istanbul, Jakarta, Herat, Lima, or Navajoland.

Salwa El-Shawan Castelo-Branco corroborated the outsider's difficulty in mapping the linguistic and aesthetic dimensions of "cassette music" by showing that in Egypt the difficulty affected even official censors, whose task it is to screen unacceptable music from the national airwaves: "Several censors I interviewed added that their university training in classical Arabic literature does not provide them with necessary preparation for evaluating colloquial Arabic texts from various parts of the country."[50] While analytical categories are helpful to the ethnographer in identifying comparative principles from the perspective of the official culture, they might not define the genre in a way that a community member would recognize.

Classification underpins social order. We "lump and split" our experiences, establishing a discourse of inclusion and exclusion out of the categories we construct.[51] How do cultural practitioners determine what is included in a category and what is not? Who sets these discursive terms? Who stands guard at the border, checking the ebb and flow of new forms and the clandestine encounters between disparate, taboo, and alien bloodlines? What motivates their exclusionary practices?

As scholars of creole culture have pointed out, new cultural forms are often characterized as impure by outsiders:[52] "Creolists see creolization as creative disorder, as a poetic chaos, thereby challenging simplistic and static notions of center and periphery."[53] This characterization of merging new forms in terms of "creative disorder" offers advantages over the purity and contamination models. This is especially true when naming music genres that cross disputed national, ethnic, and geographical borders. Such appellation is in itself a point of contention that can make the orthodox, official, and/or hegemonic order on either side of the dispute nervous.

The cassette technology provided a powerful medium for the transmission of transnational music. Here was a location through which cultural reintegration and invention could be easily practiced. Through a self-determined process of selecting and combining musical elements, musicians, composers, and entrepreneurs improvised new cultural identities.

The cassette provided not only a flexible medium but also a durable product that could weather extreme climatic conditions and accommodate longer pieces than the standard record format.[54] The medium thus facilitated two seemingly opposed directions: it stimulated musical variation and it preserved traditional elements. The increased international music dialogue generated innovation, while cassette tape provided a means of preserving "dying" local traditions, even after some members of a previous generation of practitioners had passed on. Once the traditional repertoire was efficiently "encoded" on magnetic tape, the cassettes themselves could displace older practitioners by providing an easier source of music for community events even as they preserved their music for posterity. Furthermore, the popularization of traditional genres accentuated the generational struggle. As young community members sought entrance into mainstream society, the normative sound track they created often clashed with the older familial traditions of their parents and grandparents. They could use the cassette recorder to dominate the familial soundscape and to "silence" the "embarrassing" sounds of their elders.

Cassettes assisted younger musicians in preserving traditional forms that were previously transmitted orally by elder practitioners or that had disappeared from local repertoires. For example, an oral poetry form in the Bedouin Sinai was revived in the early 1980s through cassette recordings.[55] Musicians could also record selected musical ideas from radio broadcasts of styles unavailable in the commercial market. The result was "popular music in a transcultural context."[56]

The mercurial rise of transnational music cassettes came as a surprise to both indigenous manufacturers and local commercial recording and broadcasting industries. Community producers scrambled to meet enormous demands for cassettes and mainstream executives struggled to suppress the cassette production that infringed on their previously monolithic hold on the recording market.

Economic competition took different forms, depending on who maintained control of the cassette production mechanisms. In localities such as Israel, where the cassette network was created by entrepreneurs from a disenfranchised but large subculture (over 50 percent of Israeli Jews are Mizraḥi), the mainstream industry tried to co-opt the effort by inviting the most successful local producers to set up shop within the existing recording companies. For example, after his successful cassette sales in the outdoor marketplaces, CBS Records invited Asher Reuveni to establish a Mizraḥi department in Tel Aviv in 1979.[57] In Java, foreign companies first initiated the cassette network and tried to exploit local community markets. In time, indigenous companies emerged and gained control of the domestic market.[58] In Cairo, commercial companies immediately entered the cassette market in large numbers and maintained control of it.[59]

The dynamics between mainstream recording and broadcasting industries and emerging cassette networks were different in different localities. In fact, the particular motivations that gave rise to the creation of specific cassette networks varied within each communal context. Some cassette networks were a defiant counterstatement to the existing music industry. In this case, musicians were not looking for a road in but rather for an alternative arena. "Underground" U.S. musicians converted their kitchens into recording studios and marketed their products through small mail-order catalogues. They exhibited no desire to enter the mainstream.[60] Bedouin musicians in Sinai claimed that only by producing their own cassettes and limiting their audiences to the indigenous community could they remain authentic.[61] Ḥasidic cassettes in Brooklyn and Navajo cassettes in the Southwest are further examples of alternative systems that had little ambition to enter the commercial music industry. In Israel, Mediterranean Israeli musicians aspired to enter the mainstream and viewed success in the cassette network as a viable mechanism through which they could break into the commercial industry. By the early 1990s, singers, entrepreneurs, and academic supporters founded two official federations, AZIT (*Amutat Zemer Yam Tikhoni,* the Association of Mediterranean Song) and ha-PIL (the Federation of Mediterranean Israeli Song). Through AZIT and ha-PIL, they continued to challenge mainstream rejection and fight for credibility.

The Israeli cassette network was, by virtue of the small population, a miniature version of networks in nations with more geographical space and higher population densities. In comparison to Egypt's four hundred companies, there were only three major Mizraḥi cassette companies in Israel from the late 1970s through the 1980s (Reuveni Brothers, Ben-Mosh Productions, and Azoulay Brothers), with several smaller production and distribution arms. In Israel, even mainstream success is limited by the potential consumers proficient in Hebrew. However, in a population of some five million Jews and over a million Arabic- and Hebrew-speaking Palestinian Israelis, claims that Zohar Argov's cassettes alone have sold over three million copies are staggering. It would be the equivalent of an American artist selling 150 million records.

Mediterranean Israeli music cassettes were emergent cultural forms that negotiated between an idealized past and a dislocated present. They recorded reformulated cultural identities based on new ethnic proximities. While the cassettes reacted against official authority, they simultaneously asserted local, national, and transcultural styles. Like their creators, the cassettes reflected the shifting identities and realignments of pan-ethnic experience. The creators sifted and sorted through indigenous and international musics and worked out negotiated hybrid sound tracks.

Resisting Binarism

To resist binarism is not to erase difference. It is to acknowledge that difference is constantly crystallized and dissolved. As Rebecca Solnit argues in *Hope in the Dark,* the task is to recognize "the departure of the binaries and oppositions by which we used to imagine the world."[62] This is not a passive acquiescence; it is a proposal for a new politics of the aesthetic. "Activism isn't necessarily oppositional."[63] Pointing to examples of the Zapatistas, the farm labor organizing council, and the global justice movement, she cautions us against creating either/or questions and suggests that because art and culture provide alternative models that break down binaries, blur genres, and seep across enemy lines, "symbolic and cultural acts have real political power."[64] Mediterranean Israeli music, an expression of an asymmetrical ethnic relationship, is a primary instance of a new aesthetic power.

Ethnic identity is a network of interactive and context-sensitive forces that meet at boundaries. These boundaries are both mediators of disputed territory and disputed territories in themselves. Disputed territory may be geographical or metaphorical and may involve human actors or the cultural products of human action. The problematic notion of clear boundaries can also be found within the individual, who must often barter between adversarial components of a multivocal self. The resulting friction requires negotiation as a means of clarifying the nature and position of countervailing forces. Arriving at a negotiated accommodation, whether within or between persons, groups, songs, or nations, requires reconciling the nature and the position of its constituent parts. Can music transcend, contain, or transform political relationships and boundaries in disputed territory? And if it does, how?

Understanding the relationship between ethnic identities and music genres in disputed territory—the mingling of enemy lines with musical lines—contributes to our understanding of the politics of identity and the power relationships of cultural production.[65] I propose a model of dueling nativities and appropriate appropriations[66] to trouble the prevailing concepts of indigeneity, appropriation, and inheritance in recent cultural studies scholarship, and to understand Jewish Israeli musicians with roots in Islamic countries as both insiders and outsiders to the regional soundscape. I suggest that some forms of musical borrowing, insofar as they entail the coexistence of multiple and shifting differences, can undermine political boundaries in disputed territory. In particular, I argue that a rhizomatic rather than a hierarchical analysis provides a basis for understanding how music can deterritorialize political boundaries. The rhizome, a term Gilles Deleuze and Felix Guattari made famous, is an antigenealogy. Instead of charting linear influences or flows of information or chronologies, rhizomatic mappings are weblike, similar to sound waves, both permeable and immediate. The rhizome "operates by variation, expansion, conquest, capture, offshoots."[67] Mizraḥi performances create a tension among rhizomatic multiple coexisting inheritances, polarized identity-based territorial claims to ownership, and genealogical subversion when homage and ascription flow across enemy lines.[68]

In the process of shifting alliances that produce these multiple coexisting inheritances, musics are deterritorialized and reterritorialized. Cultural, political, and social alliances are reconfigured to match the new genres just as genres are reconfigured by new coalitions. Both the European-dominated national music that became the mainstream soundscape of Israel (*ha-Shir ha-Erets Yisre'eli,* the Song of the Land of Israel) and the marginalized and excluded music genres created by Mizraḥim involved appropriation and reappropriation. Both soundscapes can be described as pan-ethnic formations that borrowed melodies and visual aesthetics from local contexts in Russia, Poland, Czechoslovakia, Greece, Turkey, and Palestine, and reconfigured them in new communal contexts.

However, as I argue, the European appropriations and reconfigurations of East European melodies with Hebrew texts and appropriated local Palestinian or Yemenite motifs that were used to create a new national Israeli sound track (from the 1880s through the first decades of the founding of the country) are significantly different from Mizraḥi appropriations of Arab, Turkish, Greek, and Persian tunes with Hebrew or Judeo-Arab texts in the 1970s–1990s. The difference depends upon claims of inheritance and the power dynamics involved. In creating the dominant new Israeli national sound track out of reconstituted Russian folksongs, European Israelis drew on their East European musical inheritance to celebrate Jewish workers tilling on ancient Hebrew soil. They appropriated local Palestinian and Middle Eastern and North African Jewish musical traditions into European styles, rather than engaging in a reciprocal musical encounter that could have resulted in a musical remixing of previously distinct Jewish communities and a musical dialogue with local Palestinian artists. Under the circumstances in which Jewish communities were state builders and Palestinian communities resisted and were often displaced by the new state, such cooperation was especially fraught.

The genre of Mediterranean Israeli music rose out of the attempts of Middle Eastern and North African Jews in Israel to create a more inclusive sound track. While European Israeli formations of national music were based on asymmetric appropriation of Mediterranean sounds, Mizraḥi musicians engaged in reciprocal pan-ethnic appropriations that created this genre against the backdrop of their political struggle for equality. Mizraḥi Jews claimed an inheritance of Middle Eastern and North African music as an extension of their centuries-old local traditions. Developments of the genre rely on rhizomatic appropriations that cross or defy political and ethnic borders, and may open spaces for political challenges to these boundaries. These rhizomatic appropriations are significant precisely because of the way their routedness/rootedness reflects the situation of Mizraḥim, who were uprooted from Middle Eastern and North African communities and rerouted to a new local context that was at war with their former homelands.

Each appropriation, each rejection, and each newly emerged style can be and is read within an emerging system of cultural values. In Israel's new musical laboratory, in which claims to origins could carry as much weight (and baggage) as claims to originality, musical appropriations mapped the confluence of several disputed territories. The dispute played out between notions of West and East, Europeanizing and orientalizing appropriations, modernity, pre-modernity, and the ancient world, but the contest itself was about participation in the national sound track of Israel.[69] Claiming a stake in the sound track meant claiming a stake in the nation. Within this context, the creators of Mediterranean Israeli music freely employed Greek, Italian, San Remo, and *ha-Shir ha-Erets Yisre'eli,* Turkish, Judeo-Arabic, and Arabic styles. The trend in the 1990s toward re-Arabizing Mediterranean Israeli music can be seen as a consolidation, not only of the music genre but also of the political coalition of Israelis from North Africa and the Middle East. This musical shift away from Greek and *ha-Shir ha-Erets Yisre'eli* tunes was also a return to the traditions of grandparents and parents who had left their homes in North Africa and the Middle East in the late 1940s and early 1950s. This reclamation of ethnic and musical specificity, whether it be Arabic, Persian, Turkish, or Kurdish, refashioned the ingathering of the exiles not as a uniform, monovocal project but rather as a sound track resounding with the hundreds of ethnic and cultural groups who had never really left their cultural and aesthetic traditions at the door of the new country.

Chapter 2

Relocation and the Emergence of Ethnicities

And if the Jews really "returned home" one day they would discover on the next that they do not belong together. For centuries they have been rooted in diverse nationalisms; they differ from each other, group by group; the only thing they have in common is the pressure which holds them together.

—Theodore Herzl, quoted in Alex Bein, *Theodore Herzl: A Biography*

Herzl's prediction is strikingly fulfilled in the bewildered observation, so frequently heard in Israel as to be something of a cliché, which many an Israeli can be heard to voice. "When I was in Hungary (or wherever) I always regarded myself as a Jew. Now that I am in Israel I feel like a Hungarian or a Pole, or a German, or a Yemenite, or an Egyptian, etc., etc."

—Michael Selzer, *The Outcasts of Israel: Communal Tensions in the Jewish State*

Three generations of an Iraqi-Kurdish family gather around the television in their Jerusalem home in Katamon Vav to watch a homemade video filmed in Zakho, Kurdistan. Some of the characters in the movie are clad in traditional white robes, though the armed guides are dressed in khaki fatigues and running shoes. The silence is broken by the occasional commentary of one of the viewers, a middle-aged Kurdish Jewish man, who also appears throughout the film. He waves from a number of landmark sites that are recognizable to those assembled, recognizable from stories that have painted images of rivers, rugged hills, and ancestral dwellings that only forty years ago were inhabited by members of this very family of Israeli Jews. The video closes with a group of Kurdish Muslims seated in a circle in the living room of the family home, hosting the Kurdish Jewish visitor with food, drink, and stories. It is one family, cousins and siblings—reunited after decades of separation. The Muslim family members had remained in Zakho; the Jewish family members had left for Israel in 1951.

Back in Jerusalem as we watch the video, it is autumn 1992, and the youngest family members comment on how small the family house actually is compared to the stories of their lost heritage that have grown large and glorious in their minds. The room is filled with a mixture of nostalgic longing and simultaneous confusion at a palpable inheritance so out of reach. The story that is not told, at least while I am present, is the clandestine nature of this dangerous journey. Travel to Kurdistan was illegal, and their family member arranged to meet a guide in Turkey, where upon arrival he stowed his Western clothing and Israeli passport. As the video concludes, the atmosphere in the room is thick, a stillness syncopated with cracking sunflower seeds and clinking coffee cups.

Ethnic Consolidation and Counter-Longings

This story narrates the subversive counter-longings for and subsequent journeys by Mizraḥi Jews to their former homelands forty years after they departed for Israel. This trend to return to former communities, some of which became enemy territory, underscores what social geographer Marie Cieri calls irresolvable geographies, "geographies that are not reducible, cannot be fixed in uncontested, unalterable meanings."[1] What is irresolvable here is the geopolitical disjuncture that maps out internally—in the aching for Kurdistan, Libya, or Iraq—a longing experienced by some aging North African and Middle Eastern Israeli immigrants. In crossing this forbidden frontier in the 1990s, they secretly reclaim and inscribe memory, cultural legacy, and inheritance on video tape.

There is no contradiction between their bold journeys to particular homes in specific Muslim countries in the 1990s and their strong affiliation with the pan-ethnic Mizraḥi community of communities that developed in Israel since the 1950s. This new Mizraḥi-ness combined groups as disparate as the Ashkenazi community against which they found themselves defined in Israel. It was at once a response to rejection and an embrace of loosely configured geo-familiarity. Yet there is an elegaic quality to Mizraḥi-ness as if in contrast to the Euro-Israeli society that failed to incorporate them, they transcended and in some cases forfeited their own differences. Returning to Kurdistan in the 1990s is an example of specific ethnic attachment that occurred alongside pan-ethnic loyalty. Furthermore, these two seemingly opposite longings were not incompatible. Both the longing for a specific former house in a particular location, such as Kurdistan, Syria, Iraq, or Lebanon, and the belonging to an emergent community of communities in Israel are expressions of personal and political reclamation.

The consolidation of disenfranchised Libyan, Moroccan, Syrian, Yemenite, and other North African and Middle Eastern Israeli Jews into a pan-ethnic community did not erase their longings and loyalties for former homes. Acting on such memories by physically returning was delayed by decades of more urgent issues in Israel—the search for adequate housing, jobs, education, and communal structures consumed daily life. The stigma attached to such trips into enemy territory may also have contributed to the long delay.

The Kurdish parents and grandparents in the chapter's opening story took part in the mass immigration of hundreds of thousands of Jews who arrived in Israel from Europe, Asia, and Africa in the late 1940s through the mid-1950s. In Zionist discourse, the encounter is referred to as *Ḳibuts galuyot* (the ingathering of the exiles), the return of the Hebrew nation that dispersed after the final destruction of Jerusalem by the Romans in 70 CE.

The conditions that contributed to the creation of a pan-ethnic Mizraḥi community of communities began with the mass immigration of European, Middle Eastern, and North African Jews to the new Israeli nation from the late 1940s to the mid-1950s. The political asymmetries that privileged European-ness presented impediments to the Zionist ideal of a unified Jewish Israeli identity.

The asymmetries among immigrant Jewish communities were complicated by the presence of traumatized Palestinian Arabs who were experiencing defeat, displacement, and disinheritance within the new Israeli nation. Under peaceful conditions, the local Palestinian population would have offered incoming Middle Eastern and North African Jews (and been offered by them) a sense of cultural commonality and aesthetic familiarity. Instead, they were positioned by the unfolding geopolitical asymmetries as defeated enemies.

Of the many intra-Jewish Israeli asymmetries, inequities in housing were particularly consequential for the immigrant communities because they resulted in North African and Middle Eastern groups living in close proximity to each other and thus building affinities of all kinds, including musical. These affinities and their cultural and artistic by-products were the subject of critique and scholarly attention in the media and the academy. Commentary was both responsive to and formative in the creation of a new Mizraḥi pan-ethnic culture.

The emerging pan-ethnic music gives voice to the mutually contradictory cultural identifications evident in Selzer's quote in this chapter's epigram and in the Kurdish family's counter-longings for Zakho and Jerusalem. These counter-longings find easy proximity at Mizraḥi weddings where the diverse musical offerings signify not only the multiple identities of the newly conjoined families but also unleash historical forces, pent-up ethnicity, and musical talent. Mizraḥi weddings are central sites for the formulation not only of Mediterranean Israeli music but of Mizraḥi-ness itself. As discussed later in this chapter, this music's matrimonial origin myth is framed by the trauma of war. What follows is a brief overview of the dual and dueling scholarly approaches to the field of Mizraḥi studies by European Israelis and Mizraḥim.

We are not witnessing a simple trajectory from an old homeland to a new homeland, or from minority group to pan-ethnic coalition. As is evident from the multiple loyalties of the Kurdish family, the formation of Mizraḥi pan-ethnicity and pan-ethnic music is a complex tripartite geometry of longings: to be part of the new Israeli society, to sustain one's history and traditions, and to resist even subtle forms of discrimination.

Jewish Mass Migration to Israel and the Formation of Asymmetrical Ethnic Groups

The creation of the Israeli state in 1948 led to a dramatic increase in immigration from Europe, Asia, and Africa. Any discussion of Israeli absorption policies must first consider the enormity of the task that confronted the new nation. With the staggering influx of immigrants, the Jewish population of the state grew from 650,000 in 1948 to 1,484,000 in 1953. At the same time, the population of Palestinian Arabs in the region was 1,358,000 in 1948 and dropped to 1,170,000 in 1950.[2] This period witnessed not only an explosion in the number of Jewish inhabitants, but also an increase in the complexity of ethnic and ideological relationships.

Against the backdrop of recent independence, international censure, economic crisis, and a state of war, the new Jewish state, mainly comprising European Jews and remnants of disenfranchised Palestinian communities, absorbed over 700,000 immigrants, divided equally between Holocaust survivors and Jews from Muslim countries. The new immigrants arrived traumatized by Nazi genocide on the one hand and by dislocation and culture shock on the other. Few European, Middle Eastern, or North African newcomers possessed vernacular Hebrew language proficiency or agricultural skills that might have prepared them for life in the new country.[3]

The Israeli Declaration of Independence proclaimed that Israel would be devoted to Jewish immigration. The Law of Return (1951) formalized this principle; by 1952 it was expanded to include the right to automatic

Each wave of immigrants has brought its unique experiences, cultural background and talents to contribute to the mosaic of Israel's society, facing the challenges of the 21st century.

Years	Asia	Africa	Europe	America & Oceania	Total*
1948-1951	237,000	94,000	327,000	5,000	687,000
1952-1960	35,000	146,000	103,000	10,000	294,000
1961-1970	49,000	151,000	139,000	45,000	384,000
1971-1980	27,000	16,000	213,000	73,000	330,000
1981-1989	10,000	23,000	60,000	40,000	133,000
1990-1994	6,000	32,000	554,000	17,000	609,000
1995-1999	39,000	12,000	276,000	20,000	347,000
Total	403,000	474,000	1,672,000	210,000	2,784,000

* 1948-51 includes 24,000 immigrants whose last continent of residence is unknown; in later years it includes a small number of such immigrants.

Immigration to Israel from 1948 through 1999. (Israel Ministry of Foreign Affairs, "Aliya and Absorption," 29 October 2002, http://www.mfa.gov.il/MFA/History)

citizenship for all incoming Jews.[4] However, for the European Jews who had controlled the pre-state institutions, the mass immigration of North African and Middle Eastern Jews represented a mixed blessing. Some scholars claim that immigrant absorption policies, while intended to promote equality and integration, were also designed to prevent the "Orientalization" of the state[5] in which the Arab cultural practices of incoming Middle Eastern and North African Jews (as well as local Palestinian traditions) might dominate the European orientation of the pre-state Jewish population.

The Zionist project of return to Palestine had been underway in several mass immigration waves since the 1880s. This transformed the centuries-long existential longing for Jerusalem and the Land of Israel that had existed since the destruction of Jerusalem in 70 CE. The shift was in imagining an actual physical return to the geopolitical location of Jerusalem rather than maintaining the ethereal connection that was deeply embedded and performed in Jewish diasporic memory through poetry, prayer, and spatial/material artifacts such as the Mizraḥ, the adornment of the eastern wall of homes and synagogues to the west of Israel and Jerusalem to indicate the direction of prayer toward the holy land/city.[6] The fact that other peoples inhabited the actual urban site did not diminish the Jewish sense of Jerusalem as an empty, shattered space, and the destruction was commemorated annually through fasting and mourning on the ninth day of the Hebrew month of Av.

The term referring to modern immigration to Israel, *aliya,* going up, reflects not only the geographical ascent to the city but also a romantic impulse pointing to the celestial direction of the project.[7] Pre-state European Jewish immigrants to Palestine created the cultural and political structures that later became national institutions. The new Israeli nation became a location in which dozens of languages, foods, liturgical traditions, and music came into intensive contact in a compressed period of time and space and created unforeseen cultural and musical collisions and coalitions. Added to this were the vast differences in experience of European Holocaust survivors and Middle Eastern and North African Jews. Each group was asked to participate in a process of suspending their past in order to transform into a shared society.

This process of "negation of the diaspora"[8] involved deconstructing former group identities regarded as contrary to the project of consolidating a new national character. Such consolidation was envisioned as a process of dissolving discrete diasporic practices into a melting pot, *Mizug galuyot.* In this way, diaspora ethnicities would be eliminated or reformed as the meltdown cooled off into an emerging Jewish-Israeli national identity. Language, dress, and other customs that would differentiate among Jews in the public sphere were considered obstacles to be left at the gate or to be featured at circumscribed folkloric occasions.[9] In this cauldron some ethnicities would be more melted than others—so that the new Israel was still grounded in the European values and practices of its Ashkenazi designers, who comprised 85 percent of the Jewish population at the time of statehood.[10]

In practice, Ashkenazim could maintain their European identities (short of the Yiddish language and shtetl manners), but North African and Middle Eastern Jews were asked to suppress their culture while at the same time providing local flavor, tokens of food, dress, and music, thereby creating an indigenous link for a Middle Eastern nation conceived by European architects. Lebanese salad became Israeli salad, one example of the absorption of customs without differentiating among former group identities.

The Kurdish ensemble Sheva Aḥayot (Seven Sisters) demonstrates their repertoire for Smithsonian Folklife Festival researchers in anticipation of participating in the Jerusalem Program on the national mall in Washington, D.C., in 1993. (Courtesy Reuven Namdar)

National policies, educational curricula, and cultural and artistic values developed under the rubric of absorption—a term that theorized a stripping away of diaspora traditions in exchange for a new Israeli identity. The emerging culture did not discard immigrant traditions, however, but soaked them up, more actively admitting European traditions (whether consciously or not) because they were more familiar to the designers of the new culture. Yiddish and other markers of an Eastern European Jewish past may have been greeted with disdain, but the intolerance resembled the patronizing of an elder family member's antiquated ways.

In contrast, European Israelis' vehement rejection of Middle Eastern and North African Jewish traditions was profoundly nonfamilial. Despite the rejection, these enemy cultural markers were passively absorbed into the new Israeli milieu. Cultural and political architects of the new nation fought the intrusion of Arab music, manner, and mentality in the practices of either local Palestinian residents or incoming Arab Jews. Nonetheless, Jewish culture that had evolved for hundreds of years in Muslim lands survived in diminished and less visible forms. The lack of opportunities for becoming proficient in Arabic language, music, and philosophy created cultural poverty without erasing the culture itself.

The Israeli ethnic problem has been rooted in the establishment's attitudes toward new Middle Eastern and North African immigrants who, under the Law of Return, should have been accorded all the rights and privileges of citizens without discrimination.[11] However, practices such as medical checks focused on North African Jews. There were instances in the mid-1950s in which Moroccan Jews were denied entrance due to health problems, although similar restrictions were not placed on Holocaust survivors, many of whom arrived in desperate physical condition.[12] Poor North African and Middle Eastern communities benefited less from free transportation, choice housing, and other incentives used to attract potential Western immigrants with professional skills and capital. Discriminatory practices also surfaced in fields of education, military service, and employment. The next generation was channeled into inferior positions that reproduced the initial social inequality.[13]

Ma'abarot, Development Towns, and Neighborhoods

One of the most significant discrepancies between European, Middle Eastern and North African immigrant groups can be seen in housing policies. This act of discrimination inadvertently created the opportunity for the creation of a pan-ethnic subculture by placing North African and Middle Eastern families in close proximity. In these neighborhoods, they had the opportunity to forge a shared culture. The rise of impoverished North African and Middle Eastern urban neighborhoods and peripheral towns is particularly important for understanding the new musical form that emerged out of this new proximity.

Several emergency responses were developed to deal with the housing crisis precipitated by the population influx. *Ma'abarot* (transit camps) consisting of army tents and tin shacks were one solution: between 1952 and 1954 over 180,000 immigrants were housed in 123 such camps.[14] Another strategy was settling new immigrants in empty Arab houses and British army compounds.[15] Meanwhile, new agricultural settlements and development towns were established in remote locations, the latter in areas without any established industry.[16] However, since the government failed to channel sufficient economic, cultural, and other resources to these areas, hindering their development, the *ma'abarot* grew into densely populated, poor neighborhoods, and the development towns grew into overcrowded, poverty-stricken cities.[17]

The establishment of *ma'abarot* and development towns in remote geographical areas was an attempt to address not only the immediate housing crisis, but also national security priorities.[18] In 1948, much of the land that formed the new state was uninhabited, in part because Palestinian Arab communities had fled or been expelled. In the Negev desert and other sparsely populated Jewish settlement areas, national security was bolstered by massive North African and Middle Eastern population influxes.[19] While many Europeans also were settled in peripheral areas, Mizraḥim were settled in these areas in larger numbers. Many Middle Eastern and North African Jews who had been urban dwellers in their countries of origin were placed in remote agricultural settlements or newly established peripheral communities. Out of the 170 new rural settlements established by the late 1950s, 120 were populated by Middle Eastern and North African immigrants.[20] Between 1956 and 1958, 22.5 percent of Polish immigrants, as compared with only 8.5 percent of North African immigrants, were assigned to preferable areas along the coastal strip.[21]

Moreover, a policy based on equal housing for all incoming families failed to take into account the fertility differentials between Ashkenazi and Mizraḥi households. Mizraḥi families averaged between six and seven children, their Ashkenazi counterparts between two and three. While both Ashkenazi and Mizraḥi families were forced to share living quarters, often a tent or a one-room shack, with several other families, the comparative size of Mizraḥi families made these living conditions untenable. In many instances, the living conditions of Mizraḥi families had not improved by the 1970s. In fact, with the Mizraḥi population growth rate being three times that of their European Israeli counterparts, the conditions actually worsened.[22]

With Middle Eastern and North African immigrants pushed to the margins of society, the ideology of blending diasporic communities became, in essence, the ghettoization of the poorest. This ironic juxtaposition of the terms diaspora and ghetto into a "linked pair"[23] suggests that while the diasporic exile was eliminated, the ghetto was resituated as a new location inhabited by Middle Eastern and North African Israeli Jews. Despite impoverished conditions, this created intimate cultural and musical exchanges among Middle Eastern and North African Jews in contrast to superficial contact with European Israelis. Army service, which was seen as one arena for cross-ethnic interaction, actually consolidated ethnic differences through asymmetrical opportunities and positions.[24] While some elementary and secondary schools were integrated, the curriculum favored Ashkenazi-oriented material and, until the shifts of policy in the late 1970s, reinforced the gap between Ashkenazim and Mizraḥim. The seeds of an ethnic underclass took firm root and continued to develop.[25]

While Yemenite, Iraqi, and Sephardi communities that had existed in pre-state Palestine maintained communal frameworks and were better able to adapt by integrating new national concepts into a preexisting structure, recent North African and Middle Eastern immigrants in the *ma'abarot* experienced profound culture shock. Lacking their former communal structures, Middle Eastern and North African immigrants came to form a pan-ethnic or Mizraḥi subclass. Distinct localized traditions that had been maintained in the homes and neighborhoods began to merge and take priority over the Euro-centered Israeli culture that had failed to integrate its North African and Middle Eastern communities. For example, the predominant music transmitted in Israel at that time, in schools, at official occasions, on the radio, as well as throughout the *ma'abarot,* was the *ha-Shir ha-Erets Yisre'eli* (the Song of the Land of Israel), a repertoire created by European Jews consisting largely of Eastern European melodies and Hebrew lyrics unfamiliar to Jews from Yemen, Morocco, Syria, and elsewhere. In the neighborhoods that grew from the original *ma'abarot, ha-Shir ha-Erets Yisre'eli* shared space with Mediterranean, North African, and Middle Eastern musics and developed new shapes through intensive interaction. Neighborhood singers received early training by performing at life-cycle and seasonal occasions. They sang *ha-Shir ha-Erets Yisre'eli* songs they learned at school along with Arabic songs and Hebrew liturgy that they learned at home and in the synagogue. As Mediterranean Israeli musician Haim Moshe explains: "My voice I got from God, it's my inheritance from God. My knowledge of music came from the synagogue, family gatherings on holidays and festivals, and from Yemenite prayers. The whole family got together around the table and sang Sabbath songs, folksongs, lots of songs that don't go easily on the radio."[26]

With the development of Ḳol Yisrael (the Israeli national radio broadcasting network founded in 1948), the local recording industry, and national television, the gap between neighborhood traditions and national folk, popular, and art musics intensified, further institutionalizing the sense of separateness and isolation.

Peripheral placement, unequal educational opportunities, housing difficulties, inexperience with "European"-style bureaucracy, and overrepresentation at the lowest levels of the army and labor force, along with underrepresentation in the more affluent urban neighborhoods and white-collar professions, sharpened ethnic lines and distinctions between Israel's European and Mizraḥi populations. As early as 1955, a government resolution

LP covers such as this 1958 album by the Oranim Zabar Troupe with Geula Gil appropriated a European-constructed Middle Eastern imaginary. The song selections were primarily Eastern European melodies, familiar to the singers, refashioned with Hebrew lyrics, forming the repertoire of *ha-Shir ha-Erets Yisre'eli*. The Oranim Zabar Troupe was a well-known band, performing not only for soldiers in Israel but also in the United States and around the world. (Courtesy Elektra Records)

called for a review of the absorption process. The findings indicated that attempts to close cultural, economic, and social gaps had failed:

> This gap, which has created two societies, holds in it the seeds of destruction and danger. It is hazardous and must be filled. We must bring down the ethnic walls, cancel differences of origin, and make all the people of the nation partners in the values and culture of the new society that we aspire to shape in Israel.
>
> This will not be done in one day or one year, but we will not become one people and we will not attain a decent cultural level for all the country's residents if the government does not make every effort to raise, both spiritually and materially, those immigrants who are deprived of education. A mass, popular volunteer movement to include pioneer settlements, intellectuals, and educators must help these new immigrants. The government will make every effort to eliminate the *ma'abarot* and poor neighborhoods as quickly as

> possible, to give the young of these impoverished communities a professional, pioneering education, and to retrain as many of these immigrants as possible as agricultural and industrial workers. We will also establish scholarships for the gifted youth who aspire to a higher education.[27]

This 1955 resolution was not an isolated effort but rather part of a growing discourse among policy makers, intellectuals, journalists, poets, musicians, and scholars who reflected, challenged, justified, or sought to correct the growing ethnic divide. Within two decades, what had come to be known as "the mistakes of the '50s" became the critiques of the '70s, '80s, '90s, and on into the twenty-first century. Although today some Israelis claim that the ethnic problem has been resolved, through policy adjustments, increased radio time, or multi-ethnic marriages, inequities are not simply echoes from the past. The increased airplay of ethnic music does not necessarily indicate an elevated position for the music makers or the resolution of ethnic asymmetries in society.

(Pan-)Ethnicity in Column Inches and on the Airwaves

Public performances of Israel's ethnic struggles have been visible and audible in media representations over the last sixty years. Radio commentators, print journalists, and later, with the development of television in the 1960s, TV talk show hosts expressed a variety of attitudes, including fear of being overwhelmed by Middle Eastern and North African immigrants. As early as 1949, journalist Arye Gelblum expressed this position in *Haaretz,* a leading Hebrew daily:

> A serious and threatening question is posed by the immigration from North Africa. This is the immigration of a race the likes of which we have not yet known in this country. . . .
>
> They will "absorb" us and not we them. The special tragedy of this absorption is that there is no hope, even with regard to their children; to raise their general level out of the depths of their existence. This is a matter of generations.[28]

Discussing the period of mass immigration retrospectively, Michael Keren notes in the 1980s that the European leadership possessed an almost missionary zeal in relation to the new Middle Eastern arrivals. Quoting Minister of Education Ben-Zion Dinur, a scholar and author, Keren wrote:

"The new immigrant 'has not experienced our spiritual development which has brought about the building of the land of Israel.' Absorption means the process by which 'the newcomer changes in spirit and gradually begins to resemble the settlers, adopting their ways of reacting, thinking, relating to each other, dressing, and values.'"[29]

Keren focuses on the central role of intellectuals in the cultural transformation underway. Israel's first prime minister, David Ben-Gurion, called upon "acknowledged articulators of ideas based on established branches of scientific, artistic, and scholastic learning"[30] to define a cultural aesthetic that would link an emerging national identity to its ancient past and strip away the residue of the diaspora: "Our former habits of thought, our internal relations, the old manners and methods and measures, no longer apply. None is exempt, not civil servants, teachers, lawyers, physicians, army officers, engineers, men of science, literature, and the arts; least of all those animated by the pioneer spirit, whether they be pioneers of labor or of settlement, or of the realm of spirit itself."[31]

Some people warned of the dangers and possible failures of this absorption policy. Author Tom Segev notes that the head of the Jewish Agency's absorption department, Giora Yoseftal, realizing the failure in the program, stated, "We are ruining these people and making them degenerate . . . but there is nothing to do but quietly cry."[32] Rachel Shazar, an activist in the women's labor movement, called on Israeli writers "to abandon the mystical assumption that the newcomers constituted a different breed of human beings, and demand that they be given better housing, work, and education. All the rest would follow naturally."[33] Moshe Shamir, a writer and, in later years, a politician, cautioned that "the spirit of a nation cannot be planned, and there is no reason why those living in the land should determine the cultural patterns for all others."[34] Not the least of these cultural patterns was music. Notwithstanding attempts to promote the music of European Israelis, the emerging musical forms that were being created in the new Middle Eastern and North African neighborhoods could not be silenced.

The Emergence of Pan-Ethnicity

The 1967 Six Day War and the 1973 Yom Kippur War altered the balance of power within Israel in profound ways and became flashpoints for increased visibility of the ethnic struggles. Ilan Halevi, a French-born self-identified Palestinian Jewish writer and analyst of Middle East affairs, points out that "the acquisition of Arab territories in 1967 was the end of the geo-cultural isolation of Israel in the Arab world."[35] While the war appeared to be a victory for Israel, it presented a fundamental contradiction for a society that had fashioned its political philosophy on a supposedly egalitarian ideal. Ammiel Alcalay suggests that for Mizraḥi Jews the new proximity to Arab territories that resulted from Israeli occupation triggered illicit recollections, what Ella Shohat has called "taboo memories"[36] of ancestral homelands, emotions that had been sealed from consciousness as Mizraḥi Israelis assumed a new national identity at war with their past.[37] On a practical level, the acquisition of new territories created more job opportunities for Arabic speakers, who were needed to help administer the occupied territories. Some Mizraḥim spoke out against these seemingly elevated yet actually untenable new social positions as interlocutors between Israel and the occupied West Bank and Gaza Strip. Yemenite Israeli poet and feminist activist Bracha Seri composed this poem in the wake of the Six Day War:

> Jerusalem
> on high
>   and
>   Sa'ana [San'a']
>   down
>   below
> are one. One is my city.
> The same oneness / the same majesty . . . I longed
> to kiss "these strangers," "our enemies,"
> to whisper my thanks
> that they exist
> as in days gone
> by, never to
> return.[38]

Seri lays bare the counter-longings for an inaccessible past in San'a', Yemen, and for her sudden access to Arab inhabitants of a now occupied East Jerusalem. She embodies the conflict as an Arab, Jewish, Israeli Yemenite woman, and her poem foreshadows the actual return to cities of longing as described at the beginning of this chapter. Seri's poems, along with the writings of many other Mizraḥi poets, received well-deserved attention through Alcalay's groundbreaking English (and later Hebrew) studies of the poetry and cultural and political forces in the '70s, '80s, and '90s.

After the Yom Kippur War, the mainstream European power grip was shaken by an anti-Labor Party outcry issuing from Israel's underclass, now consolidated into a pan-ethnic Mizraḥi coalition. Since the Mizraḥi vote was vital to the Likud victory in 1977, it seemed that society was headed on a new course in which Mizraḥi voices would be reconfigured in the mainstream equation. Earlier protests, most notably the Wādī Salīb riots of 1959, had been waged primarily on economic grounds and stood as models for a reweaving of the very fabric of society. In fact, the Wādī Salīb demonstration had resulted from a "bar room brawl" among Moroccan residents, one of whom was shot by police while resisting arrest. The shooting and subsequent arrest unleashed pent-up frustrations and culminated in demonstrations, stone throwing, and car burnings, as well as thirty-two arrests.[39]

Viewed retrospectively, Wadi Salib is an early instance of what became a directed and broad-based Mizraḥi movement both in scope and in influence. In the early 1970s, Mizraḥi youth in the neighborhoods rose to challenge what were by then widely called "the mistakes of the '50s."[40] Mizraḥi social and cultural movements sprouted. The Black Panthers, born in a Moroccan Jerusalem neighborhood of Musrara, gave voice to issues of inequality in housing, employment, and education.[41] The "East For Peace" (*Mizraḥ la-shalom*) organization claimed that only Mizraḥim would succeed in making peace with the Arabs since they had hundreds of years of shared history together in the Middle East.[42] Mizraḥi political parties began to form.[43]

Drummer/composer Shlomo Bar formed a band called *ha-Bererah ha-ṭiv'it* (The Natural Choice) and claimed, through the pointed texts of poets such as Erez Bitton, that Mizraḥi communities experienced exploitation within Israeli society and that Israel would succeed only if it recognized that it was part of the Middle East and not an extension of Europe. Moroccan filmmaker Haim Shiran journeyed back to his hometown of Meknes to show Israeli society the richness of Jewish life in North Africa and to reclaim the historic roots of holiday traditions such as the *Mimouna,* which then took on a pan-ethnic scope in Israel.[44]

The Mediterranean Israeli Music Origin Story: "It Started at a Wedding"

Like the *Mimouna,* many local traditions were emerging among Mizraḥi neighbors as shared and transformed pan-ethnic celebrations in the 1970s and 1980s. Mizraḥi-ness itself was becoming a construct formed out of these new cultural intimacies.[45] Neighborhood weddings especially were sites for merging cultural traditions in which groups intermarried, new relationships were forged, and musicians learned each other's styles and repertories. Interethnic weddings constituted an actual merging of otherwise discrete groups into a pan-ethnic culture, not only for the specific families being joined but

Music performed at festivals and weddings helps to transform these events into sites of pan-ethnic consolidation and celebration. Ethnically specific soundscapes like the Kurdish zorna player at the *Mimouna* festival take on new significance in these multicultural contexts. *Mimouna,* once a Jewish Moroccan celebration at the end of Passover, has become a pan-ethnic Mizraḥi event in Israel.

also for the guests in attendance. Therefore it is not surprising that Meir Reuveni begins his genesis story of Mediterranean Israeli music with "it started at a wedding."[46]

Under normal circumstances Mizraḥi marriage ceremonies blend centuries-old traditions and contemporary Israeli rituals. But the wedding that is considered to have been the starting point for Mediterranean Israeli music was not a typical wedding. The henna parties and traditional songs that would have accompanied Asher Reuveni's wedding were muted in the wake of the Yom Kippur War. Asher, who was wounded during the war, joined his fiancée's family as they mourned the death of her only brother, who had been killed in Sinai. The traditional mourning period took place during the Sukkot festival, normally a festive period celebrating the ancient harvest and pilgrimage to Jerusalem. In 1973 Sukkot was a somber time, not only for the Reuvenis but for families throughout Israel.

Asher Reuveni's older brother, Meir, and their friends promised him that once the mourning period had passed, they would throw a wild *ḥafla* (Arabic for party) for his wedding. Daḳlon and Moshe Ben-Mosh, two popular Yemenite musicians from Kerem ha-Temanim, agreed to perform. They played music until the early morning hours. Reuveni and his brothers, owners of a record and electronics shop in the Yemenite neighborhood of Shekhunat ha-Tiḳvah in Tel Aviv, recorded it on one of their new portable cassette recorders. After the party, they duplicated the cassette to give as mementos to all the guests. The sound mix was poor but the tape was revolutionary. It acknowledged and validated the Mizraḥi wedding singer, a musician previously considered unworthy of representation or reproduction by the mainstream. As news of the tape spread throughout the neighborhood, there was a flood of requests for copies. When someone offered a hundred lirot (Israeli pounds, approximately equal to $17 US in 1974) for the tape, Meir Reuveni knew he was onto something: "This was '74, when a lira was a lira, and don't forget, it was a '*partisani*' recording, very makeshift. So I said, 'What's happening here? My friends don't know how to read notes but they play and sing '*ala-kefak*[47] because with them it comes straight from the heart. Let them enjoy! It's good to know that the music in this country runs according to our tap!'"[48]

Meir paused after these last thoughts and leaned back in his chair behind his executive desk in the Reuveni Brothers cassette company offices, a modest walk-up in the heart of the bustling outdoor marketplace in Shekhunat ha-Tiḳvah. The phones buzzed and musicians, agents, and publicists hurried to wrap up the business of the day before the start of *Yom ha-Zikaron* (Memorial Day). Outside, the market booths were adorned in blue and white plastic Israeli flags and banners, and somber *ha-Shir ha-Erets Yisre'eli* music wafted up through the crack in his office window, the European Israeli music emblematic of a holiday of mourning creating an ironic juxtaposition to our discussion of the origins of Mediterranean Israeli music.

In his account, Meir Reuveni couples the music's rawness with its sincerity—"straight from the heart." This sentiment would pervade Mediterranean Israeli music for the next decades as a source of simultaneous outsider critique and insider pride. The very grassroots feel that outsiders condemned was embraced by insiders as genuine. Reuveni's pride in seeing the music pour out of wedding halls and proliferate via cassette to millions of Mizraḥi households is clear. Interestingly, by juxtaposing the Arabic expression '*ala-kefak* with *partisani*, a Hebrew reference to Holocaust resistance fighters, he is anticipating a broader audience of European and Mizraḥi Israelis who recognize both terms and signaling the common grassroots heritage of both movements.

It is not surprising that the story itself is built around a wedding; neighborhood singers were mainly employed as wedding entertainers. Most of the singers, who were overwhelmingly Yemenites, gained proficiency in a broad repertoire in order to perform at the parties of different ethnic groups. Mirroring the polyglot culture of the neighborhoods, they learned Greek, Turkish, and Kurdish tunes and embedded them within rock 'n' roll, light Mediterranean and Spanish popular music such as Samba, and San Remo rearrangements. They sang Eastern European Jewish tunes like "Ḥanaleh hitbalbelah" (Little Hannah Got Confused) but with Yemenite vocalization and a Mediterranean twist.[49] And as they shifted between Turkish, Kurdish, Greek, and Yiddish, the Yemenite vocal style remained at the center of the sound weave. Members of the Yemenite band Tselile ha-Kerem (Tunes of the Vineyard) point out that economics catalyzed the growth of the network beyond the summer wedding season. In the off-season, singers began to find work in the nightclub circuit. Despite increased media coverage and sporadic nightclub appearances, however, the music remained a neighborhood phenomenon that did not really threaten the status quo until the rise of Zohar Argov.[50]

Whether or not Mediterranean Israeli music began at a wedding in a Yemenite neighborhood in the turmoil following the 1973 war is not the crucial point. As with all origin stories, this tale represents a deeper set of contested issues. What is at stake in narrating this wedding tale is not only the increased audibility of a music genre but the struggle of half the Jewish Israeli population for recognition.

Politics and Aesthetics in the Media

With their homemade cassettes, the Reuveni brothers produced and distributed music that had previously been available only at live neighborhood performances, and thus were able to sidestep the state-controlled radio programs and other mainstream music industry channels. The dominant players in the music business rejected their raw combination of Middle Eastern and Mediterranean influences with Western pop music and regarded the proliferation of these cassettes as a form of aesthetic pollution. As discussed in chapter 1, the cassette production was part of a larger concern about the increasing visibility and audibility of the emerging Mizraḥi culture.

One crucial television program, often painfully remembered as an early example of negative Ashkenazi attitudes toward Mizraḥi-ness and the de-

On this double cassette release from 1983, a nine-minute-and-seventeen-second rendition of "Ḥanaleh hitbalbelah" is the third cut, sharing space with Natan Alterman and Avihu Medina lyrics, as well as Turkish and unspecified folk tunes. "Ḥanaleh hitbalbelah" is categorized as Ḥasidic folk and arranged by Yigal Harad. Moshe Ben-Mosh and Daḳlon are featured on the cassette cover. (Reuveni Brothers, courtesy Meir Reuveni)

velopment of Mediterranean Israeli music, was an interview with Mizraḥi singer Nissim Saroussi in 1978, in which the interviewer, Yaron London, belittled Saroussi before a live audience. In the 1990s, when I asked to view this segment, an Israel television archivist told me that this particular show had been lost or recorded over. The humiliation of this interview, which Mizraḥi community members still remember years later, was a contributing factor in Saroussi's decision to leave Israel for the more receptive Parisian Israeli music scene. In 1995, I interviewed Saroussi in Paris and discussed with him his decision to leave Israel. As we sat in a bustling French café, Saroussi downplayed the infamous television incident, though he was not at all surprised to learn that the television archivist had misplaced all traces of the interview. In hindsight, Saroussi thinks London's personalized attack on him backfired; he believes that London suffered more (he subsequently apologized) and that such public displays led to the consolidation of Mediterranean Israeli music and Mizraḥi identity.

In the media, politics and aesthetics merged in important ways. The media's response to the increasing visibility of Mizraḥim as a pan-ethnic

Saroussi's CD cover inscribes his black-and-white image in the foreground of a panoramic color relief of Jerusalem, including an ancient Jewish cemetery, the Old City walls, and, in the center, Jerusalem's most contested sacred site, *Haram al Sharif* or *Har ha-Bayit*. For Saroussi, now an émigré in Paris, Jerusalem's symbolic power looms large. (Courtesy Nissim Saroussi—Nes Music)

force with political teeth in the late 1970s and 1980s, when the London-Saroussi interview took place, was often antagonistic, dismissive, or trivializing. Mizraḥi pan-ethnicity challenged not only the media discourse but also scholarly discourse, where the models of immigration and absorption were insufficient to explain the multiple connections, affiliations, and loyalties of people for whom migration was neither unidirectional nor a matter of assimilation.

Shifting Perspectives in Mizraḥi Studies

The tension between tradition and transformation, rooted in a desire to understand the connections between modern Jewish traditions and ancient historical origins, informed much of Jewish musicological scholarship during the first half of the twentieth century. A. Z. Idelsohn, the founder of modern Jewish musicology, undertook a monumental research project, resulting in a ten-volume collection of the Jewish liturgical practices of Middle Eastern, North African, and European communities. Robert Lachman built upon Idelsohn's exhaustive collection by focusing on the traditions of a particular Jewish community, Djerba, Tunisia.

With the founding of the state of Israel, documentation efforts took on an accelerated pace as dozens of Jewish ethnic groups arrived in the new nation. These projects not only acknowledged but also valorized the discrete cultural contributions of the many immigrant communities. Folklorists and ethnomusicologists with preservationist agendas sought to document traditions before they were transformed in the new Israeli context. Ironically, at a time when ethnic specificity was disparaged in favor of the new Israeli identity under formation, these preservationist efforts aimed at documenting the traditions that policy makers presumed would soon disappear from the cultural landscape. Musicologist Edith Gershon-Kiwi notes:

> The mass immigration into Israel, especially from Afro-Asian countries, helped [us] to discover and closely to analyze half-forgotten Jewish tribes in their musical customs. To preserve the unwritten song of dozens of oriental communities, and to trace the musical interrelations with the musical traditions of their guest-countries, was the demand of an historic hour which in its many-coloured array of folk-styles would never repeat itself.[51]

As early as S. N. Eisenstadt's foundational work in the 1950s, scholars recognized the difficulty of absorption policies that imposed particular, in this case European, cultural values on a diverse population of immigrants. The tension between the creation of a unified culture and recognition of multiple cultural traditions persisted, but this was not the only tension. Eisenstadt questioned whether or not particular groups were predisposed to change. Later scholars recognized that even when immigrant groups were predisposed toward change and in fact desired to be integrated into the mainstream Israeli culture, there were many obstacles.

By the 1970s Israeli scholars were beginning to critically assess the impact of immigration and absorption policies in light of the emerging Mizraḥi activism. Academic articles about the Black Panthers, a grassroots Mizraḥi protest movement, coincided with news items covering the group in Israeli daily papers.[52] Studies on Mizraḥi ethnic unrest, including a number of English-language monographs, considered Israel's ethnic problem an outgrowth of the insoluble dilemma encountered by the architects of the new state who were faced with the absorption of vast numbers of Jewish communities into Israel in the 1940s and 1950s.[53] This dominant narrative contends that the overwhelming task strained the limited resources of the pre-state leadership and that the mistakes of the 1950s were honest and innocent ones made by well-intentioned architects of a newly formed and besieged country.

Works on ethnicity in the 1980s continued largely within this centrist framework. Scholars produced monographs focused on individual ethnic groups as well as edited volumes that covered a broader scope. The studies included the newest wave of immigrants from Ethiopia.[54] But the 1980s also began to see a transformation in the identity of the researchers themselves. In addition to the previously Ashkenazi-dominated scholarship, some Mizraḥi scholars became more widely known, including ethnomusicologists Avraham Amzallag (Moroccan), Amnon Shiloah (Syrian Argentinean), and Edwin Seroussi (Moroccan Uruguayan), and sociologist Sammy Smooha (Moroccan).

In the late 1980s and 1990s critiques intensified and deepened, testing the very fabric of Israeliness. New Historians (Benny Morris, Tom Segev), New Sociologists (Uri Ram, Oren Yiftachel, Sami Shalom Chetrit), Post-Zionists (Ilan Pappé, Ella Shohat), and Radical Feminists (Henrietta Dahan-Kalev, Pnina Motzafi-Haller) represented sometimes intersecting, sometimes diverging perspectives, challenging the dominant narrative that had sustained a vision of Zionist pioneers whose dream fell victim to unforeseen circumstances beyond their control.[55] The new works confronted many of the premises of Israel's founding and included an intensified focus on the Palestinian-Israeli conflict. These studies forged a new understanding of the inequities experienced by Mizraḥim in light of Palestinian discrimination and the broader geopolitical conflict. The increasing recognition of Mizraḥi inequities in Israel and the increasing visibility of their cultural and artistic contributions opened new questions that more deeply challenged the master narrative of immigration and absorption.[56]

Among their critiques was a discussion of the impetus for the Middle Eastern and North African immigration. Ella Shohat and Yehuda Shenhav argued that Mizraḥim were encouraged and even coerced into coming to Israel to fill the state's need for workers and to populate the peripheral areas for security reasons based on Palestinian, Syrian, Jordanian, and Egyptian threats.[57] They portrayed the Ashkenazi establishment as pragmatic and calculated in its motivations to populate the new nation, especially in the wake of the loss of European Jewry.

One early work focusing on Mizraḥi discrimination was Ella Shohat's groundbreaking book *Israeli Cinema: East/West and the Politics of Representation,*[58] a searing critique of representations of Mizraḥim in Israeli film. Following the publication of her book in Hebrew (like many critiques of Israeli ethnicity, the book had first appeared in English), she was interviewed on primetime Israeli television by Gaby Gazit in early 1992. In the interview, Gazit challenged Shohat's claim of racism (Shohat used the term *giz'anut,* meaning racism, rather than *haflayah,* or discrimination) against Mizraḥim. He turned to the audience, some of whom were Mizraḥim, and asked: "Do you think the Ashkenazim are trying to screw you?" To his surprise, the audience shouted back: "Yes, yes." (The moment is captured in the Swiss documentary film *Forget Baghdad.*)[59] Antagonism toward Shohat's work intensified thereafter because of her bold charge of European Israeli racism, coupled with her close affiliations with Palestinian intellectuals, most significantly Edward Said. In order to be able to do the doctoral work on which her book would be based, Shohat left Israel to study in the United States, ironically anticipating the very racism she encountered in response to it. She was a forerunner of a growing global cadre of Mizraḥi Jews who embraced the term "Arab Jew" and who considered themselves, along with Palestinians, to be victims of Zionist policies.

Israel's ethnic issues, replete with homegrown cultural and artistic forms, inhabited an expanding public arena populated by a new generation of Mizraḥi scholars armed with graduate degrees, who challenged mainstream approaches to history, sociology, political science, economics, anthropology, and literature. Mizraḥi voices were heard not only as activists or news items but as intellectuals who reflected on their experiences, and those of their parents and grandparents, through the lens of academic training. The Mizraḥi critique was a significant development in the emerging challenge to earlier approaches to Israeli history, sociology, and ethnic studies.

Sociologist Uri Ram suggests that the trajectory of Israel's ethnic studies across disciplines is constituted by two distinct approaches, a mainstream/dominant approach and radical critiques of the mainstream from outside the dominant discourse.[60] In hindsight, it is not surprising that self-determined Mizraḥi scholars and activists challenged the contours of the internal critique of Zionist history, social and cultural policies, and ethnic discrimination in the 1990s. It was during the early 1990s that the first Intifada gave way to a hopeful (albeit fleeting) period in the Palestinian–Israeli conflict. With increasing prospects for peace came a willingness to face issues that had been relegated to the periphery and to enter into dialogue with the critical work of Palestinian and Arab scholars. In 1999, the Van Leer Institute sponsored an academic conference on Mizraḥim from which an important Hebrew-language edited volume emerged.[61]

Recognition of Mediterranean Israeli music occurred in popular discourse along with the emerging debates about ethnicity in Israel. In the early 1990s, a Yemenite sociology student, Yehuda Cohen, drew on this new scholarship in order to assist the newly established Association of Mediterranean Song (AZIT, *Amutat zemer Yam Tikhoni*). The data he helped to collect culminated in a Knesset investigation of deprivation and misconduct on the part of the Israel national radio network, Ḳol Yisrael.[62]

Scholarship on Mediterranean Israeli music emerged hand in hand with popular efforts to gain air time and debates among music critics and musicians in the media. A new generation of folklorists and ethnomusicologists found themselves immersed in communities struggling for recognition. Inevitably, questions of genre, performance, and style led to a reexamination and reconsideration of issues about tradition, transformation, and appropriation.

Coexisting Repertoires of Identity

Music becomes a way of commenting on identity, especially in disputed contexts, and politics creeps into musical reviews in the form of seemingly innocuous labeling, more overt sarcastic classifications, and metaphors. Mediterranean Israeli music is always already politicized, and, not surprisingly, the media was a significant forum for the intertwining of aesthetics, ethnicity, and politics. Musicians and music critics both voiced opinions, but the conversation was rarely restricted to music itself. Because of the centrality of newspapers and television in Israeli society and their role as both creator and presenter, the mainstream media have helped shape how the Israeli public received, perceived, and evaluated Mediterranean Israeli music.

Pan-ethnicity is created through multiple modalities in a mediated response to disenfranchisement. From the home video documenting a family reunion in Kurdistan to the fight for increased representation of music genres in newspaper columns, on the radio, and on television, reenfranchisement (to coin a term) is partly about visibility and audibility. Attempts to silence Mizraḥi voices, whether in the music industry or in the academy, were met with persistent opposition. Ironically, Middle Eastern and North African

Jews wanted to be part of mainstream Israeli culture; it was exclusions on all fronts that helped to consolidate pan-ethnicity.

This brief summary provides a context through which to understand the conditions in which Mediterranean Israeli music emerged as a pan-ethnic form. It is not a simple story of disenfranchised groups finding each other and sharing cultural elements. On the contrary, as we will see in discussion of the various forms the music took, the musicians saw themselves as performing Israeliness.[63] Disenfranchisment, such as exclusion from the radio or slurs on television shows and in newspaper columns, did not prevent Mizraḥi performers from attempting to nurture a music that would be recognized as Israeli. As Nissim Saroussi pointed out, this may have contributed to the tenacity of the effort.

The formation of Mediterranean Israeli music as a pan-ethnic genre must be understood as occurring at the site of many seemingly conflicting positions. The Kurdish family we met at the beginning of this chapter saw themselves as Kurdish and longed for Zakho even as they participated fully in pan-ethnic Israeli culture in the Katamon Vav neighborhood. This continuum of affiliations maps on to coexisting repertoires of identity.

Chapter 3

The Mediterranean Israeli Music Phenomenon

> For those of us who straddle, there is a third place we go and in that place, the rules and the structures of both cultures are suspended. We negotiate a new system. It is a hybrid system. So we don't move totally from one place to the other place, but we construct a new network of rules, regulations, and standards that are a shifting blend. We walk inside of that network for the rest of our lives, if we stay sane.
>
> —Bernice Johnson Reagon, "'Nobody Knows the Trouble I See,' or 'By and By I'm Gonna Lay Down My Heavy Load'"

From the great historical movements that create the conditions for the emergence of Mediterranean Israeli music, I turn to the intimate local configurations individual singers unfold in particular pieces at particular moments. Here political forces become personal choices; aesthetic traditions become individual styles. The shift in scale is at once, musical, aesthetic, social, political and personal.

In 1992, one of the leading practitioners of Mediterranean Israeli music, Avihu Medina, divided the music into four categories:

A) *Musiḳah asli meḳorit*[1]
(real roots, the real thing),
B) *Musiḳah 'im gavan Yam Tikhoni*
(music with a Mediterranean coloring)
C) *Musiḳah 'im gavan Yam Tikhoni meḳori*
(music with original Mediterranean coloring)

D) *Musikah masortit 'im gavan Yam Tikhoni*
(traditional religious music with Mediterranean coloring)

Medina was hesitant about sharing this typology with me, not because he lacked knowledge of the music but because he was unsure how to create categories that would be understandable to an outsider researcher. To him, this repertoire drawn from diverse social contexts is seamless, but the exercise helped me understand his typology as a cultural map that accounted for more than musical styles.

Music never really fits neatly into the typologies that scholars or practitioners create. It slips over their edges, blurs their boundaries, and escapes categorization. While acknowledging music's uncontainability, I noticed that in Medina's typology, repertoire tended to cluster around what I will call nodes. I hear his categories as overlapping repertoire clusters on a cultural map rather than as distinct categories of music.

The clusters take account not only of musical styles, but also of the cultural positioning of the music, from the melodic lines performers sing, through market niches cassette sellers carve out, to critical assessments. The clusters form rhizomatic nodes of differentiation and modes of connection.[2] The singers, songs, and musical scores can all be mapped onto this system. A singer may incorporate several styles on an individual cassette, produce a number of cassettes featuring differing styles, or consistently focus on one style across his or her repertoire. Descriptive features like style, language, or cultural origin can be used to classify any item in a singer's repertoire, any cassette, the repertoire as a whole, the repertoire of groups of singers, and the Mediterranean Israeli repertoire itself according to which features it shares with other songs, cassettes, repertoires, groups, and traditions.

When musicians, impresarios, and audience members used Medina's stylistic designations in conversations, the categories appeared to be stable but at the same time resisted being pinned down. They are in fact what Bernice Johnson Reagon calls "shifting blends."[3] My goal here is to demonstrate the mutability, elusiveness, and uncontainability of the terms rather than to force songs and performances into inevitably inaccurate classifications. To this end, I focus on how musicians straddle categories and how their straddling has been received.

A) Musikah asli mekorit (the real thing) refers to the uninterrupted traditional repertoire. When performed by contemporary musicians, it evokes nostalgia.[4] The following differentiations in the repertoire are based on my conversations with Medina:

1. Yemenite *diwan:* texts by Rabbi Shalom Shabazi with traditional Jewish or borrowed Yemenite Muslim melodies that are performed in a sacred context.
2. Yemenite Hebrew or Arabic texts with borrowed Yemenite Muslim or traditional Jewish melodies performed in a secular context.
3. Sephardi and Mizraḥi *Piyyutim*[5] (non-Yemenite) with traditional Jewish or borrowed Arabic, Kurdish, or North African Muslim melodies performed in a sacred context.
4. Middle Eastern or North African folk texts with Jewish or Arabic melodies.[6] These may be folk or popular songs from various Middle Eastern or North African countries such as Turkey, Egypt, Lebanon, and Syria, where Jewish communities existed for hundreds or thousands of years. They are sung in Arabic dialects, Kurdish, Aramaic, Turkish, Persian, Hebrew, or a combination of languages.

B) Musiḳah 'im gaṿan Yam Tikhoni (music with a Mediterranean coloring) is characterized by its Mediterranean regional aesthetics:

1. Greek, Italian, and Spanish songs with reconstituted Hebrew lyrics. These may either be linked to the original lyrics or completely unrelated. They may concern love, topical, or nationalistic subjects. The Hebrew employed is often a combination of archaic literary and contemporary street styles. The songs may occasionally be sung in the original language. The tunes are preexisting popular or folksongs.
2. Mizraḥi adaptations of *ha-Shir ha-Erets Yisre'eli* songs, with their original Russian or Eastern European melodies or songs influenced by this style. To this is added Yemenite melisma and regional musical elements including Mediterranean, Middle Eastern, or North African tunes.[7]

C) *Musiḳah 'im gaṿan Yam Tikhoni meḳori* (music with original Mediterranean color) combines national and regional identity. Here, *meḳori* refers to songs that are considered to be Israeli originals but have a Mediterranean style. Topical and nationalistic themes are common as well as themes of love, all composed in a style that often features a combination of archaic literary and contemporary street Hebrew. The melodies include elements of rock 'n' roll and reflect Mediterranean and Arabic sources. Sometimes one of the musical styles, usually Mediterranean or Middle Eastern, predominates; on rare occasions, Western, Yemenite, or other Mizraḥi vocal signatures are key identity markers.[8]

D) Musiḳah masortit 'im gaṿan Yam Tikhoni (traditional music with Mediterranean color) incorporates religious elements into the *Musiḳah 'im gaṿan Yam Tikhoni* subgenre. The tunes are locally composed in a Mediterranean style: new compositions with religious themes derived from biblical, talmudic, or midrashic sources. These may be either direct quotations or reconstructions of texts.[9]

The characteristics that distinguish the subgenres described above are neither consistent nor stable. For example, the division between secular and sacred repertoire does not result in clear categories in terms of performance context or stylistic features. Instead, Medina and I constructed these repertoire clusters together in order to find a common language. The clusters were useful to him as a means to clarify the complex influences that make up his music and that of other Mizraḥi artists without pigeonholing them at the same time. As Dan Ben-Amos has noted, scholars sometimes miss what categories actually mean for their users, and how they work in practice where blurred boundaries may not matter.[10] The repertoire clusters, built out of Medina's classification system, make allowances for the way categories often become blurry where they overlap with other categories.

Medina's categories are based on continua of religiosity, place, and historical time. It is, for example, the continuity of a Yemenite *paytan* from the seventeenth century to the present that grants Shalom Shabazi's poetry its *asli,* or "real thing," status. It is important to Medina to distinguish between a tune borrowed from what he associates with Mediterranean communal aesthetics and one borrowed from a specific religious source. Medina's stylistic designations are not only about place and origins; but also about seemingly unlikely juxtapositions and how they come to make sense and sound. The categories are neither discrete nor exhaustive. They provide a way to map out affinities and differences within Israeli Mediterranean music.

Asli Meḳorit Straddlers: Zion Golan and Moshe Gi'at

Mediterranean Israeli music singers found innovative ways to combine various styles. Religious singers, often but not exclusively Yemenite men like Zion Golan and Moshe Gi'at, who would be considered *Musiḳah asli meḳorit,* drew upon popular Arab melodies to accompany sacred Jewish texts and prayers.[11] The cassettes discussed below combine liturgical texts from the medieval Yemenite poet Shalom Shabazi with contemporary religious poetry written by observant community members. The tunes range from *'amami* (folk or traditional) to tunes attributed to Egyptian musician Farid el Atrash.

The cassette covers on page 64 signal Golan and Gi'at's religiously observant identity. Golan appears in modest, formal dress, and the outline of his white *kippah* (men's religious head covering) is clearly evident against his dark hair. The title of the cassette itself, *Yemenite Hits,* in combination with Golan's visible *kippah*, marks the recording as ethnically specific and religiously focused in the context of Israeli society where most Yemenite Jews observe a *masorti* (traditional), if not Orthodox religious lifestyle. Similarly, Moshe Gi'at's recording contains liturgical texts, which are both traditional and temporally distant, in combination with contemporary compositions. The tunes blend Farīd al-Atrāsh with Gi'at's own compositions. Gi'at's cassette cover also signals religious observance and Yemenite ethnicity. He appears in a simple white Yemenite shirt holding a traditional Sabbath wine cup that is being filled by another man only partially visible on the cover. By quoting a line from the biblical text of Song of Songs, the title of the cassette, *Hashḳini yayin* (Pour me wine), ensures that the consumer understands that in this case drinking is within the ritual context. Performers of *Musiḳah asli meḳorit* appeared primarily at community events and religious occasions, although some also appeared on religious programming on Israeli Television. They saw no contradiction between their adherence to religious repertoires and the incorporation of the secular influences that kept them innovative.

The signifiers of *asli meḳorit* are both visual (the wine cup and *kippah*) and audible (the juxtaposition of Yemenite sacred texts with a wide range of traditional and contemporary tunes). What makes these songs *asli meḳorit* is the adherence to sacred text and recognizably Middle Eastern tunes combined with a Yemenite vocal style.

Particularizing the Muddle and Traversing the Clusters: Daḳlon, Tselile ha-Kerem

The migrations from disparate homelands resulted in a "muddle" of cultural recombinations. As Medina noted in one of our conversations in 1992, "It has been many years since Israelis left our Eastern or Western homelands. We have mixed together into one single, enormous muddle."[12] Yosef Levy (known as Daḳlon) exemplifies the traversing of musical styles.

In contrast to Zion Golan and Moshe Gi'at, who perform within a religiously circumscribed context, Daḳlon moves strategically among repertoire clusters and often releases seemingly counterposed cassettes simultaneously. An originator of the Mediterranean Israeli music style, he was born in the early 1940s and began his career singing religious Yemenite repertoire. Daḳlon grew up in Kerem ha-Temanim (the Yemenite Vineyard), a south

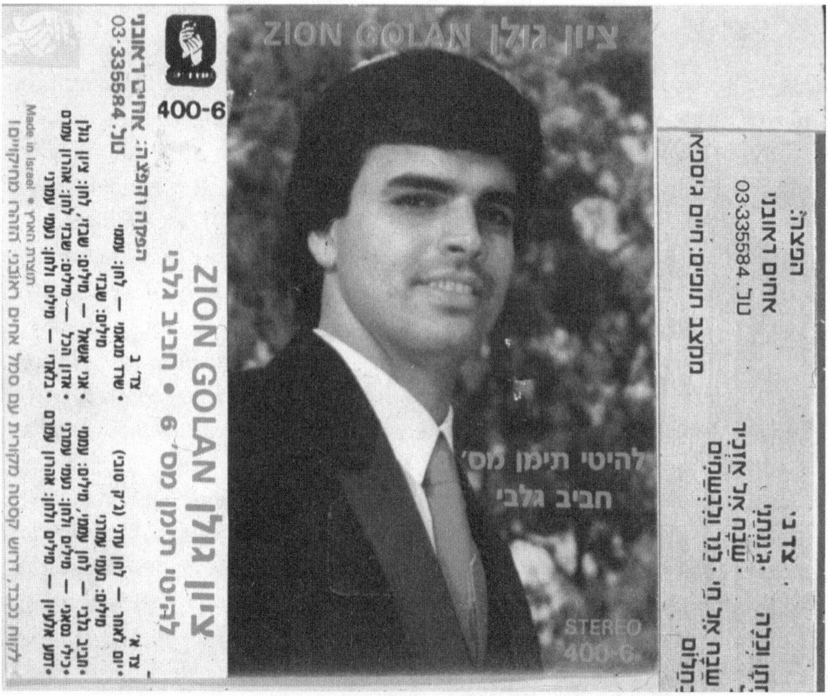

Zion Golan (*top*) and Moshe Gi'at (*bottom*) illustrate Avihu Medina's *Asli meḳorit* (the real thing) category. (Reuveni Brothers, courtesy Meir Reuveni)

Tel Aviv neighborhood founded by Yemenite immigrants in 1903. It was a tightly knit community that effectively withstood much of the ethnic upheaval that accompanied the founding of the state, and it holds a very special place in Yemenite and pan-ethnic Mizraḥi identity. As invitations to perform at Mizraḥi weddings increased, Daḳlon expanded this repertoire to include other styles. By the 1970s his band, Tselile ha-Kerem (Sounds of the Vineyard), performed *Musiḳah 'im gaṿan Yam Tikhoni, Musiḳah 'im gaṿan Yam Tikhoni meḳori,* and even Ḥasidic music and Western rock 'n' roll. The name of the band reflects their strong pride in their neighborhood and the multiplicity of tunes found there. For example, *Shoshanat Teman* contains three items from the *diwan* of Shalom Shabazi, two Yemenite traditional selections, and five *gaṿan Yam Tikhoni* selections, while *Daḳmosh* (a Daḳlon–Moshe Ben-Mosh duo) includes four *asli meḳorit,* five *gaṿan Yam Tikhoni* and one *ha-Shir ha-Erets Yisre'eli* selection.[13]

In the 1980s Daḳlon launched a solo career. He sought currency among mainstream Ashkenazi listeners by expanding his *ha-Shir ha-Erets Yisre'eli* repertoire. His recording *Mesibah im Daḳlon le-khol ha-ḥaverim* (Party with Daḳlon for all the friends),[14] which consists almost entirely of the *ha-Shir ha-Erets Yisre'eli* repertoire, uses the Hebrew title *Mesibah* rather than the Mizraḥi/Arabic slang term *Ḥafla;*[15] a subsequent recording by Daḳlon, featuring *meḳori* compositions by Avihu Medina, is called *Ḥafla 'im Daḳlon: Ahuvat levavi* (Party with Daḳlon: My beloved).[16] Though both tapes were produced in the 1980s, the cleavage between the Hebrew and Arabic terms directed them to different sectors of the marketplace.

This heterogeneous pair of recordings exemplifies the dilemma that singers like Daḳlon faced. On the one hand, they were committed to serving their own communities, whose musical preference was for *asli meḳorit* and *gaṿan Yam Tikhoni/meḳori* styles. On the other hand, they believed that in order to enter the mainstream European Israeli market, they had to demonstrate fluency in a larger range of styles beyond pan-Mizraḥi repertoire, especially rock 'n' roll and *ha-Shir ha-Erets Yisre'eli.* They did not regard this move as a shift of loyalties, but as an expansion that did not require them to choose one style or aesthetic over another.

About half of Daḳlon's repertoire was *ha-Shir ha-Erets Yisre'eli,* around a quarter was *asli meḳorit,* and the remaining quarter was *gav.an Yam Tikhoni.* Another recording, *Ḥafla 'im Daḳlon le-khol ha-ḥaverim* (Party with Daḳlon for all the friends) contains twenty-four songs: two Yemenite/*asli meḳorit,* sixteen *Musiḳah 'im gaṿan Yam Tikhoni/meḳori,* and six *ha-Shir ha-Erets Yisre'eli.*[17] *Ḳol ḳore li ba-midbar* (A Voice Calls Me in the Desert) contains nine songs: three Yemenite/*asli meḳorit,* three Mizraḥi, and three *ha-Shir ha-Erets*

Yisre'eli.[18] *Zemer be-mish'ole ha-arets* (Song in the Land's Paths)[19] is a title that, like *Ḳol ḳore li ba-midbar*, invokes a nostalgic and patriotic mood. *Zemer be-mish'ole ha-arets* features compositions by the Hebrew poet Rachel, the seventeenth-century Yemenite poet Shalom Shabazi, compositions by Avihu Medina, a Hebrew translation of a traditional Yiddish song set to music by Naomi Shemer,[20] *piyyutim,* and a well-known *ha-Shir ha-Erets Yisre'eli* lullaby.

Mizraḥi singers shared three apparently contradictory impulses: (1) to demonstrate competence in an ethnically specific repertoire (i.e., Kurdish or Moroccan), (2) to celebrate the emerging pan-ethnic Mizraḥi soundscape, and (3) to participate fully in the official European Israeli soundscape of the state (*ha-Shir ha-Erets Yisre'eli*) by Mizraḥifying canonic national songs. Daḳlon's tapes demonstrate how he straddled these impulses.

For European Israeli critics, the first two aesthetic impulses registered as abrasive. The third impulse, the Mizraḥification of canonic European Israeli repertoire, violated the sonic memory of those Israelis who held the original songs dear. The emerging Mizraḥi music did not register with European Israeli communities as part of their national, emotionally familiar sound. The Mizraḥi sound was present and, for Mizraḥim, emotional, but it was excluded from the official recognized soundscape of the state.

Daḳlon's response to emotional and economic marginalization was to straddle different genres, to find strength in a balancing act that creates a third place in which "shifting blends," as noted by Reagon, are acknowledged as the norm. Reagon points out that this third place is not a temporary safety zone but a new and permanent network. Daḳlon's range of repertoire and the graphic choices on his cassette covers illustrate his competence in the hybrid third place so central in Reagon's model of straddling. He negotiates the various elements that signify ethnicity, Arabness, Israeliness, and traditional religious and working-class identity. For Daḳlon and other Mizraḥi singers, straddling creates multiple meanings and positions. This third space created through straddling is dialogic and does not relinquish a hold on any of the component identities. This refusal to surrender constituencies creates the sturdiness of the hybrid.

In contrast to Medina's notion of the enormous muddle, the hybrid process of straddling does not obscure these components; rather, it affords the musician the possibility of being Arab and Israeli and traditional and contemporary simultaneously. The very act of straddling necessitates precarious balancing and flexible stability. Reagon has twisted an awkward posture into an artful strategy for operating in contradictory cultural spaces without abandoning homespace or pretending/performing a fabricated persona in heterospace.

Daḳlon's straddling was successful within his own community of Mizraḥi listeners. He situated *gaṿan Yam Tikhoni* selections in proximity to an equal number of *ha-Shir ha-Erets Yisre'eli* songs and consistently demonstrated a mainstream Israeli affect on his cassette covers. His simple sabra style of dress, combined with his choice of eyeglasses often worn by Israeli Air Force pilots, signal his attempt to attract an Ashkenazi Israeli following, an attempt that failed. Unlike Gi'at and Golan, who marked their appearance as religious, and unlike a number of other musicians who followed, including Haim Moshe (discussed below), Daḳlon appeared on his cassettes as an ordinary Israeli, unmarked by ethnicity or religious affiliation. His erasure of difference, underscored by the patriotic title of the cassette (A Voice Calls Me in the Desert), revealed his effort to disappear into the mainstream. What failed was not the glasses, or the clothing, but the singer's strikingly marked Yemenite vocal style, employing Greek and Middle Eastern embellishments that mainstream critics rejected.

Daḳlon's *ha-Shir ha-Erets Yisre'eli* renditions, situated among Yemenite prayers and Greek covers, resulted in a disjuncture for some Ashkenazi listeners. With Daḳlon's Yemenite voice and Greek and Middle Eastern music arrangements, their beloved Russian folksongs, previously rendered by classically trained singers, sounded unrecognizable. As with remakes or covers of classic songs from any genre, listeners are not always able to identify with subsequent interpretations. It is the contour of the original work that often triggers emotions linked specifically to an aural memory. At the same time, some covers manage to maintain a recognizable sound, as if sneaking in under the guise of the familiar. For his part, Daḳlon recast European Israeli repertoire for Mizraḥi listeners in an aesthetically pleasing form that achieved wide acceptance in the neighborhoods.

Straddling is always tricky. Suspending oneself between contradictory impulses, holding onto some while releasing others, might launch a singer into the new Mediterranean Israeli musical space but might equally exclude him or her from constituencies that regard the hybrid as disfigurement of their familiar songs.

The problem was that while Daḳlon and other neighborhood singers' sonic admixture was not familiar to European Israelis, Mizraḥim celebrated the European *ha-Shir ha-Erets Yisre'eli* repertoire recast in their neighborhood style. For European Israelis who might accept a traditional Yemenite prayer in the context of folklore or a Greek song in a Tel Aviv club, it was the infusion of these sounds into their familiar songs that sounded inauthentic. Clearly, in some sense, the exotic, in the form of the Yemenite prayer or

In this Daḳlon cassette cover, the singer's effort to reach out to diverse Israeli audiences is demonstrated aesthetically. The title *Ḳol ḳore li ba-midbar* (A Voice Calls Me in the Desert) evokes the *ha-Shir ha-Erets Yisre'eli* genre. Daḳlon is pictured wearing glasses, often referred to as pilot glasses, signifying the high esteem in which Israeli air force pilots are held. The title itself evokes the Eastern European pioneer attachment to the land characterized in many poems from the early days of the nation. (Reuveni Brothers, courtesy Meir Reuveni)

the Kurdish folksong, gets smuggled in under the guise of the authentic, but how that trick gets pulled off in any given instance proves very difficult to account for. The shifting blend blurred recognizable boundaries and fell upon closed ears.

Crossing Over but Not Getting In: Margalit Tsan'ani and Haim Moshe

Margalit Tsan'ani and Haim Moshe illustrate two distinct processes of crossing over into mainstream territory without truly getting in. They grew up in Yemenite neighborhoods near Ashkenazi communities in Netanya and North Tel Aviv. Though Moshe is considerably younger than Tsan'ani, they entered the music scene at around the same time in the early 1980s and under the auspices of the same recording company, The Reuveni Brothers.

Moshe was the Reuvenis' upcoming star just as Zohar Argov's career was in decline, and Tsan'ani was an early attempt to introduce a woman singer. The Reuvenis had briefly recorded Yemenite singer Ahuva Ozeri in the 1970s, but despite her success she soon disappeared from the scene. Raised in the Yemenite Kerem ha-Temanim neighborhood, Ozeri's short-lived career may have been partially due to family issues that intervened. Still, for a brief time she appeared on some of Daḳlon's cassettes, wrote songs, toured extensively as a solo artist, and appeared on Israeli TV in a forty-minute segment about her career. She left the music scene shortly after the controversy over her popular song "Where Is the Soldier." The song became a major hit, even though it was rarely broadcast by the media that claimed its subject, a missing Israeli soldier, was demoralizing for the public.[21] In 1982, she announced that she was leaving the music business.

Initially, Tsan'ani and Moshe both achieved tepid acceptance in the mainstream. Tsan'ani's bluesy emulation of African American style was neither accepted nor considered wholly offensive, and Moshe's Arabic renditions were tolerated, even appropriated, without really being embraced.

"Linda, Linda,"[22] Haim Moshe's first major hit, became audible in the Israeli national soundscape in the summer of 1984. Moshe's melismatic vocal style and use of Arabic, as well as the non-Hebrew name of his love song, Linda, immediately located the singer and his subject outside mainstream Israeli society. The song, which had been recorded two years earlier in New York by Samir Shukry, an Israeli Arab active in the Mediterranean Israeli network, was enormously popular in Mizraḥi neighborhoods and, as noted, among Palestinians in Gaza and the West Bank and other Arabs in Jordan, Syria, Egypt, and Lebanon. However, only when it entered the kibbutz in the form of a choreographed Israeli folk dance tune did mainstream critics deign to comment on it—disparagingly.[23] In the late 1980s the addition of Ashkenazi styles to his repertoire resulted in Mizraḥi accusations that Moshe was trying *lehit-ashknez* ("to become Ashkenazi"). At the same time, Ashkenazim resisted his attempts to penetrate their soundscape.

On Haim Moshe's cassette *Ahavat ḥayai* (Love of my Life),[24] only one of the nine selections is an *asli meḳorit* religious song, entitled "Shalom 'alai" (Peace on Me), using a liturgical tune heard in Mizraḥi synagogues in Jerusalem.[25] The other songs on the tape are contemporary *gaṿan Yam Tikhoni* and *asli meḳorit* songs sung in Arabic, including "Linda, Linda" and "Jayaguli." Moshe's next two cassettes, both released in 1984, *Lihiyot zamar* (To Be a Singer) and *Kef shel ḥafla* (What a Party), have an almost entirely *gaṿan Yam Tikhoni* repertoire, although there are scattered *asli meḳorit* Yemenite selections.

Unlike Daḳlon, who had consistently juxtaposed canonic European Israeli compositions alongside Yemenite, Arabic, and Mediterranean repertoire, Haim Moshe was accused in the press of Ashkenazification when he released similarly hybrid cassettes. (Courtesy Meir Reuveni)

With "Linda, Linda," Haim Moshe simultaneously infiltrated neighboring Arab airwaves and the symbolic center of Israel's ideological heartland and demonstrated that it was possible to straddle too far and appear to betray one's base. Margalit Tsan'ani, by contrast, was able to straddle the mainstream Ashkenazi market and her traditional audience. She did this by featuring Mediterranean Israeli music in her live performances while recording acceptable Western popular music products. Tsan'ani entered the Mediterranean Israeli music scene in the 1980s, and her construction of a style benefited from observing the struggles of other Mizraḥi singers. Like Daḳlon and Avihu Medina, she came from a Yemenite community that settled in Palestine before the establishment of the state. She grew up in Netanya, far

Haim Moshe defends his neighborhood roots in a 1986 newspaper article by Ḥavatselet Damari entitled "Lo mishtakhnez" (Not Ashkenazifying). (Courtesy Yediot Aḥaronot)

from the *ma'abarot,* and worked for many years as a wedding singer in both Ashkenazi and Mizraḥi communities. By the late 1980s she had become a crossover artist who appeared to have a foothold in Ashkenazi circles without having alienated her Mizraḥi communal base, dancing between the lines of Israel's ethnic and class divisions. Just one of the ten selections on her *Menta* recording is *asli meḳorit,* with a contemporary *gaṿan Yam Tikhoni* arrangement by Yemenite composer Tsiyon Shar'abi.[26] In "Shema' beni" (Listen My Son), the music is composed by Yemenite composer Tsiyon Shar'abi but the text comes from *Sefer Mishle* (The Book of Proverbs). Tsan'ani describes this text as *meha-meḳorot* (from the sources). The other nine songs are written by contemporary Ashkenazi Israeli composers, including Naomi Sh̨emer ("Yeled ra' Tel Aviv"; Bad boy Tel Aviv) and Uzi Ḥiṭman ("Mi-tokh ha-adam ha-afor"; From within the Gray Man). Out of forty-nine of her songs, thirty-six are mainstream Israeli popular music and thirteen are *asli meḳorit.* Tsan'ani's recordings contain only occasional selections from Mizraḥi composers such as Avihu Medina, Dani Shoshan, or Shlomo Kishur, and on *Pegishah* (A Date) she composed most of the tunes herself.[27]

How did Tsan'ani avoid the accusations of ashkenazification that threatened Haim Moshe? One reason may be that women are able to straddle boundaries and even to cross over without threatening the status quo. Perhaps women's inferior social status results in there being less at stake. It is also likely that Tsan'ani's overt identification with African American vocal styles and cultural affects did not disrupt Mizraḥi-Ashkenazi tensions. In addition, Tsan'ani grew up in an ethnically diverse neighborhood in Netanya where she acquired multiple fluencies, especially an ability to perform convincing Yiddish renditions. In contrast, perhaps Moshe's extreme range, from attempts to emulate Western rock 'n' roll to performances of Arabic popular music, elicited critique among his home base that Tsan'ani avoided through the mediating aesthetic of African American-ness. As Moshe noted, when Stevie Wonder sings microtones, he is acceptable on Israeli radio in a way that a Yemenite singer is not.[28]

Musical crossovers are not only matters of sonic penetration and reverberation but of where, how, when, and why a song occupies space and time, in Kay Shelemay's terms, as "soundscapes" or songs in context.[29] Unlike record bins in stores that require neat, somewhat artificial categories, musical events, especially weddings, bar mitzvahs, and other such occasions, require dispensing with confining bins and allowing for a mixture of disparate styles. Yet this coexistence is a temporary reprieve from the asymmetrical designations that are used to delineate the difference between acceptable and rejected styles.

The *Ma'abarah* Voices: Zohar Argov, Shimi Tavori, Avner Gadassi

There are significant differences between performers such as Daḳlon, Tselile ha-Kerem, Margalit Tsan'ani, and Haim Moshe, and the singers who grew up in poor development towns or neighborhoods such as Zohar Argov, Shimi Tavori, and Avner Gadassi. The main difference is in the fact that Argov, Tavori, and Gadassi, for the most part, do not incorporate *ha-Shir ha-Erets Yisre'eli* repertoire nor do they attempt to modify their performance, appearance, or vocal style to cater to a mainstream aesthetic. This gap may be partially explained by the fact that Daḳlon and Tsan'ani were part of Yemenite communities established in Palestine before the immigrations of the 1950s, whereas Argov, Gadassi, and Tavori are singers who were born in the *ma'abarot* and grew up in the neighborhoods and development towns that arose from these original transit camps. As such, they are products of a more intensive and rapid experience in culture contact than Daḳlon and Tsan'ani.

Like most Mediterranean Israeli singers, Margalit Tsan'ani would often perform at two or three events on a Saturday night. Traveling with her to a wedding, an army base, and a community center, I witnessed the fluidity of her live repertoire, which she seamlessly presented in these diverse settings. Here she sings at the wedding of a Maccabi Tel Aviv soccer player. (Photo by author)

The socialization process in the *ma'abarot,* neighborhoods, and development towns had a vital impact on musical repertoire. Mizraḥi solidarity grew also as a result of the realization that for many Ashkenazim their emerging style was not only illegitimate but antithetical to Israeliness. As Mizraḥim from various ethnic groups interacted, they created a contemporary style featuring Eastern vocalization and Western instrumentation. This later grew into the central feature of the *Musiḳah 'im gavan Yam Tikhoni* subgenre. This subgenre combined *asli* forms with regional, especially Greek forms.

Zohar Argov cassettes contain ninety percent *gavan Yam Tikhoni* selections with an occasional traditional *asli meḳorit* Yemenite song, Arabic or Turkish composition. On his first cassette, *Elinor,*[30] two out of nine of Argov's songs are religious selections: "Eshet ḥayil" (A Woman of Valor, from Proverbs 31:10–31) is traditionally recited before commencing the Sabbath evening meal, and "'Et dodim kalah" is based on a quotation from the Song

On the *Menta* cassette cover, Margalit Tsan'ani juxtaposes a pipe, sunglasses, and the beloved Middle Eastern mint tea. (Reuveni Brothers, courtesy Meir Reuveni)

of Songs. Argov's 1982 cassette *Hayu zemanim* (There Was a Time), contains one religious song, "Ahavat ra'ayah retsoni" (Beloved Wife, My Desire), which is a traditional text by Shalom Shabazi.[31]

To the uninitiated, including mainstream music critics, the juxtaposition of religious themes and popular Greek or Turkish music was disconcerting.[32] From an insider's perspective, however, this was a form of straddling stylistic traditions in which one remains connected to the home community within the context of innovative popular music. This straddling is, first of all, the refusal or inability to conform to the dominant European style, and, second, it is the laying of a foundation for a larger coalition, both aesthetic and political, whose common ground is a shifting of musical, political, and social influences through the process of straddling.

Writing across Borders: Avihu Medina

Avihu Medina, a leading Mediterranean Israeli music composer and an architect of the genre, maintains that his compositions embody genuine Israeliness and that mainstream society will eventually concur. This genuineness is part of his compositional process, as if his music wrote itself:

> For me, writing was simple. I have *chutzpah;* to write, what's the big deal! You need a wild imagination to start a theme, bring it to a peak, have interesting musical phrases, and not be banal but still be light. That's the music. Lyrics are harder. Lyrics to a song always come after the tune is already written. Inside the music, I don't know what I'm about to write. I know the subject. Music talks without words. That's why I'm not limited. I can go wild. I am not within the frame of words that could make me regard syllables, long and short, sentences, etc. I let the music lead me and then I adapt some words. My mood affects this. It can be rhythmic and happy or slow and quiet. Usually during the composing of the tune, some words already pop out. It's subconscious. These sentences sometimes change later but the new ones are some version of them. I know in advance the theme of the song.[33]

Avihu Medina, unlike Zohar Argov for whom he composed numerous hit songs, did not grow up in the *ma'abarot.* His childhood memories combine a strong association with Yemenite religious culture and simultaneous involvement with the emerging Israeli mainstream culture. His father was a cantor and one of his aunts was a traditional Yemenite *meḳonenet* (woman lamenter). As a gifted inner-city teenager, Medina was sent to an Ashkenazi kibbutz to study. On the kibbutz his musical talent was evident, he wrote songs, and he often led *ḳumzitsim* (Israeli campfires), where the *ha-Shir ha-Erets Yisre'eli* repertoire was sung collectively. He was also exposed to Western musical styles by Jewish American kibbutz volunteers, from whom he learned songs by the Beatles, Bob Dylan, the Temptations, and the Supremes. After serving in the army, Medina entered the diamond industry. He continued to write songs for singers in the emerging Mediterranean Israeli style. His inspiration came from the groundbreaking sounds of Aris San (a Greek singer who immigrated to Israel), Jo Amar (of Moroccan origin), and others who in the 1950s introduced Greek, Spanish, and Middle Eastern elements into their repertoires.

Despite his talent, Ashkenazi music professionals discouraged Medina from formally studying Western music. This elitist view, that classical study would destroy the authentic Yemenite character of his music, was coupled with the belief that he would have difficulty with Western notation and theory. At the same time, there were no institutional frameworks for aspiring non-European musicians. Young people such as Medina found themselves in a no-man's land beyond the official boundaries of Israeli music. Medina notes:

> Noam Sherif [the famous Israeli composer] told me once that genius is in the simple things. I don't try to be sophisticated; I write and I don't know what I write. If you try to do it by the rules you won't be special. I went to Noam Sherif because I wanted to study music. He told me it would do me only wrong. I went to another teacher, Shimon Cohen, and he gave me the same answer. He said, "Stay where you are." So I never studied music. They told me all you need are a few guitar lessons.[34]

Medina expresses regret about being discouraged from studying music seriously. There were few opportunities for talented young Mizraḥi musicians to receive musical training under the guidance of master instrumentalists, composers, or arrangers specializing in Middle Eastern techniques. At the same time, most were discouraged from receiving training in European styles. Like so many other disenfranchised musicians throughout the world, Medina was not deterred by the obstacles placed before him. He understood vocal music from his father, from his aunt, and from listening to the sacred chants in his neighborhood synagogues. He picked up American folk music from young volunteers on the kibbutz, listened to recordings of Greek, Arabic, Turkish, rock, and other styles on radio and LPs, and developed his style, confidence, and conviction. As Medina reveals:

> No one argues with me in the studio. I am the one who produces my material. I am the one who pays. Sometimes an arranger writes a phrase I don't like. "Out," I say. So he says, "But everyone likes it." But I only trust my ear and my taste. I got where I am by trusting myself only, so if I want to go on I must continue this attitude. Yet it bothers me that I can't expand musically. I cannot play all the parts that I hear in my head. My "feel" is very special and different even when I do old songs, and songs that are not my own.[35]

Despite his self-confidence, Medina also acknowledges that his lack of fluency in music composition placed limitations on his ability to enter the mainstream industry, and he is aggravated with editors who confined his compositions to Mizraḥi radio programs and other ethnic ghettos. Even in the early 1990s, Medina's songs were rarely heard on television or in mainstream Israeli music festivals. Imitations of America, Medina argues, result from an inferiority complex; appropriations of other styles, such as Greek or Turkish, are more authentically Middle Eastern:

> The difference is like between flowers and fake flowers. A real flower grows in the soil, a plastic one is manufactured. Here in Israel, if they won't play what grows in this land, we will always remain plastic flowers. They can try to sing rock and roll here for centuries. No way! What's going to stay is "Shabeḥi Yerushalayim" (Praise, Jerusalem).[36] But because of the monopoly of the broadcasting authorities on the media and the empty people who run it, they have the power to stay and brainwash us with their trashy music.
>
> If we were a real democracy, people would not be forbidden to start their own radio stations. . . . But there's no democracy here. The Israel Festival has nothing Israeli in it. My music will never be allowed to enter the Israel Festival. Not even the Israeli *Mits'ad hapizmonim* (Israeli Hit Parade). They only let in music that tries to imitate America.
>
> The media is full of people who have an inferiority complex. They don't want to sound Jewish or Mediterranean. They try to sound European or American. They are ashamed of being Jews who live in the Mediterranean. They want the illusion that they are European. The Israeli audience doesn't want this but the powers that be force it upon them. The media reports only what they want, they write that we are "bad"; they want everyone to have their inferiority complex.[37]

In other words, Medina's concept of authentic music invokes claims for indigenousness, in terms of both the land of Israel and Jewishness, in contrast with the broadcasting media, which not only has no such claims but is run by people with "inferiority complexes" because they do not have an authentic sound; instead, they "try to sound European or American" and are afraid of the indigenous (Jewish, Mediterranean, and Arabic) sound. In Medina's framework, European and American music transplanted to Israeli soil cannot last. The imported European and American sounds are inferior to the indigenous Mediterranean sounds, and a true democracy would counter the monopolistic powers that prevent the real sounds from proliferating.

There are many such conceptualizations that similarly equate indigenous origins with authenticity, in contrast to the inauthenticity of colonial aesthetics. Thus the politics of authenticity acts as a corrective to the Euro-American influences while promulgating a mentality antithetical to the colonial. This conception of Mediterranean Israeli music as more authentic is what Amy Shuman describes as "strategic romanticism," borrowing the romantic conception of the colonizer but turning it on its head.[38] The colonizer views the colonized as indigenous, authentic, but fixed in the past, not modern.

Medina, in contrast, insists on Mediterranean Israeli music as an indigenous but living, transformative tradition. He, too, uses a romantic understanding of the real and the fake, but in the service of shifting the balance and recalibrating what has become discriminatory and exclusive practice. As Medina insisted, Yemenite Israelis are no longer riding donkeys and going to synagogue three times a day. The "real flowers" as opposed to the plastic are not mere relics of the past. As Shuman argues, such romantic formulations are often in response to exclusions or discrimination.[39] If we too quickly dismiss statements such as Medina's as unproblematic or overly romantic, we not only miss his point—that the Israeli music soundscape is exclusive and discriminatory rather than democratic—but also deprive disenfranchised musicians from using the tools of romanticism strategically and persuasively against dominant or mainstream control. It would be unfair to characterize Medina as a simple romantic insisting on the authenticity of an indigenous tradition. After all, he has argued forcefully for what he calls the "muddle," the blend of styles. It is useful to attack Ashkenazi hegemony over cultural production, and Medina is correct in his indictment of the media for suppressing and ghettoizing Mizraḥi music; however, in the process, Medina reinforces a system for measuring authenticity that is counter to his practice.

I sat with Medina in his office in 1992 in North Tel Aviv, a middle-class, Ashkenazi neighborhood. He talked about his commitment to an Israel located in the Middle East and to the integrity of Mediterranean Israeli music. What he wants, he explained, is to chip away at some deeply ingrained aesthetic parameters that relegate his music to second-class status. In order for music like his to become acceptable to mainstream listeners, he claims, it would need to be played on the radio twenty times a day, fully integrated with European Israeli styles. As we talked about his song "Baladah le-Ḥaver," Medina could little imagine how quickly the tectonics of Israeli music were shifting:

> Like the song "Baladah le-Ḥaver,"[40] it is a style not sung in Israel. I once saw a Japanese movie in which an old man sat alone and

> sang a lamentation. The melody was so enchanting. He had this husky voice. I took the spirit of it; you need courage to sing like that here! It's a lamentation. Among the Yemenites when we mourn our dead, there are women whose profession is to cry at such events. The Greeks do this too. On the spot, the women compose lyrics about the person who died. Mourners sit on the floor and they cry lyrics. If you hear it once you'll be overwhelmed. I have an aunt who does this. It's heartbreaking. From this Japanese guy and my aunt and from my own feelings this song was born. It's really mourning for a friend, for Zohar [Argov].[41]

In his amazing leap from a Japanese lamentation (seen in a film) to Yemenite mourning, itself associated with Greek mourning, Medina appears to contradict his notion of real and fake flowers by replacing Western rock with Far Eastern lament. His comparison between fake and real flowers has less to do with issues of hybridization than with the question of who speaks for Israeliness: who gets to choose which kinds of foreign music become officially sanctioned and which remain outside mainstream Israeli sound. In explaining the birth of his song, Medina also explains the framework that is at the heart of the Mizraḥi understanding of legitimate appropriation. Borrowing musically is not only acceptable, but laudable when it involves true appreciation of and credit to the source of the inspiration, whether it is Japanese, Greek, Yemenite, or, for that matter, European.

As Medina explained, his song laments the death of Zohar Argov. In many ways, Medina was a father figure to Argov, who in turn served as a mouthpiece for Medina's lyrics. After Argov's death, Medina continued to write for other singers, but he soon found the experience emotionally empty and financially exploitative. Once he launched a solo performance career and began performing his own songs, he was able to interpret his own compositions and gain financial and emotional security. Although he maintained elements of his previous poetic approach, his texts became more topical. For example, "Avraham Avinu" (Abraham, Our Father) focuses on the Israeli-Arab conflict by drawing upon the biblical patriarch Abraham, who is the traditional forebear of both the Jews and the Arabs.[42] In "Lamah, El" (Why, God?), he returns again to the flower metaphor, this time neither fake nor real, but rather wild and tragic.

> I'm not talking about the lyrics now, just the music, which is what we call *Maghrabī* (North African). It's a little bit Moroccan, there's a smile in the music, a little provocative smile. Now the song talks about a big problem, the hundreds of years of wars between us and

אין דבר כזה מוסיקה מזרחית

103

מעריב 15.11.90

ואת זה קובע, אביהו מדינה, שהמציא את זוהר ארגוב ואת שימי תבורי. אחרי שדאג להם מתחיל מדינה לדאוג לעצמו. בתקליט החדש שלו "אשר אהבתי" הוא לא רק מחבר אלא גם מבצע.

מעריב

קיפר סאתרלנד ,ג'וליה רוברטס - קוין בייקון

האופנובנק שלנו הוא "כסף קטן" לעומת שודדי הבנק בניו יורק.

This 1990 *Ma´ariv* article entitled "There Is No Such Thing as Mizraḥi Music" underscores Medina's contention that the music created and performed by Mizraḥi artists is pigeonholed by the artist's ethnicity rather than by the songs themselves. (Courtesy *Ma´ariv*)

the Arabs. I took this tragedy and I turned it into a children's story. As if Grandpa Abraham looks at his children and asks: "What are you fighting about? Why not talk?" It is such a simple thing, like "What's the problem! Sit down and discuss it. It's family!"

"Lamah, El" is a song I wrote after the Lebanon War. You know in that war six hundred soldiers were killed, just like that. I compare them to the wild flowers:

Why, God, have the wild flowers faded?
They were beautiful and they are gone.
Why does love alone not burn in the hearts?
Why are the children's eyes full of fear and sadness?

Here Avihu pauses and explains, "I am talking about the eyes of children at war and the children in the bombardment." He ends with the last line from this song:

Why is it that not all thoughts are good?[43]

Avihu writes of the eyes of the children at war and the children in the bombardment, asking in the voice of the child the unanswerable question: Why? His compositions, and the loosely confederated category of Mediterranean Israeli music that he helped create, emerges in the complex conditions of war, ingathering, disillusionment, patriotisms, anger, and sadness. Mediterranean Israeli music is the aesthetic product of friction between an emerging and dispossessed Mizraḥi style and the official European Israeli forms.

To understand the relationship between music and the political forces of discrimination and hegemony is not simply a matter of mapping one onto the other. Maps, even three dimensional maps, are too static for musical processes. Instead, I suggest that in Reagon's model of straddling, the very act of reaching for a third place that is neither stable nor fixed creates sanity for disenfranchised musicians. Straddling the contentious domains of politics and aesthetics is a constant process of shifting scales.

Straddling simultaneously confounds and makes visible emergent categories. These categories temporarily conform to repertoire clusters and then shift, recalibrate, and proliferate. Each of the performers discussed in this chapter straddles the repertoire clusters that I have constructed based on Medina's categories; in a sense each has his or her own context-specific repertoire cluster. Each individual cluster is interrelated, though not identical; they coalesce into a recognizable style.

This recognition of emergent styles and the attendant disdain of many mainstream critics underscore the loaded relationship between politics and aesthetics. In part, the politics of the aesthetics of Mediterranean Israeli music stems from the fact that critics and listeners have an entirely different scale or register for measuring what makes something part of a category. What I have tried to demonstrate is that rather than naming a genre and attributing characteristics, overlapping patterns emerge. Like Wittgenstein's concept of family resemblance,[44] there is no one trait shared by all the musicians discussed in this chapter, and yet they share enough similarity to be recognized by community members and outside critics as an emerging constellation of loosely related singers. At the same time, what complicates this attempt at grouping is that the musicians themselves resist the demarcation that sets them apart from and positions them as inferior to the larger category of Israeli music. They believe that acts of exclusion prevent them from being identified solely as Israeli musicians. These repertoire clusters envision the universe of Mediterranean Israeli music; they represent a scholar's effort to locate performance distinctions within an emerging pan-ethnic genre.

Many scholars offer models for understanding the complex flow of rhizomatic cultural connections. Here I differentiate between points of multiple connections that traverse distances (or hubs), and nodes, or points of more intimate or local connection that often overlap but do not reach as far. For example, mainstream celebrity musicians are known by many and have a far reach. They act as hubs; their influence is stabilized by industry handlers who control musical territory and effectively edge others out. Grassroots neighborhood networks such as Mediterranean Israeli music are nodes; everyone is known to each other within a smaller range.

Here I articulate one piece of the complex networks that make up Mediterranean Israeli music within the larger Israeli music industry of the 1970s–1990s. Within this network, musicians came to know each other long before they achieved national or international visibility. Mediterranean Israeli musicians hoped for greater visibility and some attempted to modulate their styles to open the territory that seemed closed to Middle Eastern and North African newcomers. Interestingly, by establishing neighborhood networks before they achieved celebrity status, the Mediterranean Israeli musicians created a robust and enduring style even when deprived of national radio air time. They (and others, including scholars) expected that the absence of national radio air time would be their demise. In fact, scholars need to revise their understanding of cultural flows to accommodate nodal grassroots configurations that may create strong, enduring, and proliferating styles.

In further research, we might ask: Do the hubs that celebrity mainstream musicians construct stabilize the musical territory they command, effectively edging others out, or do they soon find themselves fatally out of fashion? Had they modulated their styles and opened the territory to newcomers, might they have held on longer themselves? Does categorizing neighborhood music, as part of an effort to gain critical authority—even into porous frameworks like repertoire clusters—diminish hybrid vigor?

According to physicist and author Mark Buchanan, networks such as Mediterranean Israeli music can gain power precisely because they contain weaker connections or nodes.[45] For example, the weak relationships between borrowed Greek melodies, Yemenite *silsul* (Hebrew for melisma), Western rock rhythms, and Arab drums create strength by proliferating in the form of multiple variations. Avihu Medina's compositional flexibility (weaving Japanese, Greek, Yemenite, and rock forms) along with his fluency in "the real thing"—the *asli meḳorit* repertoire—resulted in a supple local sound free from the constraints of time and place.

Mediterranean Israeli music proliferates and creates weak links across context; Yemenite singers master Kurdish, Syrian, and Iraqi forms to perform at diverse life-cycle and seasonal events and at club venues. In the face of exclusion from the hubs of official radio stations, Mediterranean Israeli music entrepreneurs turned to the ephemeral but paradoxically stronger locations of outdoor marketplaces. Eventually, some Mizraḥi singers outsold mainstream artists, and their increased radio time in the late 1990s helped to alter listener perception. By using the marketplace as a distribution site, the singers were vulnerable to charges of low culture. However, what they lost in public high-profile exposure, they gained in sites of local density, which also offered exposure of another kind. It is Medina's ability to juxtapose and relocalize diverse global styles that is the real thing. Medina's flowers, wherever their origin point, found fertile ground in the local soil.

Chapter 4

Sounding Right: Zohar Argov

> I sing the music with which I was raised. That's my background and the background of a million people like me. I give my audience the music it loves. I haven't invented anything new. I brought things from my father's house, from my childhood from the childhood of all of us. That's what made me.
>
> —Zohar Argov, *Haaretz,* 25 September 1981

> You cannot write original Yemenite music in Israel. In order to write original Yemenite music you have to live in Yemen and ride a donkey. We do not go to synagogue three times a day. We live in the here and now. I write about the here and now.
>
> —Avihu Medina, *Yedi'ot Aḥaronot,* 19 September 1986

> I don't think expressive culture really dies; you'd have to think of culture as a straight line evolution to believe that, and I don't. I think of it more as a spiral, changing but dipping back along the way. Even when people seem to be reviving things, that is exhuming them and breathing life into them, what they get is something new. Even Lazarus was not the same man before and after his death and rebirth. In culture, context counts for more than half of meaning, form for less.
>
> —Mark Slobin, "Rethinking 'Revival' of American Ethnic Music"

Many Mediterranean Israeli music singers are Yemenites. The reconstituted Yemenite vocal signature remains at the center of the sound mix even when the song takes on Greek or Russian melodies. Zohar Argov's vocal ability, his Yemeniteness, and the ambiguous circumstances of his tragic death conspired to transform him from a beloved community singer into a local hero.

Zohar's "Authentic Voice"

The opening bars of the orchestra's horn section prepare the ear for a Spanish bullfight. Brassy tones crest, then cool down, then pause expectantly. But the matador does not charge into the ring. Instead, a slender Yemenite in a tight-fitting Western suit appears at stage left. He walks to the microphone and fills the hall with a single, clear, piercing tone. The sound shoots out from a deep well somewhere between his heart and gut. It streams through his throat and nose, lips and cheeks, like unexpected rain winding down the interior crevices of a desert canyon. It is neither a cry nor a roar, but evokes both feelings. Overtones reverberate like the imam calling Muslims to prayer or the cantor leading a Jewish congregation. Zohar Argov is performing the opening *muwwal* of "ha-Peraḥ be-gani" (The Flower in My Garden)[1] at the 1982 *Fesṭival ha-zemer ha-mizraḥi* (Festival of Eastern Song).

Traditionally the *muwwal* in Middle Eastern music is an intricate improvisation on a sound often like "Ah" or "Yalel" with which a singer opens a vocal performance. The opening *muwwal* focuses the singer and the audience on the modes that will be used in the piece. Within the Israeli Jewish context of the 1970s, improvisational techniques such as the *muwwal* were not part of a Mizraḥi singer's musical training. Still, the employment of an abbreviated *muwwal* by singers like Argov reflected the singers' intention to draw on their own regional traditions. In "ha-Peraḥ be-gani," Argov's brief *muwwal* answers the linear horn opening with the carefully placed vocal spirals and twists of Eastern *silsulim*. His timbres soar like a bird in mid-air. His vocal lines retrace the melody outlined by the horns, creating an interior path that bends the pitches and liberates the myriad of microtones that live between the whole and half tones of Western scales. The *muwwal* lasts forty seconds and then leads into a Western drumbeat that underlines the main rhythmic body of "ha-Peraḥ be-gani." The song, written by Avihu Medina for Zohar Argov to perform at the Festival of Eastern Song in 1982, was arranged by Nancy Brandes, a recent Romanian Jewish immigrant to Israel. Avihu Medina worked with Brandes in order to create a special feel for the song, which he classifies as one of his "Spanish compositions." He notes that for him the *muwwal* marks the cultural center.[2] Between Brandes's arrangement of Spanish bullfight trumpet licks and Western drumbeats, Argov's *muwwal* assures the listener that the voice, with its Middle Eastern attitude and structure, is the signature line.

Argov's voice overtakes but does not obliterate the Spanish orchestral flourishes with a Hebrew text that emphasizes the Middle Eastern guttural letters—the deep *'ayins* and *ḥets* that persist despite the flattening of mainstream Ashkenazi pronunciation. He inserts improvisational *silsulim* where Western notation calls for rest bars. It is not only the intensity of his voice and its unlikely coalition with the musical accompaniment that shocks the listener into emotional attentiveness; it is the man himself. He has piercing black eyes and a face which he confessed was deemed "too ugly for air time" by an apologetic television producer. His movements are barely contained, a taut, controlled surface just holding back a turbulent, volcanic interior from which the sound flows. The audience is on its feet as he bows with the last note. Zohar Argov wins first place for his performance at Yosef Ben-Israel's historic Festival of Eastern Song.

Names: Zohar Orkabi from Shikun ha-Mizraḥ

Zohar Argov was born Zohar Orkabi in 1955, a few years after the Yemenite *aliya.*[3] He was raised in Shikun ha-Mizraḥ (The Eastern Neighborhood), a Mizraḥi neighborhood in the predominantly Ashkenazi town of Rishon le-Tsiyon, established by Baron Rothschild in 1882. The town was a historical center of Zionist activity; local residents are proud to share stories of their participation in the Palmach, the Jewish paramilitary in Palestine that grew into the Israeli army. According to the municipality, 160,000 residents lived in Rishon le-Tsiyon as of January 1993. The Municipal Research Department stated unofficially that the average income of local residents was among the top twenty percent in Israel.

In contrast, Shikun ha-Mizraḥ was established in 1947 as a *ma'abarah,* originally inhabited by Eastern European refugees. In 1950 the site was expanded to accommodate Yemenite and Moroccan families. As with many *ma'abarot,* Shikun ha-Mizraḥ grew into a poor Mizraḥi neighborhood. In the 1980s, at the peak of Argov's career, it housed twelve thousand residents. Until 1985 the average inhabitant lived below the national poverty level in an environment characterized by high crime and low property values.

Zohar's father, Ovadya Orkabi, worked as a milkman; his mother, Yona Orkabi, was a cleaning woman at a neighboring army base. Zohar was the eldest of their ten children, although he had an older half-brother from his father's first marriage. The Orkabis were a traditionally observant family and Zohar wore *pe'ot* (sidelocks or earlocks) until his father allowed him to cut them at the age of seven. He attended synagogue until his father's death.

Like many Yemenite boys he was trained in liturgical chanting, so that his intonations in reading the Torah were precise and clear. At the age of five, he was invited to participate in a Sabbath service. Zohar sang constantly, using tin cans as percussive backup. His classmates nicknamed him "nightingale" because of his beautiful voice. His siblings shared his love of music, and though none of them received any professional training, they sang and played drums, electric piano, and guitar. Zohar was uninterested in any aspect of school except singing. For this reason, coupled with financial problems at home, he left school at fourteen and found work with a construction company. Three years later, in 1972, he married a neighbor, Bracha Tzuberi, who gave birth the following year to a son, Gili. Zohar's father died on the day of Gili's *brit milah* (ritual circumcision held when a boy is eight days old).

I learned from the many people that I interviewed that Zohar's relationship with his father was stormy. Ovadya Orkabi's authoritarianism and drinking problem weighed heavily on him. Because of the financial responsibilities thrust on Zohar at an early age, he was excused from military service. Zohar's lack of army experience further marginalized him from Israeli society, where a military past was, at that time, a vital prerequisite for anyone entering the mainstream.

Renaming: Zohar Argov

Four years after his father's death, Zohar changed his family name from Orkabi to Argov, a mainstream Ashkenazi Israeli name shared by the renowned composer Sasha Argov (1914–1995). Argov is part of a genre of reconstituted Israeli Hebrew names chosen because of their sound rather than for their meaning. "Argov" is a biblical place name (I Kings 4:13), a site located thirty kilometers east of Lake Kinneret in the Golan Heights. It apparently stems from the Hebrew word *regev*, meaning a small mound of dirt. The act of changing his name was a pragmatic, professional move given that he was planning to record his first demo tape; as such it was an attempt to neutralize the ethnic marking that Orkabi signaled. He recorded his first demo tape in 1977 at Kolifone Studio in Shekhunat Monṭifiore (a working-class neighborhood) in Tel Aviv. It contained two compositions by Yemenite composer Moshe Nagar, "Yaldah, ḥikiti shanim" (Girl, I Have Waited Years) and "Kol yom she-'over" (Every Day That Passes).[4] Apart from Nagar and Argov's sister-in-law, who designed the cover, the team included arranger Yair Shragi, guitarist Gary Ekstein, bassist Yossi Menachem, and drummer

Ikky Levy, all Ashkenazim. The players later formed the band Brosh, which performed in Ramle rock clubs and appeared with singer-songwriter Ariel Zilber.

In 1977, Argov tried unsuccessfully to break into the commercial music industry. His demo tape was a failure when it aired during a single radio broadcast on a show featuring "musical oddities," *Maḥaṭ be-'aremat taḳliṭim* (A Needle in a Record Stack). Nonetheless, Argov began working full-time as a singer. The hours were grueling and the pay was meager. Within months Argov had incurred huge debts, all his property was repossessed, and he could no longer support Bracha and Gili. The financial strains and the pressures of late-night club engagements precipitated a marital crisis; Bracha took Gili and moved back to her parents' home. Shortly thereafter Argov was convicted of rape after he offered a woman a ride home following a bar mitzvah performance, forced her to go to his apartment, and assaulted her. He spent all of 1978 in prison.

In legendary histories about Argov, his conviction as a rapist is entirely elided. By contrast, his drug addiction is worked into the tale of his elevation to hero as the tragic flaw from which society can learn. For example, the lesson is credited with inspiring the founders of the Zoharim Therapeutic Community (a drug rehabilitation center near Jerusalem) to name their new center in his memory. Some therapists even draw upon Argov's history of addiction in the treatment of patients who are fans of his music.[5] The story of the rape, however, is rarely called into service as a tale to combat violence against women. In the matter of drug addiction, however, Argov can be presented as a victim of a disease that ultimately killed him. It is difficult to imagine what would count as posthumous rehabilitation for a rapist. The problematic intersections between racism, sexism, and cultural imperialism, central issues in current Israeli feminist theory, may be at the root of this schism.[6] Nevertheless, the Jewish Survivors blogspot, a site on which victims identify alleged and convicted perpetrators of sexual abuse, features a post in 2007 calling for action against a plan to name a street in Rishon le-Tsiyon after Argov.[7]

Yehuda Kessar: To Make a Singer Out of Him

Soon after his release from prison in 1978, Argov met Yemenite singer Jackie Makaytan.[8] Makaytan introduced Argov to Yehuda Kessar, owner of a Tel Aviv studio in the Central Bus Station district and the founder and lead guitarist of a popular Yemenite band from Kerem ha-Temanim, Tselile ha-'ūd. Kessar was immediately captivated by Argov's talent and decided "to make a singer out of him." He offered Argov a chance to appear with the band at a wedding in Be'er Sheva. "I invited him to come with us to a show in Be'er Sheva and he went to buy clothes. I remember that night he came with a shiny yellow shirt, the wet look style . . . rather tight. He wore it open to the waist. It was horrible."[9] Though Argov's outfit failed Kessar's visual inspection, he passed the vocal audition. His performance electrified the audience and Kessar sensed that in this singer Mizraḥi music could enter a new era. In 1979, Kessar left Tselile ha-'ūd to play guitar exclusively with Argov and Makaytan, and for a short time he acted as Argov's manager. Kessar introduced him to Bulgarian keyboardist Marcel Lidji and they began performing together at ha-Barvaz (The Duck), a fashionable Mizraḥi nightclub in Jaffa. Lidji's loyalty to Argov was unwavering and he helped the singer survive the rigors of his rapidly expanding career:

> There was a telepathic link between us. I would know when he was about to pass from one song to another and which song he was moving toward. He had incredible vocal power. When he started singing, the other instruments would vanish. The amplifiers could not take the overload. He had a magical control over the audience, like the Prophet Moses. Only after he died did I realize that all those years I always performed standing.[10]

The Reuveni Brothers: The Dark Side of "Glamour"

With Argov's increasing popularity in the clubs, Kessar decided that it was time to produce a cassette. In 1980 he used a portable tape machine to record a live show at ha-Barvaz. He then approached the Reuveni brothers with the homemade "master," entitled *Elinor*, and they agreed to distribute the cassette in the marketplace booths around Tel Aviv's Central Bus Station. *Elinor* was an overnight hit; requests for the cassette came pouring in from all over the country. As demands for performances increased, the pressure of managing Argov overwhelmed Kessar. By now it was obvious that Argov had the potential to become a superstar. Reuveni was now ready to negotiate a deal with him. He convinced Argov to sign a three-year contract. It was one of the first written legal documents executed in the network.

The next year Reuveni introduced Argov to Shoni Gavriel, the owner of one of the leading Mizrah̩i nightclubs, Club Ariana in Jaffa. The club became Argov's home base. Reuveni's aggressive distribution campaign in marketplace cassette booths translated into a huge increase in club and wed-

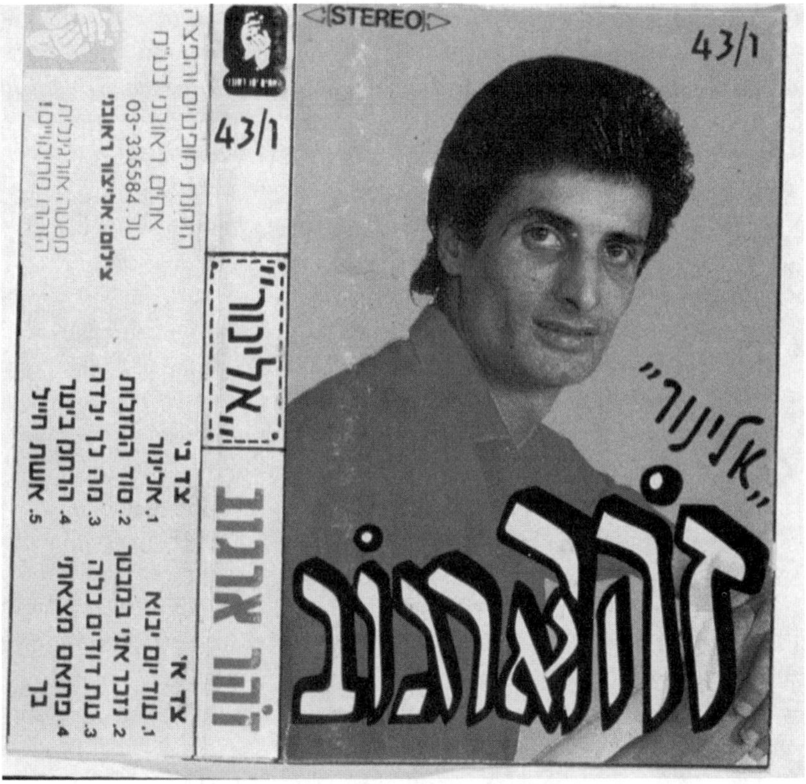

With Zohar Argov's *Elinor* cassette in 1980, Mediterranean Israeli music became audible beyond local Mizraḥi neighborhoods. A network of entrepreneurs set up cassette booths in the outdoor marketplaces throughout the country. This landmark cassette was still prominently displayed in 1984 when I bought it in the Central Bus Station marketplace. (Reuveni Brothers, courtesy Meir Reuveni)

ding engagements. Argov's audience continued to grow. In 1981 he told journalist Michael Ohad:

> I work with a wedding audience and I am not ashamed of that. Not long ago I read a newspaper article saying that Israeli singers are starving. I say, let them go down to the people. Let them go down to where they began. Let them appear in places like Tiffany's, like [the famous *ha-Shir ha-Erets Yisre'eli* group] *ha-Parparim.* A new generation has arisen. Go down to it and you will have work again. . . . I appear every night and sometimes twice a night. I must keep in touch with the audience.[11]

Argov's meteoric rise to success caught the attention of Yoel Esteron, an Ashkenazi television journalist. He produced a fifteen-minute feature on Zohar Argov in which he tried to describe the emergence of *Musiḳat ha-ḳaseṭot* ("cassette music"). The piece aired on the Friday night primetime news show *Yoman ha-Shavu'a* (Weekly Journal) on 17 April 1981.[12]

> With the cassette [Argov's first, recorded at the Aquarius Club in Jaffa] I reached the Central Bus Station and *Shuḳ ha-Karmel* (the Carmel Market). That's my radio. Who doesn't come to buy vegetables in the market? And that's where I am played from morning to night. That's my clientele. Only after I became famous and sold tens of thousands of cassettes and records, the television came to check . . . what's the noise? Who's terrorizing around here? So they took my picture and they took my mother's picture also.[13]

It was difficult for Reuveni to satisfy all the performance requests pouring in. The schedule was so tight that Argov often performed three times in one night, sometimes in different cities. The intense pressure of touring proved too much for Argov's backup players. A little less than a year into Argov's three-year contract, Makaytan, Kessar, and other band members quit. Keyboardist Lidji, who remained with Argov, averted a personnel crisis by hiring musicians for previously scheduled performances.

In 1982 Argov recorded his second cassette, *Hayu zemanim* (There Was a Time).[14] The cassette was recorded at Triton Studio in the Ashkenazi religious town of Bene Beraḳ because Kessar was busy renovating his own studio. Later that year Argov appeared in the Festival of Eastern Song, held in *Binyane ha-umah* in Jerusalem. Argov's third cassette, *Nakhon le-hayom* (Up to Date),[15] was released later that year. Like many performers who experience sudden fame and success, just at the point where Argov's trajectory looked unstoppable, he crashed.

All That Glitters: The Twin Pressures of Fame and Condemnation

Both Marcel Lidji and Asher Reuveni claim that Argov was already using drugs by early 1983.[16] This contradicts the widely held belief that he first began using drugs in May of that year, during his first performances in Los Angeles. Argov himself claimed that it was at Club Halleluyah in L.A. that he was introduced to hard drugs. By the end of the year, a demanding performance schedule and heroin addiction began to visibly affect Argov's health

On Argov's *Hayu zemanim* (There Was a Time) cassette cover, the singer evokes nostalgia for a lost past by cranking a record player. Ironically, it was the technological revolution that replaced the fixed LP format with the more accessible and mobile cassette player and duplicator that allowed for Argov's success in the marketplace. On early cassette releases such as *Hayu zemanim,* very little publishing detail is provided. Lay scholars such as Eva Broman in Sweden have provided detailed discographic information on individual songs from this early period, often linking the Hebrew renditions as in the case of *Hayu zemanim* with Greek or in this case Turkish sources. Sites such as Hebrew Song (http://www.hebrewsongs.com/?SongID=265) and Hebrew Dance (http://www.israelidances.com/dance_details.asp?DanceID=4453) offer publishing information previously unavailable. (Reuveni Brothers, courtesy Meir Reuveni)

and career. Shoni Gavriel, Marcel Lidji, and Avihu Medina took him to Eilat and locked him in a room to dry out. Their efforts were unsuccessful. By now his erratic behavior and missed engagements made him a risky investment, and the Reuveni brothers were convinced that Argov could never overcome his addiction. They therefore decided to sign a contract with promising new star, Haim Moshe.

Argov felt betrayed by the Reuvenis' association with Moshe and subsequently ended his relationship with them in December 1983. This, along with the realization that there was no chance of reconciliation with his former wife, who had recently remarried, led him to despair. On 16 July 1984, after returning from an appearance in Paris, Argov was arrested for dealing drugs. He was released on bail after two weeks but was forbidden to leave the country for six months. Argov's heroin addiction was now ruining his career and draining his income. Promoters took advantage of him by either underpaying or pretending to pay him.

In the year following Argov's break with the Reuveni Brothers, Avigdor Ben-Mosh produced two cassettes of his music: *Yam shel dema'ot* (A Sea of Tears)[17] and *Lihiyot adam* (To Be Human).[18] Argov was often dysfunctional during the recording sessions. In February 1985, during a Paris tour with Marcel Lidji, Moshe Gi'at, and Yishai Ben-Tsur, he nearly overdosed. In June 1985 he was arrested for possession of heroin and received a one-year suspended sentence.

At the end of 1985, Argov signed a fifteen-year contract with Jerusalem producer Nissim Ben-Haim. Ben-Haim distributed a cassette recorded in Paris, *Ḥafla ve-shire matsav ruaḥ, hofa'ah ḥayah be-Tsarfat* (Party and Good Humor Songs: Live Performance in France),[19] and took Argov into his home for three months, hoping that the solitude of Jerusalem would help break his drug habit. Argov performed only rarely in 1986. He was often on probation and in June he had himself committed to a drug-abuse rehabilitation program in Jerusalem. In early 1987, after he had completed his treatment, he appeared on *Mi-meni Meni* (a Friday night primetime talk show with Meni Peer),[20] where he declared that he was clean and ready to start a new chapter in his life.

In July 1987 Argov was convicted of stealing a policeman's pistol and sentenced to six months in prison. Two weeks before his release Argov was allowed to go home for the weekend. During this time he was accused of attempted rape, and his sentence was extended a few more days until the complaint could be investigated. On the night of 6 November 1987, before the investigation was completed, Zohar Argov was found hanging in his prison cell. He was thirty-two years old.

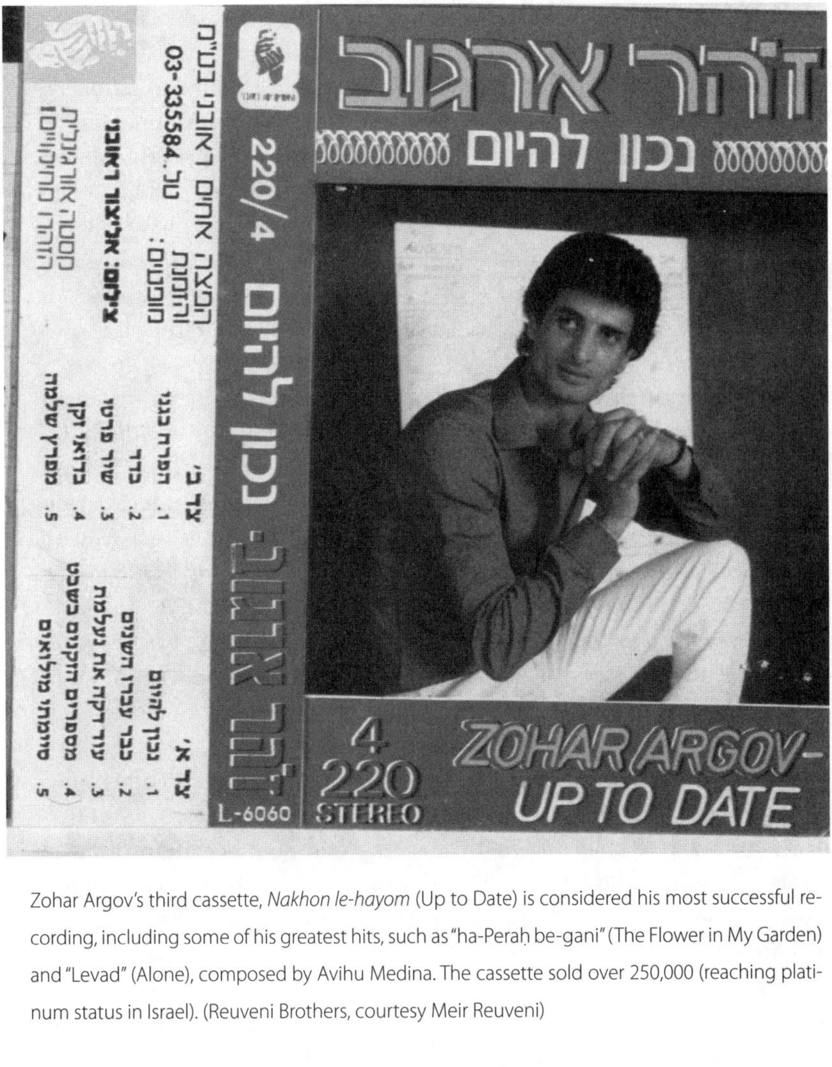

Zohar Argov's third cassette, *Nakhon le-hayom* (Up to Date) is considered his most successful recording, including some of his greatest hits, such as "ha-Peraḥ be-gani" (The Flower in My Garden) and "Levad" (Alone), composed by Avihu Medina. The cassette sold over 250,000 (reaching platinum status in Israel). (Reuveni Brothers, courtesy Meir Reuveni)

Contested Authenticities

Argov said he did not invent anything new. His vocal style was not an invention but a natural expression of the cultural cross-currents that swept through the singer himself. His innovation was in the juxtaposition and resolution of unlikely music genres. He drew his sound from his "father's house" and from the sound track of his childhood in Shikun ha-Mizraḥ, a former refugee camp for Polish Holocaust survivors that grew into a Mizraḥi ghetto of Yemenite and Moroccan immigrants. His sound was neither Eastern traditional nor Western rock; he was neither a Yemenite folk singer nor a vocalist of Mediterranean genres like San Remo, Greek, or French. He was a mediator who vocalized each of his childhood influences. He orchestrated their interactions on a conscious mission to uncover "authentic" Israeli music. When journalists and scholars attempted to analyze his music on the basis of some preexisting genre, by classifying his style as Eastern, Western, or contemporary Yemenite, he resisted. "I have never regarded my music as roots music. I am a singer with no pretensions. I don't go for roots. My purpose is that people will be turned on by my songs. And I want to state here that the Israeli audience is sentimental. They like songs that enter the heart."[21]

Not surprisingly, in Argov's claim, sentimentality cements authenticity. Sentimentality permits an invisible, unarticulated claim to "the heart," which Argov clearly differentiated from the "roots." When Argov said that he doesn't do "roots music," he meant that he refused to reproduce existing tunes so that people could nostalgically conjure up the image of a Yemenite on a donkey—he refused to submit to this stereotypical expectation of the well-behaved, authentic imaginary. He was not willing to be the model Yemenite, and by claiming to speak to the "heart," he attempted to bypass the politics of authenticity and go directly to a deeper source of "truth." What Argov and other musicians sought was not legitimacy based on identity politics but a stake in the pastiche of the true Israeli sound.

Avihu Medina composed "ha-Peraḥ be-gani" and many other songs performed by Argov. He continues to struggle with scholars who criticize the hybrid nature of his music by asserting that he never meant to create "Mizraḥi music." This label was assigned by outsiders who named the music based on the ethnicity of its leading creators and performers, which discounted the influence of arrangers like Nancy Brandes and songwriters like Uzi Ḥiṭman. As Medina explains at the beginning of this chapter, Yemenite Jews, like Argov and himself, were born in Israel in the 1950s, never rode donkeys in Yemen, and are not religious Jews who attend synagogue three times a day. Therefore, their musical style embraces the influences of contemporary Israel. He remembers:

> He [Zohar] had [pointing to his throat] a great voice. Although he did not study he was a sharp man. When he sang, he would see pictures and images before his eyes. He understood better than others the soul of the text. He knew how to use his voice in a way no one else could. Every word had a true, right sound. I wrote the

> songs for him and about him. I brought him the song "Magnolia." It reminded him of his failed marriage to Bracha. He read it and he started to choke with tears. He told me he could not sing this. He was very sensitive.[22]

The Authenticity of "Thinness and Poverty"

Zohar Argov's "authenticity" was rooted in his voicing a discomfiting musical moment. The cultural and artistic conflict itself was authentic and expressed the interface between Eastern vocalization and Western and Mediterranean musical accompaniment. Distinguished Moroccan-born composer, conductor, and musicologist Avraham Amzallag, one of the judges who supported Argov's performance of "ha-Peraḥ be-gani" at the festival, contrasts Argov's "authentic" voice with the "thinness and poverty" of the musical arrangements. This musicological observation fails to acknowledge the lack of opportunities in Israel during this period for training in Arab and other Middle Eastern musical systems that would have enhanced Avihu Medina's composition; however, this analysis is complicated by the fact that the arrangement was created by Nancy Brandes, an Eastern European Jewish arranger and musician. Amzallag elucidates Argov's vocal skill in contrast with what he considers to be the impoverished musical arrangement:

> He had an authenticity in his voice. I chose the singer, not the song "ha-Peraḥ be-gani." The music itself has nothing in it that can explain the phenomenon of Zohar Argov. The melody is simple, very melodic. The key is the performer, Zohar Argov. He felt the poverty of the material and its distance from the sources of real Musiḳah Mizraḥit. So, because of the distance of "ha-Peraḥ be-gani" from Musiḳah Mizraḥit, he put some *muwwal* here and there, or a silsul, which he borrowed from famous Oriental singers.[23]

Amzallag's comments provide an illustration of the battle over authenticity that underscored the emergence of Mediterranean Israeli music. His anxieties about simple melodies, distant origins, reconfigured pan-ethnic musical sensibilities, and "Oriental" borrowings are part of the cultural anxieties of the period. Mizraḥi music was necessarily distant from its Middle Eastern origins because the musicians had no opportunity to study the forms with masters. The new instrumental forms had to be "borrowed" while the vocals were often learned in the context of Yemenite synagogues. The music was old and new, sacred and secular, Arab and Jewish, all at the same time, thus putting pressure on any authenticity claims.

Argov's gifts were an Eastern vocal signature without exaggeration, a style that did not insist on itself and an ability to infuse Western styles with an Eastern edge. What differentiated his style from those of other Mizraḥi singers was that he neither overcompensated with superfluous *silsulim* nor refashioned his voice to fit into the Western Israeli soundscape. Amzallag notes:

> Those who want to copy him think his success is due to something material. But they are utterly wrong. The direct and authentic way in which Zohar sings that song and puts that *muwwal* into it gives the song an enormous power, even though its melody is simple. We are not only talking here about the combination of wonderful *muwwal* pieces from this or that repertoire. We are talking about a wise singer who knew the right dosage. He knew how to incorporate the real Mizraḥi elements with the "so-called" Mizraḥi elements. Other singers from this genre lacked proportion. With all the melisma the melody gets lost. Argov had a wonderful vocal instrument, clear and emotive.[24]

Yemenite musician Moshe Ben-Mosh suggested an indigenous aesthetic rationale for Argov's successful conjoining of tradition and musical competency within a blurred sacred-secular context. "Zohar presented music like it's written in the Bible, with the same *te'amim* [cantillation marks, or accents, used to chant the Torah]," noted Ben-Mosh. "When it is done with the right emphasis it makes the listener understand. And this is what came to Zohar spontaneously."[25]

Tradition

Masortiyut (traditionality) is a forgiving form of religious observance practiced by many Mizraḥi creators interviewed for this project. In musical terms, "*ani masorti*" ("I am traditional") expresses itself in the depolarization of sacred and secular generic oppositions.[26] The sacred and secular distinction is reformed as a continuum through which Mizraḥi composers and singers pay homage to ethnic, religious, national, and generational loyalties. Sacred and para-liturgical Hebrew texts with a variety of musical arrangements honor Israeli belonging and evoke the ancestral home. Arabic, Farsi, Aramaic, or Turkish texts often honor performers' parents who arrived in Israel with ancestral memories of Yemen, Morocco, Kurdistan, or Iran. Greek, Spanish, and Italian songs reflect a Mediterranean locale, and rock instrumentations and rhythms attest to a competence and grounding in contemporary Western styles. The use of *ha-Shir ha-Erets Yisre'eli* signifies national belonging and competence in the sound track of Zionist discourse. These substyles coexist within the same contexts of neighborhood events, synagogue, club, and cassettes.

In musical terms, then, traditionality is a process of negotiating and recomposing disparate musics while adhering selectively to long-established communal music practices. The goal of a traditional music practitioner is to sound right. "Sounding right," as Moshe Ben-Mosh notes, means that listeners respond emotionally and recognize the aesthetic proximity of classical Arabic tunes, Sabbath *piyyutim*, Mediterranean and Western popular musics, and European Israeli repertoire. For Ben-Mosh, Zohar Argov sounded right because he knew how to render the text with the correct vocal style used to intone the Torah—whether in a Greek love song such as "Elinor" or the para-liturgical "'Et dodim kalah," also implanted in a Greek lyrical bed.

By combining prayers, popular and classical tunes, and sacred and secular lyrics, Argov performed and embodied musical proximities. These musical proximities can be understood aesthetically as a movement among contrasts, an affinity of seemingly incongruent musical contours, proximities of contrasted and conjoined ethnicities in a political landscape. This is part of the politics of the aesthetic.

Mizraḥi singers practiced "sounding right" in the synagogue and at neighborhood seasonal and life-cycle celebrations. Weddings were locations where neighborhood singers consolidated a repertoire. They performed both ethnically specific selections and pan-ethnic blends as they reconfigured sacred and secular texts. Weddings were rituals in which *Mizraḥiyut* itself was both consolidated and transgressed as Ashkenazim and Mizraḥim entered into what were regarded as mixed marriages. Sadly, the union of European, Middle Eastern, and North African Jews in marriage, which ought to have consolidated the central aim of the "Ingathering of the Exiles," often produced strong negative reactions, typically from Ashkenazi parents who felt their children were marrying down. Mizraḥi parents also had concerns when their children entered into "mixed marriages," but their concerns were often about a loss of cultural continuity rather than status.

Ethnic Grappling and the Creation of a Pan-Mizraḥi Style

Argov's early training in the synagogue gave him the ability to incorporate liturgical elements in his singing style. His use of biblical chanting techniques in secular compositions touched a chord with community members. Argov's mass appeal is partially explained by the fact that he gave voice to the formation of a Mizraḥi pan-ethnic identity that formed as Middle Eastern and North African communities interacted in *ma'abarot* and neighborhoods. The second generation, born in Israel or brought there at an early age, was often estranged from both its traditional roots and the mainstream Israeli music milieu. It was in this environment that a new Mizraḥi identity began to develop. Argov's audience identified with his voice, which resonated with their struggle. The political took on the contours of the aesthetic. Yemenite composer/guitarist Yigal Ḥared noted, "He would start a phrase of *muwwal*; it was like a charge forward in battle. His 'lai, lai, lai' would drive the audience crazy. It was so natural with him. At the end of the line he would add Oriental variations. That was his trademark. It became a model that other singers copied. Others that tried did not succeed in doing the *silsulim* like him. Zohar sounded right."[27]

Argov practiced this musical alchemy in ghettoized neighborhoods, where the rabbi and the drug dealer competed for jurisdiction. The poverty he faced was more than economic: there were no musical institutions where he could seek support for his emerging sound. Yet the streets were filled with his voice as he mediated between dissonant musical aesthetics and formed a local style. This hybrid sound came to characterize, and even stereotype, Mizraḥi culture in Israel.

Argov personified ethnic grappling; he grew up attending synagogue, wore *pe'ot,* chewed *gāt,*[28] revered his mother, and ate *jaḥnun.*[29] He also dressed in bold suits and sported a thick gold chain. He sang lyrics that were a natural outgrowth of the cultural forces colliding in the *ma'abarah.*

From Legendary Voice to National Hero: Yemeniteness as Social Construction

Temaniyut (Yemeniteness) in Israel is a social construction forged between worlds. Communities such as Shikun ha-Mizraḥ echoed with resonances of Yemen and Israel while being neither and both at the same time. Argov's voice mirrored the Yemenite dilemma in Israel: the retention of communal memory, identification with a pan-Mizraḥi subculture, and participation in the Israeli national culture. The Yemenite project of becoming Israeli was burdened by the dichotomy between the Israeli construction of Yemeniteness and the actuality of being a Yemenite. Argov embodied the struggle to forge a contemporary Yemenite-Mizraḥi-Israeli identity.

In modern Israel, the question of authenticity and national identity was complicated by the country's relative youth. As Yael Zerubavel suggests, "In the challenging formative years of Israeli society, the Zionist settlers' revolutionary rhetoric articulated clearly their desire to depart from Jewish life in exile, and its social, cultural, economic, and political manifestations. The Zionist collective memory elevated the period of antiquity as the Hebrew nation's historic past and enhanced its commemorative density."[30]

The conventional wisdom was that Yemenites had been isolated from outside influences for over two thousand years and therefore retained unaltered the practices of the ancient Hebrews. These "unpolluted" cultural remnants were held to link modern Israelis to their ancient soil. In reality, the idea that Yemenites were protected from contact with other cultures by their geographical isolation was not entirely the case. Trade, migration, wars, and other forces brought the Yemenites into contact with other groups over the past two thousand years. The idealized Yemenite resembled neither the Yemenites who lived in the Israel of the 1950s nor their ancient forebears.

As Yemenite immigrants faced a conflict between who they were and who the Israelis imagined them to be, they confronted an unsettling disjuncture between what they imagined Israel to be and the reality that greeted them in the 1950s. Their enduring love of Zion, expressed by poets throughout the centuries as a sacred religious ideal, had little to do with the idea of building a secular nation-state.

Argov's voice and lyrics resonated with Yemenite longing for *Erets Yisrael,* yet carried the disillusionment of the *ma'abarah* and subsequent exclusion from mainstream Israeli society. Yearning for lost love may reflect not only the lyrical reality of the individual, but also the collective experience of mass migration, cultural subordination, and disenfranchisement in the new society for which the Yemenites had longed. The resonance of the song *Marlen* for Mizraḥim may be an example of this:

> For nights of eternity
> I stood in front of her window
> And a sad serenade I sang.
> I sent her flowers and a thousand smiles.
> I wrote her words of love.
> I have nourished her and tended her.
> She grew up, not a child anymore.
> She said goodbye and went away,
> No one knows where to.
> Marlen, oh Marlen.[31]

Zohar Argov belongs to this descriptive realm. He is a partner in the emergence of Mizraḥi pan-ethnicity. Yet at the same time, through his

A mural in the Yemenite Tel Aviv neighborhood of Kerem ha-Temanim (Yemenite Vineyard) depicts the immigration of hundreds of Yemenite Jews who arrived in Palestine in the 1880s, inspired by religious conviction rather than national ideology. (Photo by author)

Yemeniteness, he was empowered with a special status so that even the moment of cultural confusion reflected in his voice carried in it the aura of honesty and authenticity. As Iranian Israeli designer Shlomi Namdar put it:

> Zohar was not aware of genres. He wasn't part of the larger social context. He did what he knew how to do. He had an artistic honesty. This is what people call "putting his heart in the singing." The authenticity actually finds its expression in the lyrics' "lack of authenticity." He sings kitsch from our mainstream Israeli perspective. But for Zohar and his audience it wasn't kitsch. He was not saccharin. He was lyrical and melancholy. There was something honest about his voice.[32]

Heroics: Revoicing Communal Struggle

Zohar Argov's life and death occupy a central position in the history of Mediterranean Israeli music. While he achieved unparalleled fame in Mizraḥi

Zohar Argov and Avinu Medina at Argov's thirtieth birthday party in 1986. (Courtesy Avihu Medina Archive)

communities, he failed to overcome the personal, familial, and social hardships that challenged him. His artistic genius was set against a harsh sociopolitical climate; he was worshipped by his community but despised by national cultural brokers. His singing resonated with the emotional power of these uneasy proximities. In giving vocal expression to his community's culture and feelings, Argov challenged the very fabric of Israeli society. He battled to win space in a seemingly impenetrable system that considered his style aesthetically unappealing and politically unacceptable. He struggled to win attention for himself and those groups like him for which cultural blending was the natural extension of multivocal selfhood.

His brand of heroics not only ruffled the social fabric; it challenged the consecrated tradition of the Israeli hero. Zerubavel notes that "the establishment of [a master commemorative] narrative constitutes one of the most important mechanisms by which a nation constructs a collective identity for what Benedict Anderson calls an 'imagined community.'"[33] According to Zerubavel, the modern Israeli hero exhibits a willingness to sacrifice his life for the nation, thereby giving precedence to communal survival over individual identity.

Zohar Argov did not die liberating Jews from Nazi forces like Hannah Senesh, nor with patriotic slogans on his lips like the protagonist in Zerubavel's study, Yosef Trumpeldor.[34] He was not killed in a war against external enemies, but took his own life inside an Israeli prison. Yet Argov's melismatic sound penetrated public space and gave voice to Jews from North African and Middle Eastern communities. Argov's heroics are symptomatic of what Zerubavel calls the "shattering of the myth," the deconstruction of the monologic hold on Israeli national images and ideals of an Eastern European ethos and aesthetic. She calls attention to Trumpeldor's glorification as a "function of the hegemony of eastern European Jews in the Yishuv":

> The growing political assertiveness of groups whose voice was largely marginalized during earlier decades has gradually weakened the image of the New Hebrew, fashioned by eastern European Jews at the beginning of the century. In a society in which ethnicity has become a major political factor, a Russian Jewish hero can no longer serve as a self-evident collective representation of "the Israeli." The humorous lore articulates this discrepancy by pointing out Trumpeldor's identity as an eastern European Jewish immigrant who resembles more the Jews of Exile than contemporary Israelis. In fact his earlier glorification as the prototypical New Hebrew can now be seen as a function of the hegemony of eastern European Jews in the Yishuv; the continued efforts to preserve his mythical image can be regarded as evidence of their desire to perpetuate it. An Israeli man of Middle Eastern descent declared when I interviewed him, "Honey, if Trumpeldor were a Yemenite, no street would have been named after him!"[35]

Culture and politics are not always at odds. Both can reenfranchise marginalized communities. Discounting Argov's political contributions because of his mode of expression and lifestyle fails to recognize the potentially revolutionary role of his music and of music in general. In effect, Argov made the Mizraḥi experience audible. As Asher Reuveni remarked, "We needed a champ. If there hadn't been a Zohar, we would have had to invent one."[36] His music expresses the failure of integration. It tells a personal story devoid of national missions or historical redemption. The lyrics assert everyday love, rejection, and pain above exalted ideals. As Argov said, "I have a beautiful voice. That's from God. But the words I sing are from life."[37]

Chapter 5

The Posthumous Consecration of Zohar Argov

Zohar could not have been Baba Sali,[1] because of his lifestyle, but now that he is dead in his grave he can be holy.

—Yehuda Kessar, quoted in Merit Tobi, *"ha-Melekh"* (The King): *Research*

After his death Zohar Argov became a legendary character, mythic figure, and tragic hero. His posthumous consecration was an authoritative coproduction that brought Mizraḥi and Ashkenazi interlocutors together to create a shared national icon. Mizraḥi producers, musicians, managers, and family members cooperated with mainstream Ashkenazi journalists, playwrights, and poets to construct and promote Argov's postmortem reputation. The performances they produced of Argov defied generic classification; as repertoire clusters that exhibit similarities without being confined to rigid categories, they took on a weblike dimension.

Argov appeared in his new incarnation in disembodied performances on audiotape and in spectral performances on videotape, forming relationships between former detractors and devotees and bolstering his posthumous reputation. After his own death, he was reconstituted outside his body as a social presence. According to Katharine Young, narrative is a means for reconstituting a social presence and affording a transformation such as Argov's rise to national tragic figure. The narratives in newspaper articles, theater, and film reembody Argov in an enduring and vibrant afterlife.[2]

By the time of his death, Argov had risen from marginalized performing artist to social and cultural hero. In the ensuing years, his elevation from neighborhood hero to a tragic national figure, inhabitant of legend and myth, can be traced through commemorative events and artistic productions:

pilgrimages to his grave; the establishment of a drug rehabilitation center in his name; memorial concerts; performances of his music by mainstream artists; and theater, television, and cinema adaptations of his life.

The impact of this transmogrification from human to hero throughout the region, and indeed throughout the world, was evident in Adam Ray's declaration in 1994 that he was the reincarnation of Zohar Argov. Ray, an American Catholic from the state of Oregon with no previous knowledge of the Hebrew language, memorized Argov's repertoire (complete with correct pronunciation of *ḥet* and *'ayin* and with vocal *silsulim*) and appeared at the Arad Music Festival, where he sang one of Argov's signature songs, "Elinor."[3]

The Construction of Local Legend

By the time of his death, Argov was a hero in the Mizraḥi milieu. His afterlife found him reborn as a new Israeli subject. The processes at work refashioned the facts and fictions surrounding a contemporary artist in legend, myth, and tragedy. Stories of Argov's life were reinvented posthumously to take on the character of legend. The legend gained force through repeated performances in newspaper articles and oral stories about pilgrimages to his grave site.[4]

Argov's legendary status did not cast doubt on the generally known facts of his life, but certain threads of their subsequent refabrication are suspect. In their study of the formation of legends, Linda Degh and Andrew Vazsonyi note:

> The legend carriers, believers or nonbelievers, usually accept, pass on, and are fed back the verbal communication they themselves have launched. Thus, sometimes it might be the echo of their own statements that acts as substantial proof for the legend rather than the real facts. If this reasoning is acceptable, then theoretically we must accept that a truthful story, passed through the legend process and handed down through the legend conduit, can become a legend.[5]

Although useful for describing the relationship between actual events and legend formation, Degh and Vazsonyi's comments do not focus on the social forces that drive the emerging separation between the real and the legendary accounts. Though the singer, along with subsequent Mizraḥi performers, was instrumental in repositioning ethnicity in Israeli society, his heroic status was compromised by the scandal and crime associated with him. As in other

On this CD cover, Adam Ray hovers above New York City holding a tablet inscribed in Hebrew and English with Mediterranean Israeli songs, including Argov's "Yam shel dema'ot" (Sea of Tears). (Courtesy Oren Amram)

cases in which legends form around popular figures, scandal both fuels and threatens reputation. Both the artists and their handlers try risky strategies to promote their careers; newspapers scoop up scandals that also act as publicity, and fans get invested in flawed heroes.

The transformation of the story of Argov's life into the stuff of legend spilled over from its gestation in newspaper stories into various public performance venues. The legend took shape in Avihu Medina's commentaries during memorial concerts for Zohar Argov in the late 1980s and 1990s. The structure of the event, and especially Medina's carefully crafted texts preceding each song, elevated the problematic details of the singer's life into poetic form. For example, Medina transformed Argov's drug addiction into a larger national allegory of suffering and failed recovery. The memorial concerts became performances in their own right, gained momentum, and were institutionalized as annual events. Medina and other Mizraḥi singers initiated a series of anti-drug events at which the legend expanded. Argov's mother and sister, often seated somberly in the front row, featured prominently at these events.

From Legendary Voice to Mythic Rehabilitation

The transmogrification of Zohar Argov provides an opportunity to observe the fashioning of myth from the legends surrounding a contemporary figure. Selected historical details of Argov's life became the basic building blocks for the transmuting narrative. In posthumous conversions of humans to heroes, the boundaries between the analytical category of legend, which is rooted in history and myth and which suspends history and believability, become blurred, and the categories conflate. The conflation occurs as Argov's story outgrows the personal details of his life, allowing his frailties and his gifts to assume pan-human and ultimately mythic dimension. In myth, where the supernatural and human coexist, the taboos that would challenge the legendary or heroic figure are admissible and even anticipated. In Argov's makeover as mythic figure, we are witness to the mutation of one genre into another.

Argov emerged, after his death, both as a legendary character and as a mythic figure representing the reintegration of Mizraḥiyut into the Israeli mainstream ethos. Unlike other legendary characters that bridge ancient and modern heroic narratives,[6] Argov's mythic rise challenged Israeli origin myths about the role of the Yemenite as a link to the ancient past. Instead, Argov's story cut away from the past and insisted on a new, messy, and painful contemporary narrative replete with drugs, sexual violence, silk suits, and ethnic discrimination. The legendary element of the Zohar construction secured belief; the mythic component enchanted the psyche.

Pierre Maranda eloquently describes the power and allure of myth:

> Myth is the reluctant acknowledgment that the event is mightier than the structure. But myth is also and more than anything else the hallucinogenic chant in which mankind harmonizes the vagaries of history, the chant hummed for generations in the minds of men and humming itself in the human mind (that innate dream to reduce continuous randomness to a final pattern) as hinted by Plato and Jung, or, better, as amplified by Chomsky and Levi-Strauss.[7]

As compelling and hallucinogenic as Argov was, literally providing tunes that people hummed, his legacy failed, as legacies inevitably do, to harmonize the social discords that gave rise to it. Argov's hope was to be so fully integrated into the Israeli popular music world that he and other Mizraḥi musicians would be "scattered throughout the hours" of broadcast time or "not played at all." Argov responded to segregation by defiantly (and painfully) threatening that no airplay was better than being broadcast during restricted times and under alienating categories.[8] Not surprisingly, this hope for integration turned out to be an unsolved struggle in Argov's lifetime. This unsolvability—the creation of a diverse and yet cohesive society—is the subject of contemporary theories of multiculturalism that similarly offer as their only, and impossible, solution a recognition and even celebration of difference without redressing the social asymmetries at its root.

From Mythic Rehabilitation to Tragic Hero

In December 1990, three years after Argov's death, a memorial concert was organized in Jerusalem by local Mizraḥi neighborhood anti-drug activists. This and two succeeding annual concerts were called "ha-Peraḥ be-gani" (The Flower in My Garden) after Argov's award-winning song of the same name at the Festival of Eastern Song in 1982. The memorial concerts were produced by the Israel Broadcasting Authority and held in Jerusalem's leading convention center, Binyane ha-umah. The event was a fundraiser with the aim of establishing a center for drug rehabilitation to be called the Zohar Argov Village.

Argov's rehabilitation became more densely layered with the opening of a theater production, *ha-Melekh* (The King),[9] about the tragic elements of his life. With this play, the assimilation of Argov's life to the structure of Greek tragedy compounded the already muddied generic delineations of his biography. The actual man had been elevated beyond mortality to the realm of tragic hero; subsequently he was called into the service of theatrical/aesthetic catharsis for both Mizraḥi and Ashkenazi Israelis temporarily transported beyond the ethnic divides by their shared empathy for Argov.

Writing about fifth-century Athens, Jean-Pierre Vernant describes the tragic hero:

> Tragedy takes heroic legend as its material. The hero is no longer put forward as a model, as he used to be in epic and in lyric poetry. Now he has become a problem. The hero becomes the subject of debate and interrogation that, through this person, implicates the

> fifth-century spectator, the citizen of democratic Athens. From the point of view of tragedy, human beings and human action are seen, not as realities to be pinned down and defined in their essential qualities in the manner of the philosophers of the succeeding century, but as problems that defy resolution, riddles with double meanings that are never fully decoded.[10]

This description of the hero in fifth-century Athens is relevant in late-twentieth-century Israel where similarly realities cannot always be pinned down and meanings are never fully decoded. Yael Zerubavel has written extensively on the resuscitation of ancient figures to serve modern-day Israeli national interests. The story of Zohar Argov resembles other tragic legends and at the same time departs from them by representing a renegade Yemenite whose behavior was far from exemplary and who thus is not easily assimilated into the master narrative.[11]

The emergence of Argov as tragic hero positioned him to mediate between East and West in the national project of forming a unified society. He was both heroic and flawed, transcending the limits of his ethnic status and to an extent his criminal past. Rendering him palatable to mainstream Israelis made him of greater use for the national project. As a tragic figure, Argov not only evoked but also muted the tough ethnic issues that reverberated in Israeli society by distancing them in an ancient dramatic form.

From Local Legend to Local King

Argov was called the king of Mediterranean Israeli music. He achieved the status of king because he was acknowledged by both his audience and the Israeli art world to be the quintessential Mizraḥi singer. For Mizraḥi communities, Argov satisfied a desperate need for a local hero. For Ashkenazi media and cultural brokers, he provided an opportunity to admit a Mizraḥi singer, conveniently and tragically deceased, into the official canon. They refashioned him from what they considered to be an embarrassing example of "cheap music" into an acceptable mold, a legend out of the newspaper columns and a fallen hero in a Greek-style tragedy.

In a probing article that appeared in the Tel Aviv local paper in 1990, Amir Ben-David and Michal Zunder wrote:

> Zohar Argov died three years ago at age thirty-two. It seems to be a story about an admired star who was tempted by drugs like Janis Joplin and Elvis Presley. But it is an Israeli story about the eldest

> son of the Orkabi family from Shikun ha-Mizraḥ, who touched the dream and was the hero of hundreds of thousands. That once-in-a-lifetime voice of Argov still attracts dozens of people who try to imitate it and it continues to sell. Although the Argov myth is still alive, the full story of his life has not yet been told.[12]

A painting of Argov by a renowned Ashkenazi Israeli artist, Uri Lifshitz, was reproduced along with Ben-David and Zunder's biographical article. The authors went on to tell Argov's story by providing the background information for a feature film, *Zohar, ha-Melekh*,[13] released in 1994, two years after the theater production of *ha-Melekh.*

From Local King to National Avant-Garde Theater

The play *ha-Melekh* was written and directed by Ashkenazi dramatist Shemuel Hasfari, a former artistic director of Tel Aviv's municipal Cameri Theater.[14] Hasfari is known for his commitment to alternative theater and his sharp satire of Israeli society. The play is based on months of research by Merit Tobi. She scoured newspaper clippings and interviewed family members, impresarios, musicians, and community members. Avihu Medina was a major contributor of information on Argov's life and reflections on their musical relationship, and figured prominently in the play itself. Through the interview process Mizraḥi community members collaborated with Ashkenazi researchers to construct a fictional documentary on Argov's life. The dialogue incorporates actual quotations and memories retold through fictionalized events.

The play consists of a patchwork of flashbacks of Argov's life. In the opening scenes we hear a Yemenite child learning biblical cantillations. The child's clear and beautiful voice is juxtaposed with Argov's lifeless body hanging in a prison cell.[15] Using the framework of a radio tribute to Argov, the play documents his rise as the "King of Mediterranean Israeli Music" and gives birth to two salient speculations about Argov: that he had a death wish and felt guilty over his father's death.[16] The validity of the first idea is controversial. A number of newspaper articles from the time of Argov's death mention his wanting to die.[17] In the play, Argov's death wish appears as a recurring theme linked to guilt over his father's death. For example, an unidentified woman calls into Medina's program on Israel army radio: "He doesn't want to live. He is not interested in going clean; he wants to die. But he doesn't have the courage alone so he does it in other ways, to die on stage if possible."[18]

Playwright Shemuel Hasfari outside Beit Lessin Theatre during a dress rehearsal for *ha-Melekh* (The King) in 1992. (Photo by author)

The central scene of the play takes place in prison, where the jailer, Turjeman (who is married to Argov's fictional ex-wife, Nava), makes a deal with him. If Argov will refuse drugs for just a few hours, Turjeman will give Nava back to him. At first the deal seems to be the taunting of a jealous man. But as Argov's torment and suffering increases, Turjeman's compassion grows. He implores Argov to be strong. Argov breaks down, alluding to his sinful deed, and firmly implants the notion of his fatal course:

(Turjeman holds Zohar tightly)

Turjeman: Enough enough! You can hold on. Everything will be all right. Think of what it will be like and think of how you two will be together again and think about Nava. Think about your mother. How you'll build a house for her, a palace. Hold on, just a little bit longer. Show them who you are!

Zohar: No, I am forbidden. I do not deserve it. This is the punishment.

Turjeman: So what. You went a little bit wild. You don't have to die for that.

Zohar: Not only that. I killed. . . .

Turjeman: Who did you kill?

Zohar: Give me the pills![19]

Later in the play, a newspaper woman pushes Argov to talk about this buried memory:

Newspaper woman: Why did it all happen? Why did this misery come on you? The misery, the humiliation. The pain. Do you know why?

Zohar: From God.

Newspaper woman: That is not an answer.

Zohar: I've done something not good.

Newspaper woman: You have done something not good?

Zohar: Yes, I am sorry.

Newspaper woman: When?

Zohar: Once before everything . . . before everything. Everything that happened should have happened. Everything is a punishment for that thing. Move aside, I have to go make people happy.

Newspaper woman: What did you do?

Zohar: I can't say.

Newspaper woman: What did you do? I am not going to leave you alone. There is no crime that deserves such punishment. Maybe you are wrong. Maybe you are not to blame.

Zohar: I am not wrong.

Newspaper woman: Is this something to do with your wife? Child? Drugs?

(Zohar signals her to come closer. She comes closer and he whispers something in her ear. She freezes stiff in amazement. Then she rises and walks to the corner of the room and holds her face

> in her hands. She gazes at him and then comes back and holds his head against her body. He doesn't respond. She just stares and strokes his head.)[20]

When Avihu takes Argov to Eilat to help him dry out, they have the following conversation:

> Zohar: Life is beautiful. I breathe, I see colors. Life is beautiful. Too bad. . . .
> Avihu: (Hugs him) You deserve life too!
> Zohar: (Nods) Yes!
> Avihu: Yes!
> Zohar: No! I have done too much wrong. You see here on my forehead. There's a curse on it. The sign of Cain.[21]

Argov's voice proclaiming his guilt is countered here by Medina and the newspaper reporter's voices offering both forgiveness and the assertion that he doesn't deserve to die, no matter how heinous his crime. The play invites the viewer to take on those counter voices and find an alternative to the devastating consequences of blame and guilt. By embellishing Argov's difficult life of chronic suffering, lost love, and premature death with the notion of a death wish and a shameful deed, he is transformed from a glorified pop hero to a tragic figure. Not surprisingly, the shameful deed is not Argov's real-life rape conviction but the fictionalized though plausible complicity in the death of his father. Serving time in prison for rape may be too painful for this particular tragedy.

From Local Celebrity to Political Activist

Hasfari's theatrical depiction transforms Argov into a political activist recognizable by European Israelis. Hasfari interprets Argov's story sociologically, casting him as a victim of social inequality, seeing in Argov's life "the fundamental story of the war in Israel between two cultures. For thirty years we had here a legitimate Ashkenazi culture and an illegitimate Sephardi culture; there was a certain kind of music, way of speaking Hebrew, and style of dress that was acceptable and another one which was not. The Ashkenazim didn't want to accept the fact that they now lived in the Middle East, and in many ways they still don't."[22]

Through this reading of Argov's life, Hasfari portrays the singer not only as the "king" of his musical style but as a symbolic king of the Mizraḥi struggle. In remaking Argov into a Western-style activist, his homegrown resistance is overshadowed. For example, when asked in a real-life newspaper interview about his activism he responded with a different tone:

> I am not interested in Ashkenazim or Sephardim. Today it is already understood that 70 percent of the country loves this style. It's true that once I used to speak about discrimination in the radio. I thought it was an intended policy. Now I understand that it is all a matter of the taste of the editors. Nothing you can do about it. I cannot go to the editor of *Sha'atayim mi-shtayim* and tell him "play Avner Gadassi!"
>
> I do not know about politics. I have a "small head."[23] Why did I vote Likud? My mother said that the Labor Party was in power and no one could buy a video and a color television. Now everyone has one. You understand. That's the way I see all this nonsense. I don't know anything about it. There is nothing in it for me.[24]

Drugs and Deprivation: The White Death

Argov's genuine convictions have been refashioned in the dialogue in *ha-Melekh.* A comparison of the text of the 1986 *Yedi'ot Aḥaronot* interview, from which the "white death" monologue was derived, with the script for the play reveals some of these differences. The newspaper interview reads as follows:

> You know why they call it the white death? Because you are a living dead man, exactly a living dead man. A rag, *stam ben adam.*[25] You get up in the morning and your head is in the drug, go out to the street with the drug, eat the drug, go to sleep with the drug. You don't feel like going out at night with girls. The world stays the same, only you change. I could not perform without the drug. I would see the audience all scary all of a sudden, looking me in the eyes. Paranoia. I didn't want to give shows, to sing. I stopped believing in my power. Confidence was in the drug.[26]

In the script, the interview is transformed into a dialogue between Argov and an Ashkenazi woman journalist. In the scene, Argov's language has been reinterpreted to suit the intent of the play:

> Zohar: I can't without the drug. I see the audience as a monster, with a thousand eyes looking at me, that wants to devour me.

Paranoia. Why is it called the "white death?" Do you know? Because you are willing to die in order to be white. To stand on the stage like those *Lahakot tseva'iyot* (Army Bands). To forget that in the radio they don't play you because you are not white. To forget that in the newspapers they write that you are primitive. To forget that they wrote that the Yemenite prayers you sang were "banal, anal," I don't know what. You see me climbing the stage, going to the mike, as if it's nothing. You don't see how many monsters I have to move out of the way. Only I see them. Laughing, mocking. Doing me a favor that they bring me up on the stage with them in the same show, as if I am a chimpanzee that learned how to sing in Yiddish. I cannot beat up a radio editor to persuade him to love me. I cannot put a hand grenade in the radio in order to blow it up. Because tomorrow there will be another white guy. I cannot finish them.

Newspaper woman: So you finish yourself?

Zohar: So I finish myself, in your honor. So you will have something to put in the title, to sell newspapers on Friday to the black suckers that worry about me.[27]

While the dialogue of the play can be traced directly to the actual interview, Argov's words have been rewritten in order to sustain the Ashkenazi image of the singer as an angry "black" activist. The fictionalized references to violence and the harshness of his tone convey a rage crafted to conform to the white image of the "black" rebel. Racialized images of whiteness and blackness, purity and contamination, play throughout the script.

Suffering and Unrequited Love

Numerous meanings, both literal and symbolic, are attributed to Argov's suffering and suicide, including unrequited love, artistic torment, the Mizraḥi social condition, and irredeemable sin. All of these attributes of suffering enhance Argov's status in the eyes of both Mizraḥi community members and the Israeli cultural elite. In addition to being seen as a victim of these circumstances, Argov is invested by his audience and by Ashkenazi myth-makers with pain and love as the quintessential qualities of the artistic temperament. Blues, soul, jazz, and even rock 'n' roll artists are judged according to a criterion that includes the notion that true art emerges out of pain. Popular music, too, espouses the romantic ideal of the artist as one who suffers for his art, driven not by commercial interests but by some ineffable longing to create.

From Scandal to Tragedy

Adrian Poole writes,

> The liberating quality of tragedy is one that draws in the audience or the reader. It opens us up to a sense of possibility which we understand and feel at one and the same time to be both dangerous and necessary. The menace and promise of tragedy lies in this recognition of the sheer potentiality of all the selves we might be and all the worlds we might make together or destroy together. Through tragedy we encounter the image of futurity itself, at once so necessary and so dangerous that even as we flinch from it we are steeled to the prospect of seeing it through.[28]

In the play, Argov's artistic and personal suffering is linked to the mysterious notion of an unforgivable sin that ultimately leads to his death. With the shameful deed somehow related to his father's death, Argov's story is elevated from scandal to classic tragedy.

Classic tragedy contains several fixed phases. The first is the stage of innocence, which establishes the essential good of the hero and provides a point of departure for the tragic course of events. The second stage involves a shameful deed. The hero commits a predestined crime for which he must be punished. As with Oedipus, the crime is both intentional and inevitable. Oedipus kills his father and marries his mother deliberately, but he is unaware that they are his parents. It is the curious combination of free will and fate that makes tragedy. In this case, Hasfari creates the idea of Argov's complicity in the mysterious circumstances of Ovadya's death. The third stage, hubris, is the sin of pride, often manifested by mortals attempting to achieve the stature of gods. Argov's meteoric rise to fame climaxes in his death in prison. The final stage of tragedy is catharsis, requiring a revalidation of human values that result from a purgation, a climactic eruption of emotion that clears the psyche for the imposition of order. Catharsis restores balance to society. In this way tragedy reinforces and restores social order.[29] In the following discussion, I consider each of these categories to understand what has to be put in place (and what obscured) in order to make the transference from scandal to tragedy.

Innocence

At the beginning of the play, Argov's character is portrayed as innocent, as a simple and virtuous neighborhood Yemenite boy. The play draws from his sister's memories of the atmosphere at home on the Sabbath:

> On Friday and Saturday there was a holiday atmosphere in the house, an atmosphere of *piyyutim*. All the family would gather around the table and sing. Zohar was sensitive about making mistakes in the tune. When he went to synagogue, he always wore special Shabbat clothes. In the synagogue he would often sing. All the neighbors would come and listen to him . . . just to hear him read. He had such a beautiful voice. At the age of five he sat in the yard banging on tin cans and singing. The Polish neighbor would tempt him with sweets so that he would stop singing during her noontime nap.[30]

These images could portray any Yemenite boy with a beautiful voice who becomes a beloved participant in the weekly cycle of prayers. Yet here the image of his special Sabbath clothes, traditional style of drumming on tin objects, and perfect chanting of sacred texts are elevated to convey a uniquely prodigious child.

In a later scene, we witness Argov's first visit with manager Shimoni (a composite of Asher and Meir Reuveni), underlining his naive and innocent approach to the music business. Shimoni is bargaining with Argov as they try to establish a working agreement:

> Shimoni: We need to sign a contract.
> Zohar: What's this rubbish about a contract. I believe in you and you believe in me so we don't need a contract.
> Shimoni: So we don't need anything then. We don't do business!
> Zohar: Look, I am a good boy. I am not greedy. You will make money. Everything will be okay!
> Shimoni: I accept what you say! I am a good guy and you are a good guy right?
> Zohar: Right.
> Shimoni: So, what do you care? Let's sign a contract![31]

The image of Argov's childhood innocence, which underpins his later trust in others and invites their trust in him, enables community members to judge him as blameless for his downfall. His tragedy is seen as the inevitable outcome of the social condition of Mizraḥim in Israel. This is used to build the character as a victim of circumstance.

Shameful Deed/Fall from Innocence

For Argov's life story to be represented as a Greek tragedy, his fall from innocence must encompass more than the senselessness of drug addiction and either suicide or accidental death from a drug overdose. A shameful deed is needed to transform senselessness into inevitability.

The real cause of Argov's downfall and eventual death is contested. In spite of his efforts to escape a life of poverty and alienation, Argov dies from substance abuse. In the play, Shimoni discusses the inevitability of Argov's destiny, and Medina's character argues that Argov's addiction alone cannot explain his suicide:

> Shimoni: There is nothing we can do. It's in the genes; it's in the blood. His father was addicted to alcohol and so was his grandfather. Even God cannot help him. Destiny and God cannot help him so don't waste your efforts.
>
> Medina: I don't believe in this. I cannot accept what is written here. Not because of Zohar. Because of me. This insults me because it is racism. It is exactly what they say about blacks in America. What they say about Jews all over the world and what they say about Israelis on international radio and television. I don't believe in this. I don't believe in this. I believe that there is Man and there is the spirit of Mankind. And the spirit of Mankind breaks walls and grinds mountains.[32]

In addition to the deed being predestined and shameful, it must be a catalyst for the deterioration of events. Aristotle notes that the most horrifying of the tragic deeds are those done within the family.[33] Argov's complicity in a shameful deed, perhaps involving his father's death, remains mysterious. It is alluded to in a paraphrased summary of Merit Tobi's interview with Medina. Medina's statement as recounted by Tobi appears only in her collection of sources and is not confirmed in any other sources, including interviews with Medina, family members, and detractors. Nevertheless, the dramatic tension of the play pivots around Medina's "spirit of Mankind" quote.

In the play, the mysterious aspect of this death wish is presented as a form of complicity in his father's death. As Medina's character says:

> He wanted to die. After he reached the peak. After he became the king he wanted to die. And I know why. But all I am willing to say is that he had a guilty conscience about some matter. Some sin he committed. He wanted to die. He could not deal with the weight and he felt that he had to pay the heavy price of that sin that haunted him and sat on his conscience. He spoke to me about it a lot.
>
> He wanted to die only after suffering greatly. No one but me knows the reason. He had a large capacity for self-destruction but parallel to that an ability to hurt those who were close to him as if it was obvious to him that the whole thing was already irreversible.
>
> One thing is for sure. He did not want to die the way he died and not when he died. He wanted to live a little longer. To suffer some more and then to die on stage. Big time. As a worthy king. He wanted his death to be tragic. He wanted to kill the king, that beloved and admired king. He said it himself.[34]

Although the audience must comprehend as well as empathize with the root of the hero's suffering, *ha-Melekh* only hints at the shameful deed, leaving the audience to conjure the most horrifying of possibilities. The mystery surrounding Argov's unforgivable "act" is only seen through the nonverbal reaction of the woman journalist. Argov's character elicits empathy by stirring culpability or regretful memories in the audience itself. As Clifford Leech writes, "The tragic hero, as Conrad said of Lord Jim, is 'one of us.' He is not necessarily virtuous, not necessarily free from profound guilt. What he is is a man who reminds us strongly of our own humanity, who can be accepted as standing for us."[35]

Argov's mercuric rise to fame as well as his drug addiction and criminal record can be understood as aspects of his fall. Avihu Medina reflects on this process during one of the memorial concerts:

> Many asked why such a rare and famous talent ruins his own life and stretches his hands toward death. Hanging out in back places, seeking poisons, possessed by fits, blinded. How is it that the "nightingale," the famous one, falls in the hands of a soul merchant? Those greedy for a ready tune. Aching, addicted, tortured, humiliated, and alone. Beaten. Beaten. Overfed with heights. Wishing to die. Till when, my Lord? Till when, my spirit, will you torment my senses? I would rather be dead than alive. In his life he had only a few good days and since then years had already passed.[36]

Argov's drug-related death has been compared to the deaths of numerous popular singers, such as Elvis Presley, Jimi Hendrix, and Janis Joplin, each of whom rose from poverty and social rejection to sudden fame. The inability to survive the demands and pressures of stardom, the attempt to soar to superhuman heights, transforms victory into self-destruction.

Argov claimed that he was seduced into drug use while in Hollywood. This places culpability on an external, Western agent of corruption rather than on an intrinsic element of his character. Hasfari, drawing on an interview in *Yediot Aḥaronot,* incorporates this image in the play. The actual interview raises the issue of Argov's drug use: "When his addiction to drugs became common knowledge, Zohar Argov would say that his first acquaintance with hard drugs was in the States. In an interview he said: 'I've seen millionaires with stashes of drugs and I, little Zohar, was tempted. I saw them and I also wanted it. That's how I started. Besides crack they also brought me heroin. The way down started in glamour.'"[37]

Of course, Argov is not the only celebrity pop-star resurrected as a hero following a death from a drug overdose. The celebrity is a particular kind of hero, who lives simultaneously in the ordinary and extraordinary world, between scandal and heroism. Celebrities serve as role models, and their private lives are scrutinized in the public realm. Their fallibilities are subject to intense critique while at the same time their humanness is a reminder of the shared human condition that transcends fame and anonymity. Their drug abuse is more egregious but, at the same time, the understanding that they are ordinary people makes their mistakes forgivable. In death, the celebrity sometimes has a new opportunity for a reshaped reputation, and in fact, as in the case of Argov and others, celebrity status often changes after death.[38] I would argue that Argov's celebrity was only possible after his death when the sordid details of his life were muted and replaced with an acceptable narrative of social suffering.

Catharsis

The source of catharsis in the tragedy comes from the audience's identification with the pain and suffering of the hero. This empathic pain must give rise to purification rather than bitterness, an irony in the case of a singer of hybrid styles who rejected the attribution of authenticity or purity to Yemeniteness. Instead of anger, the audience must find release in the acceptance of the situation and the belief in human destiny. One way for this to occur is for others (in this case the Ashkenazi audience members) to empathize with the suffering of the tragic character. Redemption consolidates and reconfirms the values that were overturned in the course of the tragedy and thus, while appearing to embrace an outcast, actually confirms the status quo. Society returns, if not to how things were, then at least to a new and strengthened sense of balance and relief in the possibility of recovering from a scandal. Before his death, Argov was a celebrity within the Mizraḥi community, but, if known at all in the Ashkenazi community, it was as an increasingly visible and unwelcome intruder. After his death, the scandal of his drug abuse and sexual assault were reported simultaneously along with the belated celebration of his music. The scandal became part of the story of his personal suffering and led to the creation of the tragic story of communal suffering.

The outpouring of pain and communal loss that followed Argov's death found its cathartic release only gradually and over the course of several years. Opening five years later, *ha-Melekh* contributed to this reaffirmation by resurrecting Argov, full-bodied and full-voiced at the finale. Notwithstanding the conformist dimensions of the tragic model, change can, and in this case did, overcome constraints as Argov's voice infiltrated the Israeli soundscape. In the immediate aftermath of his death, his admirers were unable to resolve their anger and pain. Tobi recorded some of the testimony of community mourners:

> During the week in which the singer died, his fans did not shave; the girls ripped their blouses, tore out their hair. An admirer tattooed Zohar's face on his right arm. Also his name and the date of his death. Gila Golan, a friend of the Orkabi family, says: "When Zohar died, the family was penniless and in debt. I started working two extra shows a day so that on the thirtieth day he would have a tombstone. I even agreed that people put tips in my bra. The main thing is that he would be buried honorably, with a nice tombstone. Not like a dog."[39]

Yossi Blich, a man from Shekhunat ha-Tiḳvah who was thirty at the time of Argov's death, shared the following:

> When I heard that he died, I cried like a child. I did not cry like that when my mother died. He died on a Friday. On Sunday it was my sister's wedding so I tried to commit suicide. I thought there was no reason to live without him. I left a letter saying I wanted to be buried beside him. Everywhere he went to perform I went too. Even before "ha-Peraḥ be-gani." I saw him in a show in Ramle. I have his

> shirt and his pants. Someone that sat in prison with him brought them to me. I keep them in the closet until today. I hear his cassette and cry. Each of his songs is like a story from life. I go to the tomb a few times a month in the middle of the night.[40]

On 2 December 1987, *Yedi'ot Aḥaronot* reported the suicide of thirty-one-year-old Yigal Levy, who left a note claiming that he hanged himself because of Argov's suicide.[41] Cassette booth merchants in the Central Bus Station claim that people would buy the same cassettes over and over in the course of a week because they wore out the old ones. Everything that had the name of Zohar on it was grabbed. One of the sellers said: "His admirers are as fanatic as religious fanatics."[42] With time, Argov's sweeping impact penetrated outside the neighborhood boundaries and infiltrated the cultural institutions and private lives of mainstream Israel.

The concept of catharsis is barely sufficient as an explanation for the response to Argov's death. The catharsis accounts for the emotional intensity of the response, but there is something else here. The play is an aesthetic form with a sort of self-enclosure: just as it cracks open a world at the beginning, it seals it off again at the end. What we carry out of the theater is just the emotion, the catharsis as a movement through emotional states, not the transformation of a world. The something else is the impulse toward resurrection. This narrative spins itself out of the world and seems to retain the potential of spinning itself back in. It remains partially anchored in and pervious to the real, and it is therefore the world that has been changed and must be changed back to restore the social order. Perhaps what narrative makes possible, in contrast to history, is rewinding itself backward and returning the dead to the living. Turning our heroes to the stars, as in the Greek constellations, preserves in the supernatural what has died in the natural. The fragility and precariousness of the celebrity status is obvious, but so is its fabled strength. Insofar as it does not depend on anything, the status can survive the person who has it. Perhaps this is why resurrection works; celebrities live on.

The Argov narrative in its final phase as tragedy became available for the political discourse on ethnicity precisely because its ambiguities made it attractive to both the Mizraḥi and Ashkenazi sides of the debate. For instance, the Mizraḥim could regard him as their hero, who transcends them and thereby raises them above themselves; the Ashkenazim could regard him as a celebrity ceded over to them. His flaws, once a source of disdain, now signal hipness and status for his listeners. Perhaps it perversely pleased some previously European Israeli detractors to accept as a hero a Mizraḥi man so spectacularly flawed. It preserved their prejudices in the guise of overthrowing them.

Communal Reaffirmations

Avihu Medina's oral remarks, crafted for the song introductions at the memorial concerts, contributed to the posthumous construction of Argov's innocent past and inevitable destiny. They began to transform the pain and anger at his loss into a reaffirmation of community and purpose. Medina made his lyrical comments into a discourse of memorialization for a dear friend. And he passed beyond a discourse of memorialization to a discourse of regeneration. His goal was nothing less than communal rebirth:

> I am sorry for you, dear Zohar. Also the beginning of David's mourning for King Saul's son Jonathan in II Samuel 1:26. O horrible suffering and cruel fate and I cry in my heart as I remember how you screamed to me from the well . . . 'please help.' Then I sent my hand to bring you up to the light and you almost came up but again you fell back and again I pulled you away from there . . . almost pulled you away from hell but then you fell back again. And on the edge of the abyss again I called you, 'Zohar, return.' You replied, 'I wish I could but I cannot stop' and that's how the Zohar has vanished, and the light went off, and I am left here, and in my hands are my orphaned, lonely songs for my "nightingale." But know that no others will have my song. For no one but you could understand its nature and its turns and make it pleasant in its uphills and downhills. To know the meaning of the song and the melody of it at the time of its happiness and of its sadness. And now those melodies that come from me are so sad and my eyes are drowned in a sea of tears.[43]

The rabbi began the process of reaffirmation at the funeral by delivering a eulogy that elevated Argov to a golden-voiced saint. The pilgrimages to the gravesite, the anti-drug concerts, and press coverage glorify the idea of Zohar Argov, his mother, and his sister as symbols of communal redemption. Tobi recounts Argov's sister Malka's recollection as follows:

> Many admirers came to the grave on the first year anniversary of his death, thousands came. On his birthday too and on eves of holidays and on Fridays admirers come. On Rosh ha-Shanah the grave is covered with candles. People pray with yarmulkes. Sometimes it's impossible to reach the grave because there are so many people there. People are looking for souvenirs of him, pictures, personal

> belongings, clothes. Girls come to the grave and put lipstick, perfume, love letters, even gold chains there. His memories have already become a collective property. His admirers have attributed healing powers to him. In shows, they wanted to touch him as a talisman that would bring luck. They wanted a blessing from him.[44]

Tobi also recounts the recollections of a neighbor named Tova:

> The family itself is treated like royalty because of him. In every event they are respectfully welcomed. People name their children Zohar and invite the family to the brit. In Shikun ha-Mizraḥ, his mother is called auntie. People do pilgrimage to her home. She walks with food baskets. Somebody stops and offers her a ride. He says, "You are Zohar's mother." At Jackie Makaytan's and Yehuda Kessar's weddings the whole family was invited. The mother says, "I was there like a *mezuzah.*[45] All the time people came and kissed me." One of the fans was about to get married when Zohar was in jail. He postponed the wedding until Zohar's release. Eventually Zohar died. He came with the bride dressed in wedding clothes to the mother's house and from there they went to the wedding. His mother says, "When I saw them I started crying and he cried. I took an egg and I poured it on his head for *kapparah.*"[46]

Pain and Beauty: Redrawing Ethnic Boundaries

David Hume writes that the paradox of tragedy lies in its transformation of pain into beauty.[47] In the tragic work, suffering becomes an aesthetic object. Argov embodies this dialectic of suffering and beauty. Both his lyrics and popular interpretations of his life are overflowing with pain and love, with a sadness sanctified through the aura of his voice. Argov's story, because of its generic ambiguity, is not just the clean pain of tragedy; it is overloaded with sentiment, thought of as a low and indulgent form of what tragic drama is in the high, aesthetic, and refined form. These two emotions are not remote from each other as the high theorists of tragedy would like to pretend, but they are not the same thing, either. Our easy tears in a movie about a dog who dies do not meet our shock of horror and pity at the death of the young girl in Bergman's *Wild Strawberries.* The narratives that proliferate after Argov's death evoke both cheap sentiment and transcendent meaning.

But the aesthetic element alone does not render Argov's story tragedy. Central to the genre is the reaffirmation of humanity. In this case, reaffirmation occurs as Mizraḥi and (to a lesser but still significant extent) Ashkenazi communities consecrate a king. Once this consecration spills over into mainstream society, ethnic boundaries are somewhat disrupted. This spillage to the other side is an erasure of boundaries creating a temporary unity in sentiment during which the meaning can transcend the specifics of Argov's story and become an Israeli story.

Argov's existence is a series of clashes and attempted mediations between a lost past—that of the idealized Yemenite, which could not and would not be actualized in contemporary Israel—the liminal moment in the *ma'abarah,* when a pan-Mizraḥi ethnic identity was formed by the underclass, and the simultaneous efforts at integration into mainstream Israeli culture. In his lifetime Argov created a vocal weave out of the incongruous threads of his own multiple identities. His posthumous journey across ethnic lines into Ashkenazi society required that the polar elements of his existence be reconciled in a powerful form, a form capable of making a difference, of empowering change. Even closer would be in a dramatic form, specifically in tragedy, with its cathartic resolution. That sort of catharsis does not reconcile polarities; it makes them meaningful beyond themselves; it makes them allegory.[48] The cathartic effect of Argov's story resonates not only within the Mizraḥi community but throughout Israeli society. Argov is appropriated as the allegorical story in anti-drug campaigns, with an anti-racist subtext that acknowledges the injustice of the *ma'abarah.* Moreover, in providing the national imagination with a new and original tragic hero, the Argov story also contributed to the further legitimization of the Mizraḥi music subculture.

The reinvention of Argov as tragic hero offers a dramatic model for healing the schism between Mizraḥi and Ashkenazi societies. Argov's suffering is the suffering of an individual and an artist, but he also represents a culture thrust into a new society where mutual disappointment is a reality. Yemenites like Argov do not dress in traditional garb, nor do they dance and sing Yemenite *piyyutim.* This noncompliance with symbolic stereotypes of an ancient Hebrew past disappoints some producers and state arts organizers who privilege frozen cultural forms rather than the unrecognizable aesthetics created by a new generation of artists. The disappointment is reciprocated by Yemenite Israelis who feel excluded, devalued, and assigned to vestigial roles. In this moment of mutual disenchantment, Argov's music becomes a project of possible reciprocal redemption, a bridge across the rupture between communities. Strange collisions emerge among *silsulim* and Yemenite prayer structure, Italian San Remo, Western rock, Greek ballads, and *ha-Shir ha-Erets Yisre'eli.*

One element of reaffirmation is that Argov's posthumous canonization grants him entry into the mainstream Israeli discourse. Journalists seize on the Zohar craze, captivated by the outpouring of posthumous communal adoration. Even cultural elites who remain disdainful of Argov and his music are forced to address the phenomenon, thereby perpetuating the myth. As Argov predicted: "Today everybody jumps on the bandwagon. Here, now, even Dani Sanderson[49] has skipped classes and a few more of his kind have started to take our music so perhaps with time that taste will enter the head of the radio editor."[50]

The critical acclaim of *ha-Melekh* is also testimony to the increasing mainstream legitimation of Argov and the phenomenon he represents. Playwright Shemuel Hasfari commented on the audience's reaction to the play: "It's funny, because when *ha-Melekh* opened, most of Beit Lessin's regular subscribers weren't coming. I think they thought Argov wasn't 'suitable' material for the theater. Our early audiences were full of Argov fans who don't often attend avant-garde theater. Now we get both Mizraḥi community members and 'regular' [Ashkenazi] subscribers."[51]

Argov's legacy embodies Mizraḥi ethnicity and reconstitutes it as a social instrument. The Zohar myth serves to push the new pan-ethnicity from the period of cultural transition toward consolidation and reincorporation. Like the alchemist, who must first find the appropriate material to transform into gold, the cultural brokers must have a "King," a "Zohar," through which to reflect influence and transform objective cultural phenomena. On one level, Argov gave sound to a previously ignored music genre. In the process, he offered Mizraḥim a complex hero and Ashkenazim a human means of understanding the Mizraḥi revolt. The fact that Argov existed meant that he did not need to be created in order to illustrate the reality of the ethnic tectonics shifting the Israeli cultural terrain.

Chapter 6

Transgressing Boundaries: Zehava Ben

> Zehava didn't imitate Umm Kalthoum, and herein lies her greatness. She simply carried the words on the tremendous waves of her voice, bursting forth from the depths of her soul. Fifty-four minutes of unrelenting, high-voltage song.
>
> —Sami Shalom Chetrit, *Haaretz,* 12 September 1995

In the early 1990s, after more than fifty years of constant war, Israel entered what now seems an all-too-short period during which it attempted to negotiate peace agreements with its Arab neighbors and the Palestinian people. During this period, it seemed that common cultural ground might bridge the continued enmity and distrust between the parties. Mediterranean Israeli music, rooted in both Arab and Jewish cultures, was one arena of dialogue. Argov's posthumous consecration in the 1990s was only one of many indicators of the shifting ethnic terrain within Israeli society. On numerous occasions, from the period of the Washington-based peace talks in 1993 to the Oslo Accords in 1994, Arab listeners expressed a fondness for and curiosity about the music. Even earlier, in the mid-1980s, Mediterranean Israeli music stars such as Haim Moshe received numerous fan letters from Syria, Jordan, Lebanon, and other Arab countries. However, in the 1990s, the quality of these letters took on a political as well as a personal tone.

Israelis were also increasingly receptive to Arabic music. The French Moroccan Jewish singer Sappho performed to a sold-out crowd of Palestinians and Israelis in Jerusalem's largest performance hall in 1994, where she sang adaptations of "al-Atlāl," a song in the canonic repertoire of legendary Egyptian Muslim singer Umm Kulthum (1907–1975).[1] During this period, the Ministry of Culture and Science planned to open a conservatory for the study of Middle Eastern music in Jerusalem's Pargod Theater. Since that time, several schools and programs for the study of Middle Eastern music have opened in Jerusalem, Haifa, and Tel Aviv. In 1996, the Jerusalem Academy of Music and Dance initiated a full program in Eastern and Arabic musics, now under the direction of Professor Taiseer Elias.

Politicians were in the process of reiterating borders even as they were iterating border crossings. Music seeped across boundaries even when the borders stayed intact, producing sounds that insisted on, even brandished, their connections as well as their differences. Borders are differentially permeable to political and musical penetrations. The use of Mizraḥi singers as symbolic of border crossing at official ceremonies may look like, and may in part be, an effort to recognize shared culture, but it is also always a means to control the use of these volatile hybrid styles. When U.S. soldiers dropped cassettes of traditional Afghani wedding music previously banned by the Taliban into Afghanistan, it could be read as a sign of familiarity and friendship. But it also signaled occupation and aroused confusion, as villagers questioned the motives of the latest military forces trying to win over their loyalties with small tokens of cultural recognition. We should regard official recognition of music at border crossings with some suspicion. Official appropriations can be attempts to domesticate styles that might otherwise disturb their orthodoxy.

Zehava Ben made border crossings in the 1990s that seemed impossible and contradictory for people on both sides. From seemingly incongruent Meretz and Likud[2] political campaign commercials to the Jordanian-Israeli peace ceremony held at the border itself, from the official dedication of the Rabin memorial in Paris to a Palestinian beachfront casino in Jericho, from prayers at the gravesite of Baba Sali to covers of the late Naomi Shemer's "Jerusalem of Gold," Ben's trajectories revealed the ways in which musicians subvert official efforts to contain, define, or commodify them. In Ben's performances, the strong conservatism of traditional culture sustained the historical elements that challenged each other. Community-based cultural forces can help to unravel binary distinctions between sacred and secular, East and West, Mizraḥi and *ha-Shir ha-Erets Yisre'eli.*

Musical Roots

Zehava Ben was born five years before the Yom Kippur War in 1968, and her childhood years coincided with significant political, ethnic, technological, and musical revolutions out of which Mediterranean Israeli music emerged and became commercially viable. She grew up in the impoverished Shekhunah Dalet neighborhood on the outskirts of Be'er Sheva. In neighborhoods such as these, which grew from the 1950s transit camps for North African and Middle Eastern immigrants like her Moroccan-born parents, Simon and Aliza Benista, Arab music, like the songs of Umm Kulthum, coexisted peacefully with Hebrew liturgical traditions chanted in Middle Eastern vocal styles.

Simon Benista, Zehava Ben's father, was an *'ūd* player in Morocco and had hoped to continue his career in Israel. Although he did continue to perform as a neighborhood musician, he discovered that North African and Middle Eastern music was often merely raw material for European compositions. He found few opportunities as a performer outside of local weddings and other community events. However, the rejection that musicians like Benista encountered also laid the groundwork for the emergence of a Mizraḥi coalition, expressed musically and in other ways, which would coalesce during the twenty years that his daughter Zehava was growing up. This coalition arose not only from cultural and social affinities, but also in response to the shortcomings of the immigration program that treated North African and Middle Eastern Jews unfairly (discussed in chapter 2). In musical terms, Middle Eastern and North African motifs were absorbed by European Israeli composers into their stylistic frameworks. However, Middle Eastern and North African Jews did not recognize themselves in this music.

Although the music that Zehava Ben's father had performed in Morocco was rejected by the European-dominated Israeli music industry, it remained alive in Mizraḥi neighborhoods, where it merged with other styles to create new musical forms. Initially it was appreciated by neither Israelis of European descent nor all young Mizraḥi Jews. One of Israel's leading popular music singer/songwriters, Yehudit Ravitz, was, like Zehava, born in Be'er Sheva; however, she was raised in different circumstances. Ravitz shared a story about coming to terms in the mid-1980s with her earlier rejection of her Egyptian mother's culture and music. This rapprochement foreshadowed the subsequent fashionability of Mediterranean Israeli and Arab music in Ashkenazi communities:

> As a child I begged my mother to hide her Arab music in the back room where none of my friends would make ugly comments about Umm Kulthum's whiny voice. My mother loved this music, which reminded her of her childhood in Egypt. I was much more drawn to my father's Israeli folk music; he was from Poland and knew all the early songs, even those that had been composed in Europe. When

> I grew up and realized how cruel I had been to my mother, I asked for her forgiveness.[3]

In Be'er Sheva's Shekhunah Dalet neighborhood of the 1970s, Umm Kulthum's music was not confined to backrooms as in Yehudit Ravitz's neighborhood, but rather integrated into the emerging Mediterranean Israeli music genre of the neighborhoods and into the everyday lives of children. Ben came into the world as Yemenite bands like Tselile ha-Kerem were composing multi-ethnic sound tracks for Kurdish, Moroccan, or Iraqi Jewish weddings by combining Arabic music with the Eastern European sounds of *ha-Shir ha-Erets Yisre'eli*, to which they added Greek and rock 'n' roll sounds. Some musicians took the frets off their guitars in order to bend the notes. What youngsters like Ben appreciated most was that Mizraḥi singers retained eastern vocal elaborations heard only in ghettoized corners of Israeli national radio.

The journey from Yehudit Ravitz's embarrassment when her mother played Umm Kulthum to Zehava Ben's reclamation of Umm Kulthum's repertoire as her own is a retrospective story that brings into relief a history of exclusions, appropriations, and relocalizations. It is a lesson in the significance of style as a cultural map that displays the complexities of time (never a unidirectional series of influences) and space (disrupting rather than asserting the correspondence between cultures and territories).

The marginalization of musicians like Zehava Ben's father, the relegating of Middle Eastern and North African music to the category of exotic relics of the past, and the incorporation of those elements into European-derived musical compositions occurred in large measure during the 1950s and 1960s, as European Israeli cultural and artistic preferences were institutionalized in the form of chamber choirs, concert halls, and music festivals like the Abu Ghosh festival (which opened in 1957). No comparable institutions for the advancement of Middle Eastern or North African music or culture were founded. Instead, Umm Kulthum and other Middle Eastern and North African voices continued to flourish in overcrowded Mizraḥi neighborhoods like Shekhunah Dalet, where working-class people spoke primarily Arabic. North African mothers like Zehava Ben's, whose lives were overwhelmed with daily survival, had little time to attend *ulpan* (intensive Hebrew language instruction) programs.

As a young Moroccan Israeli teenager, Ben encountered Zohar Argov, whose hybrid renditions of songs such as "ha-Peraḥ be-gani" created a multiethnic soundscape. For young Mizraḥi Israeli singers like Ben, Argov was the champion whose cassette breakthrough in the *shuḳ* (outdoor marketplace)

Mizraḥi musicians, like the violinist and *'ūd* player pictured here, continued to pass down their knowledge informally in neighborhood settings like this one. Here the performers prepare for a procession from the town of Tsefat to Mount Meron during the *Lag ba'Omer* celebration. (Photo by author)

and appearances on radio and even television in the 1980s opened up the possibility of success beyond local neighborhood events. Argov provided a model for young singers like Ben by defying the limits of his own impoverished neighborhood music scene in Rishon le-Tsiyon. Ben, like Argov a decade earlier, would credit Tel Aviv's Central Bus Station *shuḳ* with providing her with her first commercial visibility.

As a singer, Ben studied Argov's performance style on television and radio and attended his occasional local shows. She was drawn to the measured intensity of his voice and incorporated his sonic juxtaposition of Jewish text with Arab vocal styles into her own emerging style; he became, by default, a music teacher for her in the absence of a formal institutional structure through which she might become proficient in Middle Eastern and North African musical systems. Young singers like Ben studied the way that Argov's sound selectively incorporated Spanish, Greek, and Western instrumentation and arrangements in order to embellish an Eastern vocal line, which remained the most resilient element of the music. In compositions such as "ha-Peraḥ be-gani," Ben copied specific components of Arab vocal style, such as Argov's adapted and abbreviated version of the *muwwal.*

By the 1980s, during her teenage years, Ben, like other young singers, studied Argov's Middle Eastern vocal style and *muwwal* on pirated cassettes. She played them over and over again in the cramped apartment she shared with her nine brothers and sisters and her Arabic-speaking parents. Youngsters like Ben imitated and improvised on Argov's captivating sound at local weddings, bar mitzvahs, and holiday parties. They bought cassettes of his music as well as that of Daḳlon, Avner Gedassi, and others, at the outdoor marketplaces in their towns and cities. These marketplaces provided them with Mizraḥi music that enjoyed scant broadcast time on radio stations largely controlled by Jews of European descent.

Zehava Ben's melismatic vocals burst into Israeli public space in 1990 against the backdrop of the fragile Middle Eastern peace process. Turkish melodies had been circulating freely in the public domain when Moroccan composer Dani Shoshan found one, reupholstered it with Hebrew lyrics, and offered it to Ben as "Ṭipat mazal" (A Drop of Luck).[4] Before radio editors even knew her name, Zehava Ben's amplified voice was blaring in all directions from dozens of cassette booths that occupied retail space between vegetable, appliance, and clothing booths in Tel Aviv's Central Bus Station marketplace. Within three months there were unsubstantiated estimates that she had sold an astounding 80,000 copies of the *Ṭipat mazal* cassette. When listeners flooded the radio with requests for the song, radio editors and record store buyers took notice.

In January 1991, Lea Inbal wrote in the newspaper *Yedi'ot Aḥaronot,* "The producers on Israel's army radio station, *Gale Tsahal,* were surprised by the requests for 'the Turkish song' by Zehava, but they didn't know who or what she was.[5] A singer named Zehava? Maybe this is all a practical joke." Inbal's "practical joke" refers to Zehava's name (meaning gold) which is also a reference to a gold record. In working-class Mizraḥi neighborhoods, Zehava Ben's Arab-style voice spoke to the residents of these neighborhoods, awakening memory and inspiring hope.

As Ben's voice continued to invade mainstream public spaces in the early 1990s, European Israelis began to comment on the eastward and specifically Turkish shift in the soundscape of Israeli popular music. The Ashkenazi Israeli writer Yonatan Gefen lamented a Turkified Tel Aviv when he indirectly referred to Ben in a May 1992 *Ma'ariv* column: "As much as I tried I couldn't avoid hearing the 'Turkish' singer whose name I intentionally deleted and who blessed the State of Israel with a medley of Turkish melodies as the audience screamed. After 44 years of solitude we have returned to the roots of Istanbul. The Turks have conquered the city."[6] Gefen's hostile response to Zehava Ben's music (to the extent that he consciously deleted her name and any notoriety that would accompany it), and his use of the metaphor of political conquest, indicate the potentially turbulent power of such boundary-crossing music in a context of ethnic polarization and disputed territory.[7]

Argov's performance of "ha-Peraḥ be-gani" remixed musical styles to form the Mediterranean Israeli music style that emerged during Ben's youth. Ben refashioned Argov's 1982 award-winning performance of "ha-Peraḥ be-gani," singing his signature song in his memory at an anti-drug concert in 1993, five years after his death. Bowing her head for a brief second at the start, she then proceeded, as Argov had a decade earlier, to captivate the audience with her opening note. But by this time, the song had become popular throughout Israel, symbolizing a growing awareness if not acceptance of Middle Eastern and North African hybrid musical forms.

Unlike Argov's hungry and piercing *muwwal,* Zehava Ben's opening improvisation at the outdoor anti-drug concert across from the *ha-Mashbir* building in downtown Jerusalem in June 1993, engulfed the listener in a sonic moment that unfolded slowly like the garden flower that is the song's central metaphor. Ben stood before the crowd that included Argov's mother and sister, eyes closed, barely moving except for her left arm, which she gently raised in beat with the soaring note that echoed off the surrounding buildings. Ben's *muwwal* charted an emotional territory through which the ensuing song lyrics could be contextualized. Sadness and hope were woven into the carefully executed melisma, as if to catch and comfort the weary

Zohar Argov's mother and sister, here seated next to a young man wearing a Black Music T-shirt, were honored guests at this anti-drug concert in downtown Jerusalem in 1993. Zehava Ben sang "ha-Peraḥ be-Gani" and other Argov hits. (Photo by author)

Zehava Ben singing at an anti-drug concert. (Photo by author)

Palestinian and Israeli audience members sitting together holding Arabic and Hebrew posters warning of the dangers of drug addiction. (Photo by author)

listener between the notes of their daily struggle. As the drumbeats signaled the beginning of the song's first verse, the audience cheered, hugged each other, and began singing in full voice. Here in a central Jerusalem park, as the Palestinian Intifada still raged and the nascent Palestinian-Israeli peace process had not yet been reduced to a CNN sound bite, European and Mizraḥi Israelis, and Israeli and Palestinian recovering drug addicts, came together, enraptured by Ben's version of the song that had brought Argov and Mizraḥi music into the mainstream Israeli canon and across the borders to Jordan, Lebanon, Syria, and the West Bank.

Like Argov's performances of "ha-Peraḥ be-gani" in the 1980s, Ben's interpretation in the summer of 1993 also straddled Mediterranean and Middle Eastern aesthetics. She framed and centered the song's Spanish and Greek arrangement with her emotive *muwwal* and convincing vocal elaborations. Her Mediterranean and Arabic musical idioms maintained a delicate aesthetic position between the Arab east and the more acceptable (more European) Greek and Mediterranean domains, both aesthetically and politically.[8]

In 1991, journalist and documentary filmmaker Rino Tsror observed that singers such as Zehava Ben were beginning to record more "risky" (read "Middle Eastern") styles, abandoning the earlier Greek and Mediterranean songs for what he referred to as "Turkish Turkish." He summed up European Israeli discomfort with the unabashed combination of musical styles embraced by Mizraḥi composers, and condemned the Arabizing of the literary Hebrew song lyrics composed by European Israelis such as Naomi Shemer (one of the best-known Israeli singer/songwriters, who composed dozens of Israeli classics, including "Yerushalayim shel zahav" [Jerusalem of Gold]):

> No one came up with a less insulting definition [of Mediterranean Israeli music] than the connection between a Greek tone and the spice of an *'ūd*, between the North African curl [referring to melismatic elaboration] and Naomi Shemer's Hebrew. So it's all over. There is no continuation of the Mediterranean experiment. The market only buys heavy Arabic, or Turkish Turkish. They want Arab stuff not Greek Hebrew. The public's request climaxes in Ofer Levi and Zehava Ben. These are the two making business boil. It is from the Be'er Sheva quarter, which is the Kiryat Ata quarter [also a poor industrial neighborhood]. Take the history of the twenty-one years that she has been living, and understand what the Shekhunah Dalet is and why they don't speak White Hebrew there.[9]

Rino Tsror was not alone in lamenting the shifting public preference away from the safety of Greek Mediterranean party music and toward the Turkified-Arabized crying songs rendered by Ofer Levi, Zehava Ben, and other Mizraḥi performers. As discussed above, Yonatan Gefen still lamented the Turkish takeover of Tel Aviv a year later. Accusatory terms such as Ashkenazification, *Shire bekhi* (crying songs), and Turkification acknowledged the dissolution of certain boundaries at the same time that they instantiated new sociopolitical entities with their own boundaries.

Moroccan Israeli songwriter Dani Shoshan, who wrote "Ṭipat mazal" by overlaying his original Hebrew lyrics on a Turkish tune, explained the appeal of the new "Turkish Turkish" trend for Mizraḥim. For Shoshan, Greek music was safely European, while Turkish folk music's unequivocal Middle Easternness resonated with Mizraḥi reclamations of their cultural roots. Shoshan also noted that Greek tunes required royalty payments whereas Turkish tunes did not, because there was no intellectual property agreement between Turkey and Israel. As a result, he was able to take the Turkish melody of "Ṭipat mazal" from the legal equivalent of public domain.[10]

Radio editor Yoel Rekem contended that it was not the "Turkish Turkishness" of Shoshan's new composition for Zehava Ben that kept it from being broadcast on Israeli radio, but the poor technical quality of the production itself. The poor quality of *Ṭipat mazal* resulted partly from Shoshan's overuse of new computer-based music compositional technologies, as well as from his lack of fluency in Turkish music. Shoshan, like other songwriters proficient in computer music technology, expanded their possibilities through the use of MIDI (musical instrument digital interface) technology. In so doing, they could synthesize the sounds of traditional Middle Eastern and North African instruments as well as those associated with European music.

Like the cassette technology of the 1970s, these new technologies provided accessible compositional tools for anyone who could learn to operate a MIDI, computer, and module. Although these techniques saved time and allowed for the incorporation of musical instruments that usually required very specialized training, in creating precise rhythmic patterns and removing rhythmic inaccuracies there was also a canned quality lacking in improvisational textures and feelings.

Despite the poor technical quality of the recording, Ben's rendition of this Turkish tune demonstrated her competence in Eastern singing. She made no attempt to sound European and the song's only Israeli sign was its Hebrew lyrics. After the *Ṭipat mazal* cassette[11] exceeded Zohar Argov's earlier record sales, a remastered version caught the attention of Israeli radio editors, who finally broadcast it on Israeli radio in the early 1990s. Increased recognition of Ben followed the release of a feature-length film in which she co-starred,[12] also called *Ṭipat mazal.* The film presents a fictionalized version of her father, portraying him as having made a difficult, ultimately fatal transition from stardom in North Africa to artistic rejection and economic ruin in Israel. During the production of this film, Ben traveled to Morocco to research her North African legacy.

Throughout the 1990s, the influence of Mizraḥi singers could be felt in Israel's shifting mainstream popular music soundscape. "Legitimate" pop and rock stars such as Yehuda Poliker had already marked the prevailing rock aesthetic with their own ethnic musical signatures. Poliker, the son of Greek Holocaust survivors, convinced his record producers to release an album featuring Greek songs.[13] Tunisian Israeli pop singer Etti Ankry, who had previously performed Western rock, added a few Arabic songs (including Safy Boutella's "Eshebo")[14] to her repertoire and displayed her skill at traditional drumming during live performances. Mainstream Israeli audiences and critics consider these singers to have successfully incorporated Eastern motifs, unlike the illegitimate versions in the so-called "cassette" music associated

The sound track for the feature film *Ṭipat mazal* was released on a major Israeli label, Helicon. The cover features Zehava Ben's co-star (and the film's director) Zeev Revach, a well-known Israeli actor. (Courtesy Helicon)

with the Tel Aviv Central Bus Station. Performers like Ankry and Poliker developed as musicians within the mainstream, often participating in military music troupes and bands or studying and performing Western music before they incorporated signifiers of their ethnic heritage.

In 1992 the popular rock band Ethnix (Ethnics) invited Ben to perform one song with them for their new recording, *Masala.* In her guest appearance on this mainstream recording, Ben shares the vocal lead with Ze'ev Neḥamah, the band's lead singer, whose parents are Sephardi Jews from Bulgaria. While Ethnix incorporated some Eastern motifs, their music was basically European pop/disco. The band's duet with Ben on the song "Keturna masala" (When Luck Returns) shifts more to the East than most of their repertoire. The meeting of Eastern and Western styles occurs mainly in the refrain, which takes the form of call and response between Neḥamah and Ben. Neḥamah sings the verses in a standard rock style, though he inserts some slow and simple trills reminiscent of his Bulgarian heritage, while Ben sings the refrain in an Arabic vocal style, demonstrating her mastery of microtones and Eastern aesthetics. Although the instrumental arrangements are almost entirely Western, an Eastern feeling is achieved through a rhythmic shift between the verses (6/4 time) and the refrain (4/4 time). This rhythmic shift punctuates the distinction between Neḥamah's Western vocals in the verses and Ben's Eastern style in the refrain. A syncopated rendering of the Hebrew word for love, *ahavah,* in Ben's vocal refrain momentarily interrupts Neḥamah's European style on the verses. The synthesizer provides an Eastern feeling by emulating the sounds of the *santur*[15] and other "indigenous" instruments.

The track "Keturna masala," from which the album takes its title, is based on the common Middle Eastern folkloric theme of searching for an appropriate gift for one's beloved. Written jointly by Neḥamah and synthesizer player Tamir Kalisky, and featuring Ben's compelling vocal line, the song was extremely popular in the early 1990s and won first place in the 1992 Israeli *Mits'ad ha-pizmonim* (Israeli Hit Parade).

Two seemingly oppositional directions met in such collaborations, in which Mizraḥi musicians performed mainstream duets with well-known Ashkenazi performers while re-Arabizing the music. The Mizraḥi vocalists maintained and even embellished their Middle Eastern vocal elaboration as a counterpart to the European styles of their vocal partners. These collaborations did not represent a true reciprocity but rather reinforced existing asymmetries and separate constituencies. At the same time, they permitted a degree of appreciation of Mizraḥi music on the part of European Israelis, who were willing to incorporate selected elements of this music into their own compositions. Although Ben's Eastern vocal refrain reverberates only faintly within the European rock frame of "Ketourna Masala," her collaboration with the Etnix, in bringing together the two styles without blending them, searches for a different kind of meeting ground.

The fact that the Etnix kept the two styles distinct may have contributed to the composition's astounding reception, avoiding blurred categories and attendant anxieties by keeping the Arab vocal style (in the refrain) separate from the European rock style (in the verses).[16] As I have argued, the question of who appropriates whom must be reconsidered so that we do not make the mistake of seeing *ha-Shir ha-Erets Yisre'eli* uses of Arab styles as "borrowing," while Mizraḥi uses of *ha-Shir ha-Erets Yisre'eli* and other Western styles are viewed as either contamination or as of inferior quality. The power brokers decided which creole forms are sanctified as the national sound track and which are disdained.

The trajectory of Zehava Ben's rise to fame in the early 1990s corresponds roughly with the trajectory of Israeli-Palestinian moves toward peace. The peace process was broken in part by the assassination of Yitzhak Rabin in 1995. It was in the course of this bold yet fragile period that the homespun sound track of Mediterranean Israeli music began shifting its position in the national landscape. In 1995, Ben, who had led the vocal journey east and was dubbed "queen of crying songs" for such numbers as "Ṭipat mazal," issued a CD of Umm Kulthum's repertoire, entitled "*Zehava Ben sharah 'Aravit*" (Zehava Ben Sings Arabic).[17] Ben's renditions of Umm Kulthum's repertoire contributed to bringing Arabic music out into the mainstream for Mizraḥim who had kept their unwavering appreciation of this iconic Egyptian singer quietly confined to neighborhood events. In the context of seemingly forward-moving peace negotiations, Ashkenazi audiences who had rejected both Mizraḥi attempts to emulate *ha-Shir ha-Erets Yisre'eli* as too Arab-sounding and the emerging pan-ethnic genre of Mediterranean Israeli music as too hybrid and confusing embraced Ben's performances of unquestionably "authentic" Arab music, a music that they could now claim as their own. Did Ashkenazi listeners of world music and high-brow repertoire consider the Egyptian songs of Umm Kulthum more generically "pure" than hybrid Mizraḥi popular music? World music, a marketing concept and emergent genre that took hold in the late 1980s, had resituated Arab music as legitimate for Ashkenazi music consumers who might own a copy of an Umm Kulthum recording without personally appreciating the music itself. In a way, the world music boom prepared the European Israeli ear for Ben's reclamation of Umm Kulthum.

At this moment in early 1995, Zehava Ben chose to showcase her mastery of Umm Kulthum's repertoire. While her then-manager, the savvy Eli Banai, no doubt saw the commercial potential of producing an Israeli cover of a renowned Egyptian singer, Ben's performance was more than a successful marketing ploy. She presented her performance of Umm Kulthum and other Arab singers as homage to revered masters. The album cover of her Arabic recording merges a drawing of her own face with Umm Kulthum's, and includes photographs of her pilgrimage to Umm Kulthum's grave in Egypt. In the feature documentary *Zehava Ben, Solitary Star,* director Erez Laufer juxtaposed footage of Ben's pilgrimage to Umm Kulthum's grave with a television news item announcing restricted travel to Egypt for Israelis.[18] She defined herself as a daughter of Arab music rather than an outsider, evidenced by her Egyptian pilgrimage and her choice of a title, *Zehava Ben sharah 'Aravit,* that emphasized her reclamation of the Arabic language. Consistent with that tradition, she learned and emulated the style of her forebears. Although this move was contested by some Israelis (as either too Arabic or too transparently exploitative of the opportunities of the peace process) and by some Arabs (as thievery and fakery), many Arabs and Israelis appreciated both her boldness and the quality of her performance of decidedly Arab music.

Several months later in the fall of 1995, following Rabin's assassination, Ben released a sequel, *Zehava Ben sharah 'Aravit: Inta 'Umri* ("You are My Life"), on the mainstream Helicon label.[19] Umm Kulthum's *Enta Omri* was a classic within the Arab world and among Mizraḥi Jews in Israel. Written by Mohammed Abdul Wahab, a composer who intentionally mixed European and Arabic forms, *Enta Omri* sounded like Arab music, even when rendered by a Moroccan Israeli, who reduced the fifty-seven-minute classic to a five-minute cover. In the time between her first two Arab CDs, Ben had studied classical Arab music, language, and performance, developed competency in Umm Kulthum's repertoire, and employed the Arab Orchestra of Haifa to accompany her. As many Israelis and Palestinians grieved together over Rabin's death and the unsettled prospects for peace, Ben's CDs and her appearances in Nablus and Jericho and at ceremonies marking the cold peace with Jordan acquired new meaning.

With these Arab CDs and live performances of Arab songs, Ben defied single-voiced categorizations and claimed conflictual identities and multiple indigeneities. Her encounter with Umm Kulthum's life story and artistry was personal and emotional. Umm Kulthum's flexible religious identity and poor rural background resonated with Ben's own traditional religious upbringing, impoverished childhood, and cultural marginality.

That this bold revoicing of Arab Jewish heritage should emanate from a woman is particularly important in the context of the Israeli-Palestinian conflict.[20] Women's coalitions such as Women in Black, Bat Shalom, Machsom Watch,[21] and many others have created personal, grassroots, institutional connections of the sort Hannah Naveh calls "women's ethics of proximity,"[22] which have served as parallel, dissenting, or intersecting channels in relation to the male-dominated official diplomatic process. Often women's efforts have been more durable and able to cross lines more successfully. As Ben herself said, "I am braver than a man and so I went to perform in Arab communities. I was always treated with great gentleness and kindness."[23]

Ben's bravery is unmistakable, and her risks to her own career and to her person cannot be underestimated. At the same time, her statement evokes the sexist system in which a woman is treated more kindly and allowed to pass across dangerous borders. Although this is a real border crossing, it is also a reminder of borders yet to be dismantled. In 2003, Ben's travel to Palestinian communities was made impossible by escalating violence. Still, her cassettes and CDs continued to be sold on the streets, even by Muslim vendors in Jerusalem, and she continued to perform Umm Kulthum's repertoire for Israelis, claiming, "I will always sing in Arabic. I pray that my music, my

A Palestinian Israeli woman, Amal Markus, performs a peace song in Hebrew and Arabic at the "Women Go for Peace" conference, Jerusalem, 1990. (Photo by author)

The Women in Black movement demonstrates at a crowded intersection in Jerusalem every Friday afternoon at the height of the week's traffic. (Photo by author)

singing can bring real peace. I wish it were so. I wish my music would create some sort of connection. That is the most important thing right now."[24]

Perhaps as an example of the kind of connection Ben envisioned, on 12 November 2003 the *Jerusalem Post* announced that al-Jazeera, the Arab TV network, planned to feature her in a celebration of the one hundredth anniversary of the birth of Umm Kulthum.[25] Even if this invitation represented only a token acceptance of her work, it had meaning for both audiences and performers. Minority artists the world over are often acclaimed as token representatives of their group, at the same time as the group itself remains marginalized. Zehava Ben has responded to this accusation by challenging the opposition between authentic and hybrid, traditional and contemporary, marginal and mainstream. Ben's performances defy such compartmentalized identities. Her music charts soundscapes that challenge geopolitical maps of disputed territories, where affiliations and loyalties have heightened significance and life and death consequences.

As a Moroccan Israeli Jew, Ben vocalizes the space between the Jewish Israeli *shuḳ* and the Muslim Arab *sūq* (Hebrew and Arabic words from the same root, both meaning open marketplace) and returns us to my original point of embarkation, the marketplace in Tel Aviv surrounding the Central Bus Station. The *sūq* and the *shuḳ* are, as Mikhail Bakhtin puts it, places of heteroglossia, hybridity, and polyglot exuberance.[26] Here Ben's cassette first took fire. In the Israeli *shuḳ* and the Arab *sūq* she is operating in the borderlands and thereby demonstrating that these are not opposites facing off across a border, that there is no border, just this ramifying territory of emerging formations between older fixed formations. That is the hope aesthetics offers politics: not solutions or resolutions or dissolutions, but this space of reformations.

Sonically, we return to the opening *muwwal* of the story in which Jews from Islamic lands lovingly carried Umm Kulthum's music to their new home in Israel. We return to a woman's voice—though now Moroccan Israeli singer Zehava Ben reconfigures and re-covers Umm Kulthum. Why does Ben perform Israeli reconfigurations of Umm Kulthum's songs in Arabic? Despite its surprising commercial success, Ben's venture was politically risky. By reclaiming Arab music as her heritage, she opened herself up to criticism at home and in the Arab world.

Umm Kulthum taught Ben more than proper classical Arab music; she was an opening for Ben into her own Arab-Jewish heritage. Each of Ben's multiple identities is native to her yet contradicts some others so that she herself, her body and the music it produces, is the site of what I call "dueling nativities."[27] She is emblematic of the contradictory selves that are played out

Zehava Ben's second Arabic CD was produced by Helicon, a major Israeli recording label. She is pictured in Egypt, where she journeyed to pay homage to Umm Kulthum. (Courtesy Helicon)

on Israeli bodies, in Israeli music, and, by extension, in Israeli politics and in its social order. Israeli Jewish musicians with roots in Islamic countries are both insiders and outsiders to the regional soundscape.[28] In the context of an emerging peace process, Ben hoped to resolve her multiple identities: woman, Jew, Israeli, Arab, North African, Moroccan. This hope met a longing that arose out of the strange dislocations and relocations of her childhood: acceptance as a Jew among Jews coupled with denial of her North African Arabic heritage. There is danger in romanticizing Ben's musical reach across hostile national boundaries. Audio penetration of enemy territory does not create peace, even if it demonstrates arenas of aesthetic common ground. This is what Quaker coexistence worker Gene Knudson Hoffman describes as "compassionate listening," the ability to not only hear but listen to that which is other, foreign, distasteful, objectionable, or confusing.[29]

The disparate sounds of the marketplace are not enough to create new formations, whether social or musical. In fact, my first experience in the marketplace was typical of many Ashkenazim like myself. I didn't know what I was hearing, and perhaps, had I not gotten lost and stopped to ask for directions, I might have tuned it out. What has happened over the course of time (approximately twenty-five years since I began this project) is that Israeli popular music has begun to absorb these disparate sounds. What Haim Moshe told me in the 1980s in the offices of the Reuveni Brothers, in the Shekhunat ha-Tiḳvah neighborhood, is taking place in 2010. As Moshe

Although the peace process that had gained momentum in the early 1990s was derailed, Zehava Ben's cassettes continued to be showcased alongside Arabic singers and Koranic recitation in the Palestinian East Jerusalem marketplace. (Photo by author)

predicted, the soundscape has changed and Israeli music is enfolding the multitudes of Eastern and Western local styles into itself. Mizraḥi musicians, once consigned to restricted airtime and ignored as performing either "cheap music," "Central Bus Station music," "party songs," "crying songs," and so on, can now be heard in mainstream venues. It is this embodied absorption of that which was once other that leads to new aesthetic formations. At historical periods on the cusp between enmity and unity, amid tentative alliances such as those in Israeli society in the mid-1990s, aesthetics takes on the cast of politics, or perhaps art's political cast becomes perceptible in it.

Musicians like Ben make audible this political aesthetics, to suspend together in the same composition, in the same historical moment, difference—not to create new forms but to hold together old forms in a harmonic matrix, literally and figuratively, which does not dissolve difference but announces it. It is this announcement that makes the aesthetics of Mediterranean Israeli music political.

Zehava Ben performs not quite a new musical formation but the fraught fermenting moment just before it becomes one, when it is still perceptible, audible, as a political aesthetic. Ben and other Mediterranean Israeli music performers make audible their personal histories that are also political histories, social histories. Their music moves hearers, not just because it carries sentiment, but because the subtle, fragile way its alien elements are held together, poised on the edge of both coalescing and disintegrating, yields emotion: hearers feel in this music, anxiously, irritably, resistantly, hopefully, exhilaratingly, ecstatically, the great political movements of their time. They are at that moment, in this music, drenched in meanings that exceed the music, meanings of which they are aware and which move them. And this can be so precisely because a musical argument is not a rhetorical one. They do not think the argument; they feel it.

The Politics of the Aesthetic

All music absorbs other musics. What it has internalized will initially remain perceptible as a foreign body, but eventually it will be incorporated into the music and become imperceptible; the music will become a new musical genre. Or, under certain sociopolitical pressures, the music will be purged of and disgorge its foreign elements. At the moment of its formation, the sort of moment with which this book is concerned, the appropriateness of music's appropriation of foreign elements is at issue. Its aesthetics, that is to say, become political.

An Israeli soldier wearing a Moroccan fez demonstrates what Haim Moshe and Asher Reuveni predicted when I met with them in their offices in the 1980s: that in twenty years Israeli music and culture would absorb Middle Eastern and North African aesthetics. (Photo by author)

Not only has the appropriateness of certain appropriations been at issue in the formation of Mediterranean Israeli music in the 1980s, but also a revisionist history of "appropriate appropriations" has been legitimated by scholars, media commentators, and the musicians themselves.[30] All embrace the idea that *ha-Shir ha-Erets Yisre'eli* "borrowed" from Middle Eastern and North African musical styles. This understanding, in which the European performers are the borrowers and the "indigenous" Yemenites are those borrowed from, proposes a sociocultural map of the region that draws Africa into the Middle East and positions Yemen as its ancient cultural core. By contrast, centering *ha-Shir ha-Erets Yisre'eli* pulls the "Middle East" toward Europe, positioning it along a North African–Southern European littoral as a Mediterranean culture. Thus a historico-geographic imaginary foreordains and legitimates a real social asymmetry. In fact, neither group is indigenous, but in the absence of a large, longstanding, local Jewish culture, Yemen has become the regionally situated site of continuous indigeneity.

Indigeneity is always strategic. Such maps of the indigenous imaginary strategically attempt to create hierarchies of proximity, distance, and cultural value. To unpack rather than reproduce these hierarchies, it is necessary to suspect both cultural forms representing contiguities and those referring to dislocation. In music as in politics, it is precisely through the dialogue between continuity and dislocation that we can begin to dismantle the binary of conflict and resolution.

At the moment of the formation of Mediterranean Israeli music, the aesthetic had *become* political. There was no innocent music. Nobody implicated in it could hear the music without hearing its political resonances. The aesthetic exceeded itself; on some reckonings, the aesthetic betrayed itself; it became the more-than-aesthetic, and also perhaps the other-than-aesthetic; it was expanded by the political. It was not that musical harmony could in some idealistic, romanticized, magical way open a path to political harmony. But all performances of this music resonated beyond themselves, not programmatically, as if musical resolutions offered political ones, but emotionally. The music moved people. It was for Mizraḥi communities a great, deep, sad, joyous confluence of sounds, bearing the weight of their disparate and conjoined histories. It lifted them beyond themselves. This expansion of spirit composed, or coalesced, or configured an audience's emotional readiness to imagine itself also as a political coalition that might entertain political solutions.

Ben's rhizomatic appropriations map out the multidirectionality of uprooted and rerouted communities. In the case of Mizraḥim, who were uprooted from Middle Eastern and North African communities and rerouted to a new country that was at war with their former homelands, rhizomatic appropriations represent more than dueling homelands. Put another way, there is a stand-off between dialogical imaginaries in which the Mizraḥim find themselves suspended between their confabulated memories of the homelands they left behind and their unrequited expectations of the homeland to which they both turn and return. Mediterranean Israeli music holds together the sounds of these spatially dislocated, temporally anachronistic, and thematically conflicting imaginaries locally, simultaneously, and harmoniously.

Framing the relationship between appropriation and inheritance properly will illuminate this question of dueling nativities. Such a framework begins to emerge from an account of how music makes its way across both temporal and geographic borders. Temporally, as Peter Seitel demonstrates, genres are places involving appreciation for accepted and familiar forms as well as places for new configurations.[31] Traditionality is always emergent; tradition and innovation are not oppositional. In the case of the interethnic formation of the genre of Mediterranean Israeli music, I have observed both the creation of pan-sonic categories as the musicians share styles and the recontextualization of particular ethnic forms at life-cycle events.

In this redistribution of histories and localities, Zehava Ben's musical covers of Umm Kulthum are appropriate appropriations. Unlike the asymmetrical borrowing that characterized *ha-Shir ha-Erets Yisre'eli* use of Palestinian, Yemenite, and other regional stylistic elements, Ben sees a fluid, if troubled, line of descent between Umm Kulthum and herself that connects Egypt, Morocco, and Israel.

What Ben accomplished in her performance of Umm Kulthum was to expand, perhaps even reconfigure her inheritance. She inherits both from her Israeli predecessors, like Zohar Argov, and her seemingly more distant Arab predecessors, like Umm Kulthum. In her repertoire these inheritances are treated equally as homage to and respect for forbears.

What legitimates musical takeovers, or covers of songs, as inheritance proper or appropriate appropriations, or delegitimates them as theft or inappropriate appropriation, is a matter of what Amy Shuman calls entitlement.[32] In entitlement claims, the temporal is no less fraught than the geographical; they are dialogically involved in a complex process of negotiation. The composers of *ha-Shir ha-Erets Yisre'eli* draw from biblical, Palestinian, and Mediterranean sources to relocalize their European repertoire within their new geographical context. What is inappropriate here is the actual disempowerment of the local and regional music makers, not the desire to relocalize.

Despite the intensity of the struggles with Palestinians, Zehava Ben received little critique for her covers of Umm Kulthum.[33] Although official

Israeli media rejected Arab music, the iconic Egyptian singer was a sonic staple in Ben's childhood neighborhood. One way to understand Ben's success would be to observe that, in this case, inheritance claims trump entitlement challenges. As a Moroccan, Ben draws on her North African Arab inheritance. In North Africa, Jews, Muslims, and Christians shared a civilization for over a thousand years; Ben's father was a Moroccan musician who performed Arab music as an indigenous member of the culture. Ben, then, can claim indigeneity; she can claim Umm Kulthum as part of her own musical heritage. However, Ben is also an Israeli. In this climate, the Arabness of a Moroccan Jew spars with her Israeliness. Ben does not perform Umm Kulthum without attracting notice and critique. But interestingly, that critique does not overwhelm her success. She is not charged with impersonating the other; instead, to the extent that she performs well, she performs Arab music as a daughter of the tradition. Although this is an instance of aesthetics outweighing politics, Ben is nonetheless a profound political symbol of border-crossing.

Arab music is a part of the sound track of modern Israel. Ben's covers of Umm Kulthum enabled Arab music to waft out of the circumscribed ghettos where media efforts at containment had proved ineffective. Regardless of critical evaluations, whether by academics or journalists, about what belongs where or to whom, the music already had seeped across the borders and it was too late to send it back "home," wherever that was. Mediterranean Israeli music relocated the other in the self, them in us. Ofer Levy's attestation, "I am a Syrian, Turkish, Iraqi, Israeli," spoke linearly, thinly, what Mediterranean Israeli music presented inarticulately but thickly as a shifting configuration of soundscapes coming into dialogical relationships with each other. Levy's list did not illuminate how performers and audiences understood the relationship between their musical affinities and their political affiliations. The political and the aesthetic were, for Mizraḥi performers at that specific moment, interpenetrated domains. Though they might at other historical moments pull themselves apart into separate domains, aesthetics and politics refuse containment, plunging themselves, with all their complexities, over each others' borders. This reminds us, in Suheir Hammad's words, that in crossing borders we must "pack lightly, because you see I already have to carry so much with me."[34] In a political space that requires people to narrow their complex identities into impossibly bifurcated and polarized categories, music offers an opportunity for them to continue to transcend that schism and experience auditorially one of the most tragic ironies of the conflict, the sense that a part of their own being is the enemy.

Chapter 7

Disputing Territories

> Cultural identity is not a fixed essence at all, lying unchanged outside history and culture. It is not some transcendental and universal spirit inside us on which history has made no fundamental mark. It is not once-and-for-all. It is not a fixed origin to which we can make some final and absolute return. Of course, it is not a mere phantasm either. It is *something*—not a mere trick of the imagination. . . . It is always constructed through memory, fantasy, narrative and myth. Cultural identities are the points of identification, the unstable points of identification and suture, which are made, within the discourse of history and culture. Not an essence, but a *positioning*.
>
> —Stuart Hall, "Cultural Identity and Diaspora"

Absorbing Binaries

New formations, musical and political, get entangled. But to interpret music solely as politics trivializes the creativity of music, the way in which music is work, the way in which it is self-referential, as opposed to the way it refers to its political context. Although new musical formations can arise out of political situations, they are not political in kind. They are nearer a cultural pathos than a cultural politics.

These musical insights record a long history in which emerging sound tracks preserve their connection to other and older music cultures and at the same time forge a new one. Each new sound track absorbs and sometimes dissolves inherited binaries. I intend both senses of "absorbing": dissolving and taking in as well as fascinating. These processes of absorption create sound laminations, each with its own closure or uncontainability—a wound in the body of the text—some set against others, in the music itself as well as in my writing about it.

Mediterranean Israeli music enters into a dialogic relationship with politics and society. Each resists, evades, and exceeds the other as much as it succumbs to, transforms, celebrates, or demonizes the other. Music and politics enter into relationships with each other, proper and improper, unholy alliances and holy wars. By 1995 Mizraḥi musicians took up more radio time, attracted more diverse audiences, and sold more CDs than they once did, but this triumph did not reflect social or political triumphs of the same magnitude. The diverse audiences were still separate, even if they had more CDs in common on their living room shelves. The cassettes that lacerated the soundscape in the marketplace in the 1980s have been domesticated to the public order of the radio establishment, becoming a sound among sounds, a music among musics. Although the greater cassette sales of Mediterranean Israeli music did not facilitate economic redistribution, the new forms of cultural circulation made possible by the cassettes created greater audibility/visibility for Mizraḥi communities. Mizraḥim and Ashkenazim are still not social equals, but Mizraḥim now are recognized as having a contemporary culture rather than as representing either an imaginary/exoticized past or a sordid present. Whether or not cassette sales had an impact on politics, hearing one's own music on the radio during regular broadcast time has implications that cannot be easily measured. Even if cassette sales did not inspire social movements, the circulation of goods created an economic and cultural exchange.

In this final chapter, I bring into focus the intersections, overlaps, and divergences between the story of the music and the story of Mizraḥi social struggles. Though Mediterranean Israeli music is not overtly political, the political and social identities that surface in the music find new footholds there and make new tracks in the music.

Founding Territories

Amnon Shiloah notes that the Israeli national anthem, Naftali Herz Imber's "ha-Tiḳvah," written in 1878, instantiates the peculiarly diasporic Jewish dialectic between the East and the West as both the future and the past. For European, Middle Eastern, and North African Jews, the present, the diasporic spread, is outward and westward; the future, like the past, is inward and eastward, so that going east (though of course some Middle Eastern Jewish communities traveled west to Israel) is both going forward and going back, the myth of the eternal return.[1]

The refrain of Imber's ballad captures this equation: *Ule-fa'ate* (turn) *mizraḥ* (east) *ḳadimah* (forward!), "Turn forward, toward the east." This concept of turning forward, eastward, characterized by movement forward, toward a cultural future, was also a turning back to a historical memory, a religious past. Shiloah further notes: "*Ḳadimah* on its own is a call for action: 'Forward.' Yet in the synonymous pair *Ḳedmah-Mizraḥah,*[2] it is simply an intensification of *mizraḥ* with the emphasis not on action, but on place. *Ḳadimah* may also be understood as an allusion to the land of the Jews 'in days gone by,' *Yeme ḳedem,* further distancing itself from any implied movement forward."[3] The relationship between the future and the past, between *ḳadimah* and *mizraḥ,* was already controversial when Imber wrote his ballad in the late nineteenth century, during the period in which European Jews began to settle lands they regarded as the once and future Israel. It is still controversial.[4]

All this can be traced musically. In Mediterranean Israeli music, as in all emergent cultural styles, traditional elements are being rearranged and foreign elements are being introduced to create a new musical formation. Sounds that used to be outside a musical tradition begin to trouble its edges and wedge themselves in, because communities once separated become neighbors, because those who used to be outside marry into families. When for reasons of politics, propinquity, or sentiment, musical styles get forced together, new possibilities become available, not all of which get exploited. When they are exploited, the musical result is not a copy of the social landscape but a new aesthetic space undergoing its own formation, which may in turn play back into politics or be recognized there, but which neither foreordains nor reflects it.

If the actual musical elements were to be mapped out, they would bear traces of the reconfigured family, neighborhood, and global territories. The vocal line is a melismatic signature that centers the music. Orbiting this are various shifting musical elements: bass guitar is a Western sound mode; a Greek melody is Eastern enough without going too far, the bent guitar notes are Blues enough to evoke the micro-tonality of an *'ūd*, and the drum machine can be programmed for either Arabic *darabukka* or rock 'n' roll drums. Hebrew lyrics based on biblical texts, the modern Hebrew poets Haim N. Bialik or Natan Alterman, and street slang tie the vernacular, the ethnic, and the biblical into one big hybrid knot. Arabic, Kurdish, Yemenite, Turkish, and Persian texts subvert the unified ideology of the blended exiles, revealing a patchwork of unmelded identities and reverberating with fresh counter-memories and affinities that developed over centuries in Islamic societies.

The pan-ethnic music Mizraḥi musicians created from the 1970s through the 1990s was both unabsorbable and accommodative: the language,

הגטו לא מת

טוען אביהו מדינה, הלוחם הגדול להחררת הזמר המזרחי לתקשורת האלקטרונית • בשיחה עם חוה אלברשטיין: שום דבר לא השתנה, רק הרחיבו את הגטו. ברדיו ובטלוויזיה עדיין מעדיפים סנדרסון ומתי כספי • למה לא מדברים על הזמר הרומנזי של שלמה ארצי?

תצלומים: שאול גולן

ראיינה חוה אלברשטיין

In this newspaper article, drawn from an interview that Chava Alberstein conducted with Avihu Medina on Israel's army radio station, *Gale Tsahal*, Medina contends that "the ghetto is not dead." He claims that Mizraḥi artists are creating songs from the present and not from "some tribal archeology." (Courtesy *Yedi'ot Aḥaronot*) arrangements, vocal lines, distribution, and audience all placed it outside mainstream channels. Yet the incorporation and reworking of canonical European-Israeli lyrics, tunes, and themes were clear markers of Mizraḥi fluency in the dominant culture.

Defining Mediterranean Israeli music was not an objective question of its relative placement on an East-West continuum. The music behaved like a lightning rod that attracted the conflicting social currents rumbling in the air. Economic and social terms that described Mizraḥi inequality, such as *kipuaḥ* (deprivation), *ha-geṭo* (the ghetto), and *Sheḥorim* (blacks), were also applied to the performance culture. Like lightning, the emerging music not only attracted but also conducted the social currents and provided a site that forced the confrontation between aural polarities and revealed them as interconnected sound clusters.

In the 1980s, the ghetto was a central image in the discourse surrounding Mediterranean Israeli music. What was ghettoized was not a closed-off geographical space but a sealed pocket of airtime in which Mizraḥi musicians were detained and isolated from "normal" listening hours. These temporal ghettos in the broadcast radio were, of course, associated with the spatial ghettos of Israeli ethnic neighborhoods.

The charge that Mediterranean Israeli music was being ghettoized afforded the media an opportunity to debate whether the ghetto had been broken, who had broken out of the ghetto, and what new and unlikely musical juxtapositions had penetrated the airwaves. For singers such as Haim Moshe, Margalit Tsan'ani, and, posthumously, Zohar Argov, the word "ghetto" was used to describe the social conditions from which they rose, and to preserve the stigma of "Central Bus Station music." That the term "ghetto" itself carries the history of European antisemitism makes ironic the importation of ghettoizing practices into the new nation. The use of the term unmasks the yet unrealized dream of the blending of the exiles, the social order of a Mizraḥi pan-ethnic community, formed out of the "ingathering of the exiles." Doubly ironic, given the vernacular uses of the term "ghetto" in the United States, this new ghettoization resembled the North American ghettoization of poor people of color more than it did the medieval isolation of Jewish communities. Diasporic ethnicity was not erased on arrival in Israel but rather consolidated in unexpected ways. Argov raised this issue in an interview with Michael Ohad:

> Now, 55 percent of the Israeli public is my audience, but if they want to hear me on the radio they have to wait until 2:00 pm on Wednesday in the *Mi'edot ha-Mizraḥ* (From the Easterners)

> broadcasting corner or in the show *Aṿirah Yam Tikhonit* (Mediterranean Feeling) on *Gale Tsahal.* We live in 1981 and those programs were old ten years ago. When I was a kid I would listen to Ahuva Ozeri on that show. Enough!!! We are fed up!!! This is old fashioned. It's primitive. It's insulting. They play ten black singers in a row. This is really disgusting. Why this separation. Why are we being locked in a . . . I didn't say ghetto . . . that's your word! I only said it hurts and it's humiliating. Scatter us on all the hours with all the programs or don't play us at all.[5]

Barbara Kirshenblatt-Gimblett notes that historically, "the terms *diaspora* and *ghetto* often form a linked pair. What is not blamed on one is attributed to (and often entailed by) the other—stranger and marginal man flow from them."[6] It is precisely the creation of ethnically specific Jewish ghettos within a Jewish state that uncouples this seemingly linked pair. No longer in the diaspora, newly ghettoized Mizraḥi populations in contemporary Israel were estranged within the homeland by marginalization, extrusion, ejection, and hence subjugation.

Throughout the course of my research, I heard repeated claims that the music ghetto no longer existed and that Israel's ethnic problems had been solved. Ethnic bias is more easily recognized retrospectively. So musicians, citizens, community leaders, journalists, even scholars often rewrite the history of the present. The music is played on the radio, on television, and in festivals, and Mizraḥi and Ashkenazi intermarriages abound; Mizraḥi musicians, however, still carry the label of "pan-ethnic" and with that the old judgments of "inauthenticity" (they sing a hodgepodge of sounds rather than a clear world-music rendition of "traditional" Kurdish repertoire) render it inferior. But it is only because Mediterranean Israeli music was broadcast that what was previously rejected as too different was repositioned within a hierarchy of distinctions.

In its ongoing rewriting of the history of the present, each constituency values difference differently. Whereas scholars read the emergence of Mediterranean Israeli music into the public sphere as a triumph of their values of diversity, hybridity, defetishization, and decommodification, many Mizraḥi musicians themselves yearned for the erasure of all borders.

To put the argument in these terms is to imagine that once the spatial problem of Mizraḥi exclusion is solved (which it is not—inferior housing, education, and employment persist), the asymmetry will be solved. As my story demonstrates, even increased integration of musical forms does not reflect a shift in social power dynamics. However, it is an indication that Israeli culture is moving eastward and that mutual influences/audibilities can be read as political aesthetics. When does a sound that has been there all along become audible to a specific community of hearers as foreign or their own?

Inventing Boundaries

In Israel, Jews from North Africa and the Middle East, each bringing their own traditions, comprise a larger Mizraḥi community. Mediterranean Israeli music mediates their variant strands of selfhood, revealing a trans-ethnicity that forms and transforms itself within a pluralistic and asymmetrical society. Ethnomusicologist Adelaide Reyes Schramm describes ethnic identity as a repertoire of identities that continuously shift their "center of gravity."[7] She traces her argument to Frederik Barth's concept of "ascriptive identity," that is, the interplay between identities ascribed to us by others and identities we ascribe to ourselves.[8]

Musical genres are contested sites in which people negotiate their identities and territorial claims. Singers negotiate between cultural memories of Arab or Islamic countries and Jewish national loyalties to create what Haim Moshe calls "the new, authentic, Israeli expression." This renewal subverts the previous "new Israeli authenticity" formulated by Eastern and Central European immigrants, whose own search for national identity and authenticity privileged European styles and embellished these with Middle Eastern, and particularly Yemenite, elements. This attitude manifested itself in the exoticization of localness,[9] and the adoption of "native" elements such as Bedouin dress, Yemenite dance, and Arabic tunes.[10] On the other hand, many Mizraḥi singers' cassettes resolved a different need for "authenticity" by including in their pieces one or more Middle Eastern or North African song in their family's local dialect. Next to these traditional elements they incorporated Western elements such as harmony and major keys, which, according to Peter Manuel, signify power and modernity to the non-Western listener.[11] Musical instruments such as the bazouki and *'ūd* resided next to the electric bass and synthesizer. According to Richard Middleton, popular culture is neither pure resistance nor superimposition but rather an arena of negotiation.[12] This arena of negotiation is illustrated by Yemenite singer Haim Moshe's comments in 1984:

> The truth is, we are in the Middle East, surrounded by Lebanon, Syria, Iraq and strongly influenced by Arabic music. We are also strongly inspired by England, America, and France. So maybe in another twenty years we'll have a music style and people will not say,

"This is Eastern; this is Western." In another twenty years it will be known as original, authentic, Israeli music.[13]

Now, more than twenty-five years later, Moshe's prediction appears prophetic. Israelis no longer categorize music as Eastern or Western as much as they did in 1984 or in the same way, but they still invent claims of indigeneity and authenticity to privilege some music and disparage others. So although Mizraḥi musicians who were silenced in the 1970s and 1980s have found voice and new Mizraḥi styles have emerged, a political aesthetics is still at work.

A Politics of the Aesthetic

The details of the musical formation—how sounds are held to each other, which ones get taken up, their hierarchies, dissolutions, interfoldings, in short, their aesthetics—are influenced by politics. Music does not mirror politics, nor are politics influenced in some romantic or sentimental way by music. Politics offers music a context in which its cultural appropriations can become foregrounded and contested, that is to say, that aesthetic choices in music are not made exclusively for aesthetic reasons; some of them are made for political reasons. To say that music makes aesthetic moves is precisely not to say that it makes a political argument. Musical performance participates in the dichotomies created by political contestation and can also be one force for resisting the hegemonic hold of dominant powers.

Eviatar Zerubavel demonstrates how dichotomous thinking works in both politics and social life and explains why this sort of thinking creates dissonant categories and border disputes. He begins by observing that dichotomies are culturally produced: "Reality is not made up of insular chunks. . . . Most boundaries . . . are therefore mere social artifacts."[14] He insists that categories are not just arbitrary and constructed but that differences in classification systems "touch the deepest emotional as well as moral nerves of the human condition."[15]

Abstract dichotomies, such as that between Mizraḥim and Ashkenazim, become at once concretized and malleable when we consider music. Put another way, the categories of Mizraḥi and Ashkenazi music are not entirely dichotomous. Musicians themselves do not think dichotomously; they freely insert "foreign" elements into their compositions and make them native. A steel drum tune heard by a Kurdish drummer in passing on a radio show is attributed to Trinidad even as it becomes Kurdified. The Kurdification of a steel drum tune is not so much a matter of compatible musical scales or lyrical poetics as it is of the competency of a Kurdish musician to relocalize Trinidadian sound through performance. In Zerubavel's terms, these chunks of music may appear insular to an insider, but they are at the same time accessible to outsiders in other communal contexts. In other words, classification describes an ongoing process; instead of Mizraḥi or Ashkenazi music, we can observe how music is Mizraḥified or Ashkenazified according to the context.

Under what conditions do people accept or reject each other's (or their own) music, and how does that rejection/acceptance map onto political affiliations across lines of conflict? Music does not create borders inside itself, nor does music create or reconcile conflict. Instead, people create both aesthetic genres and political boundaries, and each realm influences the other. People create musical categories and assign meaning based on what sounds familiar and what sounds foreign, what is recognized as part of a category and what is considered outside. These musical processes of familiarization, recognition, alienation, and foreignness are connected to other public discourses. But they are not the same.

Nancy Fraser argues that multiple public discourses should be the goal of democratic participation and that scholars such as Jürgen Habermas are mistaken in their urge for greater participation in a single public forum.[16] Music styles are sites of multiple public discourses, instances of coexistence of aesthetic elements rather than the domination of one overarching paradigm. For a musical composition to succeed, the composer must understand the goal as not so much consensus as mutual respect and coexistence among constituent elements.

The acceptance or rejection of musical categories (whether by insiders or outsiders, musicians or listeners) cannot be entirely (or even mostly) explained by political affiliations. Even an Ashkenazi activist who fights for greater social equality between Mizraḥim and Ashkenazim might still reject Mizraḥi music aesthetically while promoting it ideologically. Mizraḥim who politically reject "all things Arab" embrace what they consider to be their own music, which often incorporates Arab elements or is wholly Arabic.

Eviatar Zerubavel moves us from a conversation about boundaries as social artifacts to a discussion of border disputes. "The prototypical border dispute is a battle over the location of some critical line in actual space, as manifested in disputes ranging from local turf feuds between neighbors to full scale international wars. It is the original on which numerous battles over the location of various partitions in mental space are modeled."[17] Zerubavel contends that "when sociology conference organizers debate about whether to include a single 'Race and Ethnicity' session, or two separate ('Race' and

'Ethnicity') ones, they are actually fighting over whether or not being Black or Oriental is different than being Irish or Italian."[18]

These are only a few of the cases of "fine lines" Zerubavel describes in which "labeling politics reveal how attitudes toward (protecting or defying) boundaries and distinctions betray deep sentiments (conservative or progressive) toward the social order in general."[19] Zerubavel is suggesting that territorial disputes are not just another example of dichotomous thinking but are instead the literalization of a vast array of conceptual borders. Territorial boundaries are also social artifacts. The material world presents perceivers a surface over which things are distributed unevenly but the things are not unambiguously separated from each other. Segmenting this rough terrain into chunks rests on social convention. Because people treat their own cultural classifications as natural and immutable, they cannot recognize others' classifications as anything but strange and unnatural. As a consequence, classification systems create as much distress as they do order. The mutual regard of the other as strange and unnatural, especially where power asymmetries exist, is a basis for many border disputes.

Examining musical encounters, interchanges, and blends suggests a way to understand border disputes as genre differences and to regard ambiguous classifications as hybrid combinations. Musical aesthetics (or formal relationships among elements) create unlikely juxtapositions which operate differently than the proximities of conflicting political issues. Music at times permits the coexistence of proximal juxtapositions that would, in the political arena, be intractable conflicts. The asymmetries that coexist in music, like the negotiation between a Yemenite vocal line and a western rock beat, play out simultaneously with the political struggles across ethnic, racial, national, and religious lines. As Rebecca Solnit argues, "Often the road to politics lies through culture. It was, for example, the 1976 persecution of the Czech band the Plastic People of the Universe that sparked Charter 77."[20] In fact, many of the leaders in the democracy movement that developed after the Soviet invasion of Czechoslovakia in 1968, including Vaclav Havel, were artists, musicians, and writers.

If we grant, then, the role of culture in disputed territories, and if we understand a link between political processes and musical aesthetics, the question becomes how new musical coalitions work as sites of resistance to existing power structures, especially those that marginalize and disenfranchise groups and perpetuate conflicts among them. My question here is how various dimensions of music, from performances to listeners to the cassette industry, served to shift centers of gravity and recalibrate asymmetries and reciprocities. The model of asymmetries and reciprocities can suggest that the cultural objects or performers are fixed entities in fixed positions and that the relations between them are what changes. Instead, I am proposing that the cultural objects themselves—the music, the performers, the producers, and the consumers—can be identified or identify themselves only in relation to shifting centers of gravity. The appearance of stability, of gravity as stability, is transient, and though we can map those transient moments and even trace, in some instances, the movement from one to another, they elude our grasp. In documenting these performances as if fixed, we participate in the same acts of exclusion, inclusion, and misrepresentation as the officials we accuse of discrimination. Instead, my goal is to describe performances as unstable mutating assemblages that coalesce into a new musical style.

What elements of a performance, a style, or a repertoire become identifiable (audible) as one category or another, and under what conditions? It's not just a matter of what one hears but about modes of discrimination (in the political as well as aesthetic realm). Political discrimination (that produces injustice and inequality) is based on ignorance. Aesthetic discrimination is based on the ability to discern and recognize significant differences. In terms of music, discrimination is the art of hearing, listening, and having a finely tuned ear.

Music's relationship to politics is sticky. It attaches itself to politics without mirroring or representing it. Aesthetics can move politics just as politics can flavor aesthetics. I do not propose some sort of untenable equivalence between politics and music; rather I uncover the linkages that exist between them. Musical multiplicities and shifting centers of gravity can unseat dominant power positions.

The accommodation of differences in the musical context varies greatly, from coexistence in which styles mingle without discernable distinctions to the juxtapositions of styles that are alternatively perceived by a hearer to be a mingled, hybrid style. Some would detect or decipher or hear in a piece of music its elements as disintegrative. Music sets out, juxtaposes, and interplays sounds it has picked up out of a political soundscape so that they operate with respect to each other, playing off each other, arousing passions, including passionate rejections, because they are resonant with political meanings, not because they replicate the political structure. This is the politics of the aesthetic, a politics specific to music as it exists within communities and not a politics imprinted on music from the organization of the political arena. In music, whatever is political has a different flavor, pattern, and significance, derived from its musical resonances as much as from its political ones.

Mediterranean Israeli music is an unstable assemblage of hybrid forms. This music is neither an alliance nor a coalition (political terms) but a different node of meaning, a hybrid genre in political-cultural space. This unstable position parallels Bernice Johnson Reagon's analytic framework for the continuity and innovative vitality of African American musics within the asymmetrical context of American society.[21] Both the emergence of African American music during the civil rights movement and the emergence of Mediterranean Israeli music during ethnic struggles in Israel occur in the context of social asymmetries. They differ in this respect from the proliferation of world music in the context of post-colonialism, which is not always about resolving social inequity. Hybrid music does not necessarily resolve or even address power asymmetries, though it can. The appropriation of other peoples' traditions can, for example, be a conservative gesture designed to keep them in the past, or it can be an activist move to preserve the values of a culture that have been excluded.

Because Mizraḥi musicians were either relegated to state-controlled folklore ensembles or excluded by the music industry until the early 1990s, a spontaneous cassette network developed in Israel. It was this contemporary music, created by Jews from Muslim lands and therefore perceived as Arabic, that came to redefine the margins of Israeli national identity. The movement of Mediterranean Israeli music between illegitimate network and acceptable genre comes out of and enters into its relationship with official Israeli institutions. Anthropologists Ivan Karp and Steven Lavine argue that cultural representation by state institutions affects local community arts.[22] Consequently, understanding community membership and the complex relationship between people negotiating disputed territories requires documenting how they perform their identities through the genres of artistic expression and how (and whether) those genres are recognized. Studies of the politics of recognition need to take into account not only institutional resources and inequities but also the imaginary and ritual practices that intersect both private and public domains in everyday life.[23]

As Mizraḥi pan-ethnic identity became more consolidated and visible, representatives from authoritative institutions sought publicity at Mizraḥi community events. Many politicians appeared at ethnic festivals and music events such as the Moroccan Passover season celebration of the *Mimouna* and the Kurdish *Saharana.*[24] In order to assure that the two events did not compete with each other, and therefore to enable state officials to attend both, the Kurdish festival was moved to coincide with the holiday of Simḥat Torah.[25]

As anthropologist Guy Haskell noted:

> In fact, [the *Mimouna*] is nearing the status of a national festival. In addition to the display of Moroccan ethnicity, it has become a mandatory stop for Israeli politicians, and other ethnic groups display

> their dances, songs, wares, and foods, as well. On St. Patrick's Day, all Americans are Irish. On the *Mimouna,* all Israelis are Moroccan. But the *Mimouna* also carries with it the message that all members of the various *ʿedot* (ethnic groups) are Israeli.[26]

At the 1991 *Saharana* festival in Ashkelon, the leader of the opposition in the Knesset, Shimon Peres, gave a public address about the Kurdish community's important contributions to Israeli culture. During the performance of Kurdish singer Itzik Kala, a top-ranking Kurdish Israeli Defense Force general, Yitzhak Mordekhai, appeared on stage to join in a duet. These gestures are always strategic; they extend recognition in multiple directions among the performer, politician, and community. The appearance of decorated military officials on concert stages is not always an indication of a singer's increased recognition. It is sometimes a veiled attempt by the political parties to gain recognition and votes among ethnic constituencies. Yemenite singers Avihu Medina, Haim Moshe, and Margalit Tsanʿani, who in the 1990s maintained their appeal to Mizraḥi constituencies while becoming acceptable in some Ashkenazi communities, were frequently invited to participate in official state celebrations such as Independence Day and Jerusalem Day. The shifting and blending of ethnic positionings matched the hybridization of Mediterranean Israeli music's multiple styles.

The tension between the illegitimacy and acceptability of Mediterranean Israeli music intensified in the mid-1980s through the 1990s, by its exhibition of aesthetic markers that identified it with hostile musical forms. These aesthetic border skirmishes, involving adversarial musics, were particularly charged within the context of a politically disputed territory such as Israel. The permeability of national borders and the penetration of music across "enemy" lines was illustrated in an article that appeared in an Egyptian opposition newspaper, *Sawt al-Shaa,* in 1985. The essay, by Wafa Ahmad, asserted that Israeli music had a detrimental effect on Egyptian youth and warned that the growing popularity of black-market Israeli cassettes in Egypt would diminish the nation's standing in the Arab world.[27] At the opposite extreme of such detractors were Mizraḥi and Ashkenazi seekers of regional normalization between Israelis, Palestinians, and neighboring Arab countries. Many who subscribed to this ideal saw the music revolution as one of several examples of shared artistic (as well as, perhaps in the future, political) domains. However, some Ashkenazi activists regarded shared music as a political tool but did not appreciate or even understand the music itself. In other words, they shared political but not artistic domains.

The appearance of decorated military officials like Kurdish IDF general Yitzhak Mordekhai, in duet with Kurdish Israeli Mediterranean musician Itzik Kala, is not always an indication of a singer's increased recognition. The strategic performance of ethnic specificity is celebrated in carefully orchestrated contexts—such as this at the *Saharana* in Ashkelon—and is not seen as counterproductive to the emergence of a coherent Israeli culture. (Photo by author)

Despite the protests of detractors on both sides of the border and the advocacy of supporters who viewed the music as ideologically if not aesthetically acceptable, the music itself continued to cross political borders without political motives attached. There were successful Arab performers of Mediterranean Israeli music, of whom one of the earliest and most renowned contributors to the genre was singer/violinist Samir Shukry. Shukry's performance of "From Moses to Muhammed" (*mi-Mosheh ṿe-'ad Muḥammed*) won second place in the 1989 Children's "FestiGal" (an acclaimed children's music contest and show that takes place annually during Hanukkah; the *gal* in "FestiGal" is Hebrew for "wave"). On his web site, Shukry proudly highlights his father, Sodki Shukry, a professor of Arabic music, who taught generations of musicians in Israel and also taught music at the Teachers Seminar in Haifa. The elder Shukry was actively involved in the fledgling Israeli television of the early 1960s and performed on Israeli radio.[28]

In the early 1990s, Haim Moshe spoke of his music's ability to transcend the boundaries between Israeli Jews and Arabs: "Last Friday I performed at Tamra in the Galilee, where Jews and Arabs are together. It was quite successful, with everyone together. The truth is, Arabs listen to our music."[29] During the same period, Shafik Salmon, then a popular Arabic-speaking Israeli deejay, whose radio program "From Israel with Love" broadcast Mediterranean Israeli music over the Arabic channel of Israel's national radio channel Ḳol Yisrael, claimed to receive over one hundred song requests and fan letters per month from Syria, Jordan, Lebanon, Egypt, the West Bank, and Gaza. One letter, from a young Muslim woman in Syria (sent via Europe to his office in Jerusalem), began with the Hebrew words *shalom u-verakhah* (peace and blessing) and continued: "If the Syrian people requested, do you think Israeli singers would come to perform for us personally? Without the Syrian ruling family stopping it? I am trying to learn Hebrew so I will know what they say in their beautiful songs. I ask God that an agreement will be reached between our two countries so that we will be able to see you. What is the feeling of the singers when a Syrian writes to them?"[30]

As this plea for peace demonstrates, political borders do not keep Mediterranean Israeli music in. Even as the music seeps across these boundaries, at its root it is the product of an Israeli process: the cultural and ethnic struggles among European Israeli Jews and Middle Eastern/North African Israeli Jews. The seepage into Syria does not resolve the border dispute, just as the internal ethnic struggle, despite official claims to the contrary, continues even in the context of musical rapprochement. The local struggle between Jewish ethnicities within Israel emerges in the context of this larger struggle over disputed territories in the Middle East. Asymmetries of power between

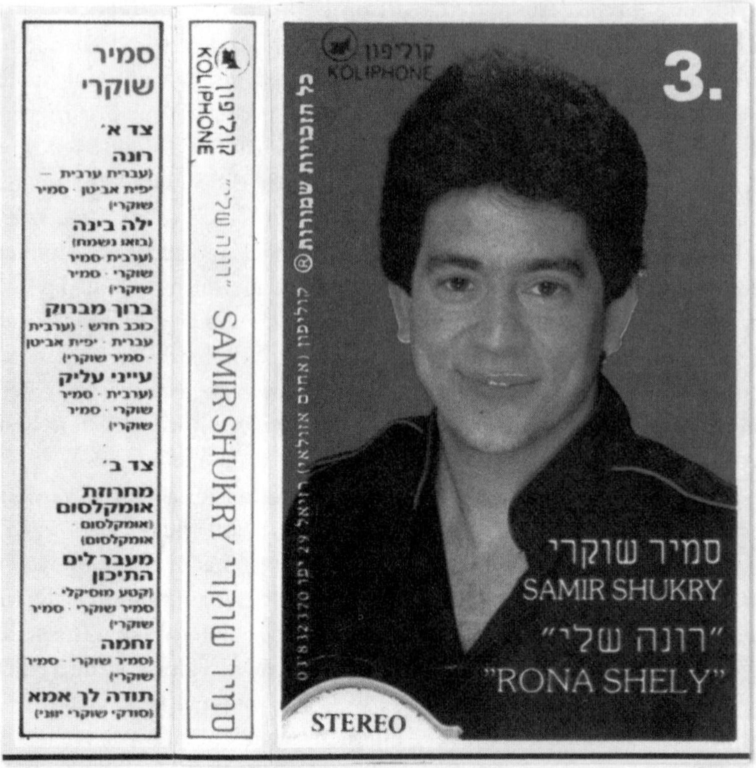

Raised in a musical family in Akko, singer/violinist Samir Shukry is a renowned Israeli Arab who performed within the Mediterranean Israeli music network. *Rona Shely,* an example of what Shukry calls his musical intermarriage of East and West, was also popular in Egypt, Syria, Lebanon, Jordan, France, and the United States. (Courtesy Azoulay Brothers)

Israeli ethnic groups parallel asymmetries of power between Israelis and Palestinians on a much reduced scale. But the parallels are imperfect. Though their ethnic status varies, Jews of all ethnic groups are legal citizens of Israel, and even the more disenfranchised of these groups enjoy a more privileged status in Israel than Palestinians. While some Palestinians are also citizens of Israel, many others live in a patchwork of occupied territories under Israel's dominion. Israeli occupation of Palestinian lands, cultures, and communities, while not the focus of this study, may have contributed to Mediterranean Israeli music's status as itself a territory under dispute.

Transgressing Boundaries

Even in the 1980s, when Mediterranean Israeli music was still held at the margins of Israeli radio, it was passing across the boundaries of Israeli political space into the Palestinian communities of the West Bank and Gaza, to Arab listeners in Syria, Jordan, and Lebanon, and from these spaces to Israeli and Arab communities in Europe, the United States, and South America. Territorial boundaries are not necessarily auditory boundaries. Sound travels differently than politics and makes different alliances. Music sometimes slips through barriers bodies cannot. And this airborne, disembodied audio slippage—of music creeping across hostile borders—can open up more physical passage for border crossing by musicians themselves. Israeli politicians, often at the suggestion of Palestinian, Jordanian, or Egyptian politicians, invited singers like Zehava Ben, Ofra Haza, and Haim Moshe to perform at peace negotiations or, in the case of Jordan, at the border ceremony marking their peace treaty with Israel. These performances were seen not as mere entertainment but as profoundly symbolic gestures of inclusion. The singers themselves were also quietly invited to Tunisia, Morocco, and Hebron.

As Israel began to embrace its Arab heritage in the mid-1990s, Mediterranean Israeli music went mainstream. Discussing what he described as Israeli society's growing inclination to accept "the Arabic" within it, Alan Sipress of the *Philadelphia Inquirer* quoted a seventeen-year-old Russian Jewish immigrant to Israel as saying that newly arrived immigrant youth "don't like American-style music. Most of the time they listen to this Oriental music. In Oriental music, they talk about life as it really is. They give you what's in the heart."[31]

The fact that Sipress's article appeared in a mainstream daily American paper testified to the growing popularity of this music not only in Israel but in the United States as well. Partly because of its popularity abroad, the music had become increasingly prominent in Israel. In 1990, when I interviewed Yardena Houja, a second-generation Iraqi-Kurdish member of the Houja family in Jerusalem's Mizraḥi Katamon Vav neighborhood, she professed disdain for Mediterranean Israeli music; by 1995, she had changed her mind. Frequent radio broadcasting of the music had "opened her ear" to these sounds.

It is tempting to suppose that music is politics in a new key. As we see in the case of Mediterranean Israeli music, music and politics influence each other, but their influences are complex and reciprocal rather than unidirectional and causal. While in some sense the opening of mainstream Israeli audiences to Mediterranean Israeli music may have presaged political advances for the Mizraḥi community, in another sense these political advances opened the way for increasing acceptance of the musical form. Music and politics are interlaced, perhaps especially so in disputed territories, but they are not one and the same, and their interconnections are multifaceted. Music suffuses politics with passion and presence; politics expands music beyond itself and gives it gravity and import. At the time of the peace negotiations in the mid-1990s, Mediterranean Israeli music was dialogically related not only to politics but also to itself. It embraced both affinities and antipathies. It was not just political; it was musical. Musicians described themselves as "freely" drawing upon their diverse inheritances, carefully juxtaposing soundscapes representing their internal disputed territories.

Take, for example, the 1975 renditions by Yemenite bands *Tselile ha-karem* and *Tselile ha-ʿūd* of "Ḥanaleh hitbalbelah." The bands adapted a *nigen*[32] that used to be performed by Klezmorim,[33] with lyrics from a poem by Polish-born Natan Alterman, a renowned author of modern Hebrew poetry, and rendered it in a Yemenite vocal style. To this unlikely mix they added Greek rhythms and Western rock beats. The poem itself is an ironic and humorous narrative about a wedding between a Mizraḥi man and an Ashkenazi woman. Things continually turn upside down in the story—the least of which is the baby's arrival prior to the wedding. In short, the song mirrors the confusion of Mizraḥi/Ashkenazi encounters and reflects what could be called (to riff Alice Walker) "the aesthetics of my familiar."

Despite having been assigned to broadcast corners and heritage displays (as a relic of the past rather than a living art), a disenfranchised neighborhood music that had flourished at a grassroots level blasted out of the ghetto to become the sound track to an emerging pan-ethnic political coalition. At the heart of the conflict over this increased audibility in mainstream media were questions of appropriation and the claim to Arab musical inheritance. Initially, renditions of Arab music (such as Haim Moshe's "Linda Linda") crossed both borders within Israel's ethnically divided society and the borders between Israel and Palestine, Syria, Lebanon, and Jordan. Mizraḥi musicians, like Zehava Ben, touched the hearts of Arab listeners everywhere. Truly reciprocal interactions between Mizraḥi and Ashkenazi singers were no longer surprising, and media attention shifted from the ethnic issue to the music itself. The proliferation of cable channels and decentralized "local" radio stations reconfigured and expanded access to broadcast channels, and local papers regularly reviewed new releases and concert appearances. By the late 1990s, Mediterranean Israeli music was, as Argov had wished, "scattered throughout the hours" rather than ghettoized in Mizraḥi corners of radio and television.

Even as Mediterranean Israeli music reached the mainstream, a new generation of Mizraḥi musicians were returning to the ethnically specific, rural and urban, classical and folk, Middle Eastern and North African music styles their parents and grandparents had been asked to abandon in the late 1940s, when ethnicity itself had been regarded as illegitimate and the national musical task was to blend exilic soundscapes. In the context of a burgeoning world music industry and of the increased acceptability of Middle Eastern and North African musics, Moroccan, Kurdish, Iranian, and other particular traditions began to find favor in the mainstream Israeli marketplace. The popularity of specific ethnic musics may have grown from the nostalgia that came with the consolidation of Mizraḥiyut (Eastern-ness). As Mizraḥim became more integrated into Israeli society, Mizraḥi ethnic communities experienced a longing for their specific ancestral diaspora homelands. At the same time, Ashkenazi communities embraced North African and Middle Eastern music roots, of the sort Yael Zerubavel calls "recovered roots." These new stylistic innovations were appealing in their seemingly aesthetic coherence grounded in the appearance of indigeneity contrasted with the hybrid Mediterranean Israeli music style.[34]

Recoveries of ethnic specificity are sometimes regarded as uncontaminated in contrast to appropriations across cultural boundaries. Yet recoveries are another form of borrowing even if they are from the imagined coherence of one's own heritage. All these complex appropriations[35] are forms of power relationships. Appropriation can involve the loss of control by official culture or by the manufacturers of meaning (to use Bourdieu's phrase) and the proliferation of emergent styles that contest pure categories. Music is regarded by some as inevitably contaminated as it travels through the airwaves across national boundaries, transgressing customs, checkpoints, and security zones. Hybrid borrowings, appropriations, cultural recoveries, stylistic survivals, and inheritances create relationships across geopolitical conflict lines and the performance of cultural identities confirm, ignore, realign, transcend, and/or defy those borders. Uncontested appropriations belie their invented nature and can be deployed to create powerful political affiliations across enemy lines. Uncontested status is always temporary, always open to suspicion. How porous to such infiltration a particular political landscape may be depends on the nature of its cultural and political boundaries.

People lament the loss of their traditions and speak about their culture in terms of survival or disappearance, but we have to note that the survival

A Moroccan Israeli soldier affixes Zehava Ben's *Tipat mazal* (A Drop of Luck) cassette cover on his weapon in a display of ethnic, musical, and aesthetic irony. (Photo by author)

of culture is not coterminous with the literal survival of people in war-torn places. At the same time, the overlapping discourses of cultural and physical survival are not only figuratively interwoven but literally inseparable. In this study, I have documented the ways in which innovative negotiation and change in both the musical and the political arenas became necessary for survival, not only of musics in their constantly mutating forms, but of the people who create, inherit, transmit, and cherish these war torn soundscapes. Survival is not the transport of fixed immutable forms over time. Rather, in music as in life, innovation and tradition are linked in both dispute and resolution.

National and musical boundaries continue to unravel, travel, and reform in unexpected ways. Although analysis of Mediterranean Israeli music's consolidation in the 1970s–1990s cannot answer global questions about these contested terrains, it can contribute to our understanding of how these aesthetic and political struggles arise in cultural terms. I propose this analysis at the interface of art and politics as song wars and war songs, peace tracks and sound tracks, echo in the thick air of disputed territory. Mediterranean Israeli music is the voice of people who live in this thick air. We have something to learn from their homespun sound track.

Notes

Chapter 1

1. These would grow into a five-part radio series: Amy Horowitz, *Side by Side: Creators on Restless Soil,* ed. Ziv Yonatan, 1986.

2. A melisma is "a group of more than five or six notes sung to a single syllable." Richard L. Crocker, "Melisma," *Grove Music Online,* ed. L. Macy, http://www.grovemusic.com.

3. Yael Amsha-Reyyn, "Lo shir shel tshaḥatshaḥim" (Not the Song of *tshaḥatshaḥim*), *Yedi'ot America* (New York), 9 November 1990, S12–14. *Tshaḥatshaḥim* is a pejorative slang term for Jews of North African and Middle Eastern origin. Oded Ahiassaf, Ra'anan Ahiassaf, and Radad Goni, eds., *Leksikon ha-sleng ha-'Ivri veha-tseva'i* (The Lexicon of Hebrew and Army Slang) (Tel Aviv: Prolog Printers, 1993).

4. Unless otherwise noted, translations throughout the book are my own. I have consulted with Reuven Namdar, who was my research assistant during the ethnographic process. Yossi Galron provided editorial corrections and refinement of transliterations.

5. The *'ūd* is a "short-necked plucked lute of the Arab world, the direct ancestor of the European lute, whose name derives from al-'ūd ('the lute')." Christian Poché, "'Ūd," in Macy, *Grove Music Online.* The *qānūn* is a "plucked box zither psaltery of the Middle East, North Africa and parts of Asia; it is trapiziform in shape, two of the sides forming a right angle." Christian Poché, "'Qānūn," in Macy, *Grove Music Online.* The *darabukka* is "a single-headed goblet drum. It is made from pottery, wood or metal; the bottom is open and the skin head is directly attached by nails, glue or binding." William J. Conner, Milfie Howell/Tony Langlois, "Darabukka," in Macy, *Grove Music Online.*

6. John Hutnyk, *Critique of Exotica: Music, Politics and the Culture Industry* (London: Pluto Press, 2000), 115. I use the term "hybrid," while acknowledging the critique of the concept of hybridity. This critique highlights the difficulty of finding vocabulary to address multivocal forms. See Hutnyk's critique of the concept of hybridity. "The criticism of hybridity can be collected into several categories: the heritage of hybridity's botanical roots, the sterility of the hybrid mule, and its extension to mulatto, mixed race, half-breed and other obscene races, the reclamation of the term reconfigured as creativity at the margins, and as advent of vibrant intersections that cannot be otherwise incorporated; the hegemony of the pure that co-constitutes the hybrid; the inconsequence of hybridity in the recognition that everyone is hybrid, everyone is 'different'; the commercial co-option-option of multiplicity, and that if everyone is hybrid, then the old problems of race, class, gender, sex, money and power still apply. All of this is the terrain of hybridity-talk made fashionable in the salons of social commentary" (115). Rey Chow writes that "the enormous seductiveness of the postmodern

hybridities's discourse lies . . . in its invitation to join the power of global capitalism by flattening out past injustices." Rey Chow, *Ethnics after Idealism* (Bloomington: Indiana University Press, 1998), 156, quoted in John Hutnyk, *Critique of Exotica,* 115. Also see Deborah A. Kapchan and Pauline Turner Strong, eds., "Theorizing Hybridity," *Journal of American Folklore* 112, no. 445 (1999).

7. Erik Cohen and Amnon Shiloah, "Major Trends of Change in Jewish Oriental Ethnic Music in Israel," *Popular Music* 5 (1985): 199–223.

8. Jeffrey Halper, Edwin Seroussi, and Pamela Kidron, "Musica mizrakhit: Ethnicity and Class Culture in Israel," *Popular Music* 8, no. 2 (1989): 131–41.

9. Mordechai [Motti] Regev, "The Coming of Rock: Meaning, Contest and Structure in the Field of Popular Music in Israel" [in Hebrew] (Ph.D. diss., Tel Aviv University, 1990), 175.

10. Pierre Bourdieu, "The Field of Cultural Production, or: The Economic World Reversed," *Poetics* 12 (1983): 311–56.

11. In the Israeli context, one of the avenues for elite acceptance is previous participation in the various military entertainment ensembles (*Lahaḳot tseva'iyot*). "Membership in the Army Bands was . . . an almost essential prerequisite for authorization and recognition in the popular music field in Israel. This sort of authorization enabled . . . Arik Einstein, Shalom Hanoch, Dani Sanderson, and others to integrate rock and 'Israeliness' through this process to be accepted as 'authentic.'" Regev, "The Coming of Rock," 175. Another way of becoming accepted is by collaborating with already "consecrated" composers, singers, and arrangers. Ibid., 167–68.

12. Gilles Deleuze and Felix Guattari, *A Thousand Plateaus: Capitalism and Schizophrenia* (Minneapolis: University of Minnesota Press, 1987).

13. Although sabra is often used simply as a term for a native-born Israeli, it has a deeper and more complex connotation in Israeli culture. As Oz Almog notes in his landmark work, *The Sabra: The Creation of New Jew* (Berkeley: University of California Press, 2000), "Leaders of the Yishuv imputed great importance to the education of their children, the Sabras, and kept a vigilant and concerned eye on how the young natives developed and behaved. . . . The Sabra was expected to solidify and broaden the achievements of the first generation, yet remain loyal to its values" (23–24). Linguistically, sabra is related to the Hebrew word for cactus pear, and refers to a tough or thorny exterior covering a sweet interior.

14. Ilan Halevi, *A History of the Jews* (London and Atlantic Highlands, N.J.: A. M. Berrett, 1987), 208–9; Ammiel Alcalay, *After Jews and Arabs: Remaking Levantine Culture* (Minneapolis: University of Minnesota Press, 1993), 36–37.

15. Edward Said, *Orientalism* (New York: Random House, 1978), 3.

16. Ibid.; Gabriel Piterberg, "Domestic Orientalism: The Representation of Oriental Jews in Zionist/Israeli Historiography," *British Journal of Middle Eastern Studies* 23, no. 2 (1996): 125–45. Ivan Kalmer Davidson argues, "In fact, orientalism was a complex, ambiguous mixture of admiration and denigration that reflected the West's preoccupation with its own 'soul.' The West defined itself in contrast to an Orient imagined as its opposite-utopian or dystopian or both at the same time, and importantly as the origin of its defining religion, Christianity." Kalmer, "Research," 30 June 2004, http://www.chass.utoronto.ca/~ikalmar/research/research.html.

17. The expression *Samekh Ṭet* is the abbreviation of "*Sefaradi Ṭahor*" (pure Sephardi). For a discussion of the issues surrounding the definition of the term Sephardi in an

academic context see Rachel Simon, "Reference Sources for Sephardic Studies," 1994, http://www.princeton.edu/~rsimon/jl.html.

18. Erik Cohen, "The Black Panthers and Israeli Society," *Jewish Journal of Sociology* 14 (1972): 94.

19. Hussein M. Fahim, ed., *Indigenous Anthropology in Non-Western Countries: Proceedings of a Burg Wartenstein Symposium* (Durham, N.C.: Carolina Academic Press, 1982); Emiko Ohnuki-Tierney, "'Native' Anthropologists," *American Ethnologist* 11, no. 3 (1984): 584–86.

20. James Clifford, "Introduction: Partial Truths," in *Writing Culture: The Poetics and Politics of Ethnography,* ed. James Clifford and George E. Marcus (Berkeley: University of California Press, 1986), 9.

21. There are problems in what Clifford describes as the shift from objective to subjective voice ("Introduction: Partial Truths," 13). "Literary approaches have recently enjoyed some popularity in the human sciences. . . . In their quite different ways they have blurred the boundary separating art from science." Clifford, "Introduction: Partial Truths," 3. The dilemma is not resolved by refashioning ethnography as fiction recounted in novel form.

22. Alessandro Portelli, *The Battle of Valle Giulia: Oral History and the Art of Dialogue* (Madison: University of Wisconsin Press, 1997).

23. Following recent interest in exposing the cooperative nature of ethnographic ventures in folklore, ethnomusicology, and anthropology, Ruby and I discussed the extent to which he would appear in the book. The pretense of equality of scholars' interlocuters is as problematic as their erasure. Ruby was not only a crucial research associate who changed the shape of the work, but also an insider and a student for whom the project was both familiar and strange. It was his decision to remain a minor voice in the actual text.

24. Clifford, "Introduction: Partial Truths," 7.

25. Shimon Parnas, interview by author, tape recording, Jerusalem, 12 August 1984.

26. Horowitz, *Side by Side.*

27. Haim Moshe and Meir Reuveni, interview by author, Tel Aviv, 5 August 1984.

28. *Pa'ame ha-Mizraḥ* (Footsteps of the East), produced by Yosef Ben Israel, "*Mits'ad ha-pizmonim ha-Mizraḥi be-Ḳiryat Gat*" (The Eastern Hit Parade in Ḳiryat Gat), singers Haim Moshe, Zohar Argov, Moshe Hillel, and Tsiyon Golan (Jerusalem: Israel Television, 12 October 1983); *Od lahiṭ* (Another hit), hosted by Regi Bitlin and Kobi Rekht, "Performances by Margalit Tsan'ani, Etti Ankri, Zohar Argov, Ester Shamir, Shlomo Artzi, Ofer Akerling" (Jerusalem: Israel Television, 1 September 1983); *Sha'ah ṭovah* (Good hour), Daniel Peer, interview with Zohar Argov (Jerusalem: Israel Television, 7 January 1983); *Yoman ha-shavu'a* (Weekly Journal), Yoel Esteron, interview with Zohar Argov (Jerusalem: Israel Television, 1981).

29. Shemuel Hasfari, *ha-Melekh* (The King) (n.p., 1992); Merit Tobi, comp., "*ha-Melekh*" (The King): *Research,* Background Research for the Script (n.p., 1992).

30. Dan Caspi, *Media Decentralization: The Case of Israel's Local Newspapers* (New Brunswick, N.J.: Transaction Books, 1986); Dan Caspi and Yehiel Limor, *The In/Outsiders: The Mass Media in Israel* (Cresskill, N.J.: Hampton Press, 1999).

31. Kessar used the term quarter tone, which is "an interval that is one half of a semitone or half of a half-step. This interval in not commonly used in Western music." Virginia Tech Multimedia Music Dictionary, 1996–2007, http://www.music.vt.edu/

musicdictionary/textq/quatertone.html. In actual use by Mizraḥi musicians, these intervals can be considered microtones, as they are not always exactly quarters and often vary in size and differ from standard Western measurements and terminology. Microtones are commonly used in Arab music, and many instruments have to be modified in order to be able to play all of the twenty-four tones used in the scale.

32. Amnon Lord, "Anaḥnu tsrikhim la-tset meha-ḥor ha-ze" (We Have to Get Out of This Hole), *Iton Tel Aviv*, 17 January 1992, 38. See http://www.ugly-things.com/churchills.html for an interview with Miki Gabrielov conducted by Mike Stax.

33. See their web site at http://www.emi.org.il.

34. See their web site at http://www.acum.org.il.

35. See Select Discography for information on some such cassettes. One example is the song "Elinor," performed by Zohar Argov.

36. Raḥel Mehagar, "Yafah shetiḳah" (Silence Is Beautiful), *Kol ha-ʿIr* (Jerusalem), 12 April 1991, 55.

37. Lea Inbal, "Zehava," *Yediʿot Aḥaronot* (Tel Aviv), *Musaf Shivʿah Yamim* (Seven-Day Supplementary), 1 April 1991, 32–33.

38. Tal Peri, "Salamat Zehava," *Maʿariv* (Tel Aviv), 14 June 1991, 50.

39. Natan Shahar, "The Eretz-Yisraeli Song 1920–1950: Sociomusical and Musical Aspects," Ph.D. diss., Hebrew University, 1989; Motti Regev and Edwin Seroussi, *Popular Music and National Culture in Israel* (Berkeley: University of California Press, 2004), 49–89.

40. For a detailed account of this process in Northern India, see Peter Manuel, *Cassette Culture: Popular Music and Technology in North India* (Chicago: University of Chicago Press, 1993); Roger Wallis and Krister Malm, *Big Sounds from Small Peoples: The Music Industry in Small Countries* (London: Constable, 1984).

41. Robin James quoted in Jon Pareles, "Cassette Culture: Home Recording or Original Music on Cassettes," *Whole Earth Review* 5 (Winter 1988): 110–11.

42. Amal Bakir, "Hadhihi al-Sumum al-Masmuʿua" (These Are Aural Poisons), *Al-Ahram* (Cairo), 11 February 1983, 8.

43. Houston A. Baker Jr., *Black Studies, Rap, and the Academy* (Chicago: University of Chicago Press, 1993), 41.

44. Bakir, "Hadhihi al-Sumum al-Masmuʿua," 8.

45. Thomas Kuhn, *The Structure of Scientific Revolutions* (Chicago: University of Chicago Press, 1970), ix.

46. Salwa El-Shawan Castelo-Branco, "Some Aspects of the Cassette Industry in Egypt," *World of Music* 29 (1987): 39–40.

47. Lila Abu-Lughod, "Bedouins, Cassettes and Technologies of Public Culture," *Middle East Report*, no. 159 (1989): 7.

48. Amy Shuman, "Dismantling Local Culture," *Western Folklore* 52 (1993): 345–64.

49. The *zurna* is a "folk shawm of West and Central Asia, south-eastern Europe and parts of North Africa. Its general form is a conical wooden tube 30–45 cm long, but its length may extend to 60 cm. It is played with a double reed and usually has a pirouette." Christian Poché with Razia Sultanova, "Surnāy [sornā, surla, surle, sūrnā, surnāī, srnāy, zournas, zukra, zurla, zurna, zūrnā," in Macy, *Grove Music Online.* A *muwwal* is an Arabic term for the opening introductory segment of a song in which a performer often introduces the modes (*maqamat*) that will be heard. The San Remo style is part of an Italian popular music form emerging from the San Remo festival that draws upon "Mediterranean-ness"

and a juxtaposition of cosmopolitan and traditional models in the formation of a national popular music. See Franco Fabbri, "Nowhereland: The Construction of a 'Mediterranean' Identity in Italian Popular Music," *Journal of Musical Anthropology of the Mediterranean* 6 (2001), http://research.umbc.edu/eol/ma/index/number6/fabbri/fab_0.htm.

50. Castelo-Branco, "Some Aspects of the Cassette Industry in Egypt," 39.

51. Eviatar Zerubavel, *The Fine Line: Making Distinctions in Everyday Life* (New York: Free Press, 1991), 1–4.

52. John F. Szwed, "Metaphors of Incommensurability," *Journal of American Folklore* 116, no. 459 (2003): 9–18; Robert Baron and Ana C. Cara, "Introduction: Creolization and Folklore—Cultural Creativity in Process," *Journal of American Folklore* 116, no. 459 (2003): 4–8.

53. Baron and Cara, "Introduction: Creolization and Folkore," 5.

54. Pareles, "Cassette Culture," 110–11.

55. Abu-Lughod, "Bedouins, Cassettes and Technologies," 8.

56. John Bailey, "Cross-Cultural Perspectives in Popular Music: The Case of Afghanistan," *Popular Music* 1 (1981): 120.

57. Amir Ben-David and Michal Zunder, "Ekh 'avru ha-shanim" (How the Years Have Passed), *Iton Tel Aviv*, 2 November 1990, 44.

58. R. Anderson Sutton, "Commercial Cassette Recordings of Traditional Music in Java: Implications for Performers and Scholars," *World of Music* 27, no. 3 (1985), 28.

59. Castelo-Branco, "Some Aspects of the Cassette Industry in Egypt," 37.

60. Pareles, "Cassette Culture," 110–11.

61. Abu-Lughod, "Bedouins, Cassettes and Technologies," 9.

62. Rebecca Solnit, *Hope in the Dark: The Untold Story of People Power* (Edinburgh: Canongate Books, 2004), 91.

63. Ibid., 97.

64. Ibid., 122. It is in this sense that Amy Shuman describes folk groups as political action coalitions (Shuman, "Dismantling Local Culture").

65. Disputed territory refers to both a geographically situated regional struggle with national, religious, and political dimensions as well as a metaphorical way of describing dissonant spaces such as exist between Israeli ethnic groups.

66. Amy Horowitz, "Dueling Nativities: Zehava Ben Sings Umm Kulthum," in *Palestine, Israel, and the Politics of Popular Culture,* ed. Rebecca L. Stein and Ted Swedenburg (Durham, N.C.: Duke University Press, 2005), 202–30.

67. Deleuze and Guattari, *A Thousand Plateaus,* 21

68. Territories assume a coterminous relationship between people, identities, places, ownership of culture, and self-determination. Deterritorialization is accomplished by taking apart any of these naturalized associations. Thus, the concept of rhizome substitutes endless nodes of connection for overdetermined associations (ibid., 10–11). Similarly, Bahktin/Volosinov's concept of reported speech deterritorializes by taking apart the association between the speaker and the owner of the words spoken. See Mikhail Bakhtin, *The Dialogic Imagination: Four Essays by M. M. Bakhtin,* ed. Michael E. Holquist, trans. Caryl Emerson and Michael E. Holquist (Austin: University of Texas Press, 1981), 270.

69. Itamar Even-Zohar, "The Emergence of a Native Hebrew Culture in Palestine: 1882–1948," *Poetics Today* 11, no. 1 (1990): 175–91; Itamar Even-Zohar, "The Emergence of a Native Hebrew Culture in Palestine: 1882–1948," *Studies in Zionism* 4 (1981): 167–84.

Chapter 2

1. Marie Cieri, "Irresolvable Geographies," Ph.D. diss., Rutgers University, 2004.

2. Of these, 873,600 of the 1948 Palestinian population resided within what became the borders of Israel, with 485,000 outside those borders. In 1950, only 165,000 Palestinians resided inside Israeli borders. Justin McCarthy, "Palestine's Population during the Ottoman and the British Mandate Periods," 8 September 2001, http://www.palestineremembered.com/Acre/Palestine-Remembered/Story559.html.

3. Joseph B. Maier and Chaim I. Waxman, eds., *Ethnicity, Identity and History: Essays in Memory of Werner J. Cahnman* (New Brunswick, N.J.: Transaction Books, 1983), 274.

4. Tom Segev, *1949: The First Israelis,* trans. Arlen Neal Weinstein (New York: Free Press, 1986), 95.

5. Hannan Hever, Yehouda Shenhav, and Pnina Motzafi-Haller, eds., *Mizraḥim in Israel: A Critical Observation into Israel's Ethnicity* [in Hebrew] (Jerusalem: Van Leer Institute/Hakibbutz Hameuḥad, 2002); Yehouda Shenhav, *The Arab Jews: A Postcolonial Reading of Nationalism, Religion, and Ethnicity* (Stanford: Stanford University Press, 2006); Erez Tzfadia, "Public Housing as Control: Spatial Policy of Settling Immigrants in Israeli Development Towns," *Housing Studies* 21, no. 4 (2006): 523–37.

6. Galit Hasan-Rokem discusses the physical and meta-physical Jerusalems in her article "Dialogue as Ethical Conduct: The Folk Festival That Was Not," in *Research Ethics in Studies of Culture and Social Life,* ed. Bente G. Alver, Tove I. Fjell, and Ørjar Øyen (Helsinki: Suomalainen Tiedeakatemia, 2007), 149–61. Hasan-Rokem discusses the personification of Jerusalem in "Not the Mother of All Cities: A Feminist Perspective of Jerusalem," *Palestine-Israel Journal of Politics, Economics and Culture* 2, no. 3 (1995), http://www.pij.org/details.php?id=627. See also Barbara Kirshenblatt-Gimblett, "Spaces of Dispersal," *Cultural Anthropology* 9, no. 3 (1994): 339–44.

7. Amnon Shiloah, "Eastern Sources in Israeli Music," *Ariel* 88 (1992): 4–19.

8. Amnon Raz-Krakotzkin, "Diaspora within Sovereignty: Critique of 'Negation of the Diaspora' in Israeli Culture" [in Hebrew], *Te'orya u-viḳoret* (Theory and Critique) 4 (1993): 23–55.

9. Ella Shohat, "Invention of the Mizraḥim," *Journal of Palestine Studies* 29, no. 1 (1999): 5–20.

10. R. Mendlezweig and N. Magor, *Aliyah u-ḳeliṭah, hitpatḥut u-megamot* (Immigration and Absorption, Development and Trends) (Jerusalem: Government Press Office, 1984), 14.

11. The Law of Return, adopted in 1950, grants all Jews automatic citizenship upon immigration to Israel. For a discussion of the paternalistic attitudes and the lack of understanding of the cultural dimensions of absorption, see Jeffrey Halper, "The Absorption of Ethiopian Immigrants: A Return to the Fifties," *Israel Social Science Research* 3, nos. 1–2 (1985): 112–39.

12. Sammy Smooha, *Israel: Pluralism and Conflict* (London: Routledge and Kegan Paul, 1978), 87.

13. I. Adler, N. Lewin-Epstein, and Y. Shavit, "Ethnic Stratification and Place of Residence in Israel: A Truism Revisited," *Research in Social Stratification and Mobility* 23 (2004): 155–90; H. Ayalon and A. Gamoran, "Stratification in Academic Secondary Programs and Educational Inequality in Israel and the United States," *Comparative Education Review* 44 (2000): 54–80; Uzi Rebhun and Chaim Isaac Waxman, eds., *Jews*

in Israel: Contemporary Social and Cultural Patterns (Hanover, N.H.: Brandeis University Press, 2003).

14. Mendlezweig and Magor, *Aliyah u-ḳeliṭah, hitpatḥut u-megamot,* 18.

15. For Palestinians, memories of ancestral homes now either destroyed or occupied by Jewish Israelis are palpable and ongoing. Many Palestinians pass their keys to family homes to their children along with the stories of their lost inheritance. See Yara Bayoumy, "Father to Son, Keys to Palestinian Home Cherished," *Reuters,* 23 November 2007, http://www.reuters.com/article/worldNews/idUSL22373092007 1123. See "Return to Jaffa" in Suad Amiry's memoir, *Sharon and My Mother-in-Law: Ramallah Diaries* (New York: Random House, 2003), 19–28; and the cover photograph of Salim Tamari's collection of essays, *Mountains against the Sea: Essays on Palestinian Society and Culture* (Berkeley: University of California Press, 2009). See Susan Slyomovics, *The Object of Memory: Arab and Jew Narrate the Palestinian Village* (Philadelphia: University of Pennsylvania Press, 1998).

16. Smooha, *Israel: Pluralism and Conflict,* 86, 94.

17. Halper, "Absorption of Ethiopian Immigrants," 121.

18. Oren Yiftachel, "Social Control, Urban Planning and Ethno-class Relations: Mizraḥi Jews in Israel's 'Development Towns,'" *International Journal of Urban and Regional Research* 24, no. 2 (2000): 418–38; Rachel Kallus and Hubert Law Yone, "National Home/Personal Home: Public Housing and the Shaping of National Space in Israel," *European Planning Studies* 10, no. 6 (2002): 765–79; Sammy Smooha, "The Mass Immigrations to Israel: A Comparison of the Failure of the Mizraḥi Immigrants of the 1950s with the Success of the Russian Immigrants of the 1990s," *Journal of Israeli History* 27, no. 1 (2008): 1–27.

19. Smooha, *Israel: Pluralism and Conflict,* 87.

20. Mendlezweig and Magor, *Aliyah u-ḳeliṭah, hitpatḥut u-megamot,* 19.

21. Smooha, *Israel: Pluralism and Conflict,* 91.

22. Calvin Goldscheider, "The Demography of Asian and African Jews In Israel," in Maier and Waxman, *Ethnicity, Identity and History,* 280–81.

23. Kirshenblatt-Gimblett, "Spaces of Dispersal," 340.

24. Maurice M. Roumani, "The Military, Ethnicity, and Integration in Israel Revisited," in *Ethnicity, Integration, and the Military,* ed. Henry Dietz, Jerrold Elkin, and Maurice Roumani (Boulder, Colo.: Westview, 1991), 51–81.

25. Nissim Yosha, "The Heritage of Oriental Jewry in Israeli Education and Culture," in *Encyclopedia Judaica 1983–85 Yearbook,* ed. Geoffrey Wigoder (Jerusalem: Keter, 1983), 106.

26. Haim Moshe, interview by author, tape recording, Tel Aviv, 6 August 1984.

27. David Ben-Gurion, quoted in Mosheh Yitsḥaḳ Imanu'el, *ha-Pa'ar* (The gap) (Holon, Israel: Ami, 1968), 158.

28. Arye Gelblum, quoted in Raphael Patai, *Israel Between East and West* (Westport, Conn.: Greenwood, 1970), 294–96.

29. Ben-Zion Dinur, quoted in Michael Keren, *Ben-Gurion and the Intellectuals: Power, Knowledge and Charisma* (Dekalb: Northern Illinois University Press, 1983), 126.

30. Keren, *Ben-Gurion and the Intellectuals,* 4.

31. David Ben-Gurion, "The Call of the Spirit of Israel," in *Rebirth and Destiny of Israel,* ed. Ben-Gurion (New York: Philosophical Library, 1954), quoted in Keren, *Ben-Gurion and the Intellectuals,* 10.

32. Segev, *1949: The First Israelis,* 126.

33. Rachel Shazar, quoted in Keren, *Ben-Gurion and the Intellectuals,* 126.

34. Moshe Shamir, quoted in ibid.

35. Ilan Halevi, quoted in Ammiel Alcalay, "Israel and the Levant: 'Wounded Kinship's Last Resort,'" *Middle East Report* (July/August 1989): 18.

36. Ella Shohat, *Taboo Memories, Diasporic Voices* (Durham, N.C.: Duke University Press, 2006).

37. Alcalay, "Israel and the Levant"; Ammiel Alcalay, *After Jews and Arabs: Remaking Levantine Culture* (Minneapolis: University of Minnesota Press, 1993); Ammiel Alcalay, ed., *Keys to the Garden: New Israeli Writing* (San Francisco: City Lights, 1996).

38. Bracha Seri, quoted in Alcalay, *After Jews and Arabs,* 250.

39. Howard M. Sachar, *A History of Israel: From the Rise of Zionism to Our Time* (New York: Knopf, 1976), 422.

40. Jeff Halper, interview by author, in *Side by Side: Creators on Restless Soil,* ed. Ziv Yonatan (Jerusalem, 8 September 1985).

41. Erik Cohen, "The Black Panthers and Israeli Society," *Jewish Journal of Sociology* 14 (1972); Sammy Smooha, "Israel and Its Third World Jews: Black Panthers-the Ethnic Dilemma," *Society* 9, no. 7 (1972): 31–36; Sami Shalom Chetrit, "'Either the Cake Will Be Shared or There Will Be No Cake.' 30 Years to the Black Panthers in Israel," *Kedma–Middle Eastern Gate to Israel,* n.d., http://www.kedma.co.il/Panterim/PanterimTheMovie/EnglishArticles.htm; *The Black Panthers (in Israel) Speak,* written and directed by Eli Hamo and Sami Shalom Chetrit (Israel, 2003), videotape.

42. Sheli Elkayam, interview by author, Jerusalem, 10 August 1985.

43. Sami Shalom Chetrit, "Mizraḥi Politics in Israel: Between Integration and Alternative," *Journal of Palestine Studies* 29, no. 4 (2000): 51–65; Y. Peled, "Towards a Redefinition of Jewish Nationalism in Israel: The Enigma of Shas," *Ethnic and Racial Studies* 21, no. 4 (1998): 703–27.

44. Amy Horowitz, "Resetting Ethnic Margins, Sephardic Renaissance through Film," *Jusur* 5 (1989): 91–104. *Mimouna* is a North African Jewish celebration of the first baking of leavened bread immediately following the last day of Passover. It has become a pan-ethnic Mizraḥi festival in Israel.

45. Michael Herzfeld defines cultural intimacy as "the recognition of those aspects of cultural identity that are considered a source of external embarrassment but which nevertheless provide insiders with their assurance of common sociality." Herzfeld gives the example of Greeks banning plate smashing because it is embarrassing. He quotes Andrew Shyrock as saying, "Whether Germans really do look down on Greeks for smashing plates does not matter; the intimacy that emerges in this context of self-recognition is decidedly Greek, as is the embarrassment that comes with the realization that cultural difference, yet again, upholds a larger system of ranking in which Greece is not quite modern, not quite Europe." Herzfeld, *Cultural Intimacy: Social Poetics in the Nation State* (New York: Routledge, 1997), 3.

46. Michael Ohad, "Libi ba-Mizraḥ" (My Heart Is in the East), *Haaretz* (Tel Aviv), 25 September 1981, 16; Motti Regev and Edwin Seroussi, *Popular Music and National Culture in Israel* (Berkeley: University of California Press, 2004).

47. An Arabic phrase that has entered Hebrew slang, *'ala-kefak* literally means "very good," "wonderful," "excellent."

48. Meir Reuveni, interview by author, Tel Aviv, 5 August 1984. Asher Reuveni recounted a similar version of this story to journalist Michael Ohad (see Ohad, "Libi ba-Mizraḥ," *Haaretz*, 25 September 1981).

49. Edwin Seroussi, "Ḥanale hitbalbela (Hanale was rattled)," in *Fifty to Forty Eight: Critical Moments in the History of the State of Israel*, ed. Adi Ophir (special issue of *Te'oryah u-viḳoret*, vols. 12–13; Jerusalem: Van Leer Institute, 1999), 269–78. See also Regev and Seroussi, *Popular Music and National Culture in Israel*, 213–14, for a brief history of this song, composed by one of the most renowned Hebrew poets, Natan Alterman, who remembered a *nigen* (Yiddish, tune) from Eastern Europe that he used in the song. The best-known recording is by Naftule Brandwein under the title "Bulgar alla Naftule" in 1927.

50. See chapter 4.

51. Edith Gershon-Kiwi, "Musicology in Israel," *Acta Musicologica* 30, fasc. ½ (1958): 23.

52. Smooha, "Israel and Its Third World Jews: Black Panthers—the Ethnic Dilemma"; Cohen, "The Black Panthers and Israeli Society."

53. Shlomo Deshen and Moshe Shokeid, *The Predicament of Homecoming: Cultural and Social Life of North African Immigrants in Israel* (Ithaca: Cornell University Press, 1974); Harvey Goldberg, "The *Mimouna* and the Minority Status of the Moroccan Jews," *Ethnology* 17, no. 1 (1978): 75–87; Nitza Druyan, *Without a Magic Carpet: Yemenite Settlement in Eretz Israel (1881–1914)* [in Hebrew] (Jerusalem: Ben Zvi Institute, 1981); Moshe Shokeid, *The Dual Heritage: Immigrants from the Atlas Mountains in an Israeli Village* (Manchester: Manchester University Press, 1971).

54. Goldscheider, "The Demography of Asian and African Jews in Israel"; Halper, "The Absorption of Ethiopian Immigrants: A Return to the Fifties."

55. Benny Morris, *The Birth of the Palestinian Refugee Problem*, 1947–1949 (Cambridge, UK: Cambridge University Press, 1988); Ilan Pappé, *The Making of the Arab–Israeli Conflict*, 1947–1951 (London, I. B. Taurus, 1992); Henrietta Dahan-Kalev, "Tensions in Israeli Feminism: The Mizraḥi Ashkenazi Rift," *Women's Studies International Forum* 24 (2001): 1–16; Henrietta Dahan-Kalev, "Breaking Their Silence: Mizraḥi Women and the Israeli Feminist Movement," in *Studies in Contemporary Jewry: Sephardic Jewry and Mizraḥi Jews*, ed. Peter Meding (Oxford: Oxford University Press, 2007), 193–209. See also Ruth Tsoffar, "'A Land That Devours Its People': Mizraḥi Writing from the Gut," *Body & Society* 12, no. 2 (2006): 25–55. All other authors mentioned in this section are cited elsewhere in this book.

56. Alcalay, *After Jews and Arabs;* Alcalay, *Keys to the Garden.*

57. Ella Shohat, "Sephardim in Israel: Zionism from the Standpoint of Its Jewish Victims," *Social Text* 19/20 (Autumn 1988): 1–35; Yehouda Shenhav, "Ethnicity and National Memory: The World Organization of Jews from Arab Countries (WOJAC) in the Context of the Palestinian National Struggle," *British Journal of Middle Eastern Studies* 29, no. 1 (2002): 27–56.

58. Ella Shohat, *Israeli Cinema East/West and the Politics of Representation* (Austin: University of Texas Press, 1989).

59. *Forget Baghdad,* written and directed by Samir (Switzerland, 2003), film.

60. Uri Ram, "Postnationalist Pasts: The Case of Israel," *Social Science History,* 22, no. 4 (1998): 513–45.

61. Hever, Shenhav, Motzafi-Haller, *Mizraḥim in Israel.*

62. Amy Horowitz, "*Musiḳa Yam Tikhonit Yisraelit* (Israeli Mediterranean Music): Cultural Boundaries and Disputed Territories," Ph.D. diss., University of Pennsylvania, 1994; Regev and Seroussi, *Popular Music and National Culture in Israel,* 222–24.

63. Regev and Seroussi, *Popular Music and National Culture in Israel.*

Chapter 3

1. *'Asli* is an Arabic term that connotes originality and authenticity; it literally means "true" or "praiseworthy." Oded Ahiassaf, Ra'anan Ahiassaf, and Radad Goni, eds., *Leḳsiḳon ha-sleng ha-'Ivri ṿeha-tsevaʼi* (Lexicon of Hebrew and Army Slang) (Tel Aviv: Prolog Printers, 1993), 20, 578. "*Meḳori/t*" is Hebrew for "original." Here both terms are used in their emotive rather than analytical context and should not be confused with the musicological term that refers to tunes by Israeli composers in the network. The subjective feeling of "realness" may contradict analytical categories.

2. Gilles Deleuze and Felix Guattari, *A Thousand Plateaus* (Minneapolis: University of Minnesota Press, 1987). 9. Also, see Patti Lather's discussion of the rhizome in "Fertile Obsession: Validity after Poststructuralism," *Sociological Quarterly* 34, no. 4 (2005): 673–93.

3. Bernice Johnson Reagon, "'Nobody Knows the Trouble I See,' or 'By and By I'm Gonna Lay Down My Heavy Load,'" *Journal of American History* 78, no. 1 (1991): 115.

4. For example, see Zion Golan, *Lahiṭe Teman #1* (Hits of Yemen #1) (n.d.), Reuveni Brothers 1048/1074; Zion Golan, *Lahiṭe Teman* # 2 (Hits of Yemen #2) (n.d.), Reuveni Brothers 1048/1075; Zion Golan, *Ayumah be-har ha-mor* (Awesome at the Mount of Myrrh) (n.d.), Reuveni Brothers 222/23; Zion Golan, *Be-lahiṭe zahav* (In Golden Hits) (n.d.), Reuveni Brothers 131/37; Zion Golan, '*Et ratson, ya jamaʼa* (Good Times, Gang) (1988), Reuveni Brothers RC 240.

5. A Jewish liturgical poem.

6. Tselile ha-Kerem, *Shoshanat Teman* (Rose of Yemen) (n.d.), Yasu Reuveni Brothers.

7. For examples of Greek, Italian, and Spanish songs with reconstituted Hebrew lyrics, see Ofer Levy, *Eheyeh lakh le-me!ekh* (I'll Be Your King) (1992), Lin Productions: Michaeli 92; Haim Moshe, *ha-Ḳolot shel Pireus* (The Voices of Pireus) (n.d.), Reuveni Brothers RV272; and Avihu Medina, *Mah yihyeh* (What Will Be) (1992), AM Productions 004.

8. For an example of Mizraḥi adaptations of *ha-Shir ha-Erets Yisreʼeli* songs, see Eli Luzon, *Ezo medinah* (What a Country) (1987), Ben-Mosh Productions.

9. For example: Avihu Medina, "Shabeḥi Yerushalayim" (Praise, Jerusalem), composed by Avihu Medina, *Pirḥe gani* (The Flowers in My Garden) (1988), AM Productions 001–02; Haim Moshe, *Tsaʻad Temani* (Yemenite Step) (n.d.), Reuveni Brothers RC 8–399.

10. Whereas ethnic genres are cultural modes of communication, analytical categories are models for the organization of texts. Ben-Amos notes that as folklorists we often abandoned the cultural reality and strove to formulate theoretical analytical systems. We transformed traditional genres from cultural categories of communication into scientific concepts. Dan Ben-Amos was among a new generation of folklorists in the 1960s and 1970s who envisioned performance theory as a means of studying text in context. See Ben-Amos, "Analytical Categories and Ethnic Genres," in *Folklore Genres,* ed. Dan Ben-Amos (Austin: University of Texas Press, 1976), 216–41.

11. For a discussion of the practice of borrowing popular Arabic and other melodies as tunes for liturgical music in Middle Eastern and North African Jewish communities,

see Kay Kaufman Shelemay, *Let Jasmine Rain Down: Song and Remembrance among Syrian Jews* (Chicago: University of Chicago Press, 1998); Mark L. Kligman, *Maqām and Liturgy: Ritual, Music, and Aesthetics of Syrian Jews in Brooklyn* (Detroit: Wayne State University Press, 2008).

12. Amy Horowitz, "*Musiḳa Yam Tikhonit Yisraelit* (Israeli Mediterranean Music): Cultural Boundaries and Disputed Territories," Ph.D. diss., University of Pennsylvania, 1994.

13. Tselile ha-Kerem, *Shoshanat Teman* (Rose of Yemen); Tselile ha-Kerem, *Daḳmosh #2* (n.d.), Yasu Reuveni Brothers.

14. Daḳlon, *Mesibah 'im Daḳlon le-khol ha-ḥaverim* (Party with Daḳlon, for All the Friends) (1980), Reuveni Brothers, Levitan Studios CR 306.

15. *Mesibah* is the Hebrew word for party, although *ḥafla*, the parallel Arabic term, has entered Israeli slang and is associated with *Mizraḥi* culture.

16. Daḳlon, *Ḥafla 'im Daḳlon: Ahuvat levavi* (Party with Daḳlon: My Beloved) (1988), Reuveni Brothers, Kessar Studios AC 305.

17. Daḳlon, *Ḥafla 'im Daḳlon le-khol ha-ḥaverim* (Party with Daḳlon for All the Friends) (1978), Reuveni Brothers BC 130/8.

18. Daḳlon, *Ḳol ḳore li ba-midbar* (A Voice Calls Me in the Desert) (1990), Reuveni Brothers.

19. Daḳlon, *Zemer be-mish'ole ha-arets* (Song in the Land's Paths) (1991), Reuveni Brothers.

20. The Yiddish song "Oyfn veg shteyt a boym" was translated by Itzik Manger into "Al ha-derekh 'etz 'omed." There are several other translations into Hebrew, including those by Naomi Shemer and Natan Yonatan.

21. Ozeri, who suffered from throat cancer in the 1980s, made a comeback in the late 1990s, reissuing many earlier cassettes on CDs and recording new material.

22. Haim Moshe, *Ahavat ḥayai* (Love of My Life) (1984), Reuveni Brothers.

23. Merav Moran, "Linda Goes to the Kibbutz," *Ḥadashot,* (Tel Aviv) 7 October 1986, 19. In 1982 Samir Shukry recorded "Linda, Linda" on his first cassette *Etmol, ha-Yom, u-Maḥar* (Yesterday, Today, and Tomorrow). Shukry's version was also popular but did not receive the notoriety of Moshe's subsequent hit.

24. Haim Moshe, *Ahavat ḥayai.*

25. Medina, interview.

26. Margalit Tsan'ani, *Menta* (Mint) (1988), Reuveni Brothers: Sigma.

27. Margalit Tsan'ani, *Pegishah* (A Date) (1991), Reuveni Brothers: Galkol.

28. Haim Moshe, interview by author, tape recording, Tel Aviv, 6 August 1984.

29. Kay Kaufman Shelemay, *Soundscapes: Exploring Music in a Changing World* (New York: W. W. Norton, 2001).

30. Zohar Argov, *Elinor* (1980), Reuveni Brothers 43/1.

31. Argov, *Elinor*; Zohar Argov, *Hayu zemanim* (There Were Times) (1982), Reuveni Brothers.

32. Although mainstream audiences listened to Greek or Turkish music and employed it in their popular styles, the aesthetic formulation by Mizraḥi composers and arrangers was considered "cheap" and low quality.

33. Avihu Medina, interview by author, tape recording, Tel Aviv, 1 June 1992.

34. Ibid.

35. Ibid.

36. Medina, "Shabeḥi Yerushalayim" (Praise, Jerusalem).

37. Medina, interview.

38. Amy Shuman, "Strategic Romanticism," paper presented at the Feminist Rhetoric Conference, Corvallis, Ore., 1997.

39. Ibid.

40. Avihu Medina, "Baladah le-ḥaver" (Ballad to a Friend), *Asher Ahavti* (That I Loved) (1990), AM Productions 003.

41. Medina, interview.

42. Medina, "Avraham avinu" (Abraham, Our Father), *Mah yihyeh* (What Will Be) (1992), AM Productions.

43. Medina, "Lammah, El" (Why, God), *Mah yihyeh* (What Will Be) (1992), AM Productions.

44. Ludwig Wittgenstein, *Philosophical Investigations,* 50th Anniversary Commemorative Edition, trans. G. E. M. Anscombe (Malden, Mass.: Blackwell, 2001).

45. Mark Buchanan, *Nexus: Small Worlds and the Groundbreaking Theory of Networks* (New York: W. W. Norton, 2003).

Chapter 4

1. Zohar Argov, "*ha-Peraḥ be-gani*" (The Flower in My Garden), composed by Avihu Medina, *Nakhon le-hayom* (Up to Date) (1982), Reuveni Brothers 220/4.

2. Avihu Medina, interview by author, tape recording, Tel Aviv, 1 June 1992.

3. The following biographical information is compiled from interviews with Avihu Medina, Yehuda Kessar, Yigal Ḥared, and Argov's family members, as well as from interviews with Argov that appeared in the Israeli press. See chapter 2 for a discussion of Israeli ethnicity and ingathering.

4. Zohar Argov, "Yaldah, ḥikiti shanim" (Girl, I Have Waited Years), composed by Moshe Nagar, *Demo Tape* (1977), Kolifone Studio; Zohar Argov, "Kol yom she-'over" (Every Day That Passes), composed by Moshe Nagar, *Demo Tape* (1977), Kolifone Studio.

5. T. Horesh, "Music Therapy, Regression and Symbolic Distance in Substance Abusers and Their Preferred Music," *Music Therapy Today* 8, no. 3 (2007).

6. Deborah Gordon, ed., *Feminism and the Critique of Colonial Discourse,* special edition of *Inscriptions* 3–4 (1988): 1–154.

7. See their Call to Action at their web site, http://jewishsurvivors.blogspot.com/2007_08_01_archive.html.

8. Amir Ben-David and Michal Zunder, "Ekh 'avru ha-shanim" (How the Years Have Passed), *Iton Tel Aviv,* 2 November 1990, 39–52.

9. Yehuda Kessar, quoted in Tobi, *"ha-Melekh"* (The King): *Research.*

10. Marcel Lidji, quoted in ibid.

11. Zohar Argov quoted in Michael Ohad, "Libi ba-Mizraḥ" (My Heart Is in the East), *Haaretz* (Tel Aviv), 25 September 1981, 16.

12. Yoel Esteron, "Interview with Zohar Argov."

13. Argov, quoted in Ohad, "Libi ba-Mizraḥ," *Haaretz* (Tel Aviv), 17. (This is also the source of Argov's quote in the first epigraph of this chapter.)

14. Zohar Argov, *Hayu zemanim* (There Was a Time) (1982), Reuveni Brothers.

15. Zohar Argov, *Nakhon le-hayom* (Up to Date) (1982), Reuveni Brothers 220/4.

16. Ben-David and Zunder, "Ekh 'avru ha-shanim," *Iton Tel Aviv,* 39–52.

17. Zohar Argov, *Yam shel dema'ot* (Sea of Tears) (1985), Ben-Mosh Productions: Kessar.

18. Zohar Argov, *Lihiyot adam* (To Be Human) (1985).

19. Zohar Argov, *Ḥafla ve-shire matsav ruaḥ, hofa'ah ḥayah be-Tsarfat* (Party and Good Humor Songs: Live Performance, France) (1985), Tal Productions.

20. *Mi-meni, Meni* (From Me, Meni), Meni Peer, interview with Zohar Argov (Jerusalem: IBA, 1987).

21. Argov quoted in Ohad, "Libi ba-Mizraḥ," *Haaretz* (Tel Aviv), 17.

22. Medina quoted in Tobi, *"ha-Melekh"* (The King): *Research.*

23. Avraham Eilam Amzallag, "*Musiḳat ha-ḳaseṭot—lo musiḳah Mizraḥit*" (Cassette Music—Not Eastern Music), *Musika* 9 (1987): 34–35; Tobi, *"ha-Melekh"* (The King): *Research.*

24. Amzallag, "*Musiḳat ha-ḳaseṭot—lo musiḳah Mizraḥit,*" 34–35.

25. Moshe Ben-Mosh, quoted in Liat Amran, *Aliyato u-nefilato shel elil ha-zemer ha-mizraḥi Zohar Argov* (The Rise and Fall of the Mizraḥi song idol Zohar Argov), unpublished research paper, archived in the Edwin Serrousi collection, Bar Ilan University (1991), 53.

26. I thank especially the Houja family for illustrating the problematic binary opposition of sacred-secular in the Mizraḥi context. See Yehouda Shenhav, "No Room for Misfits," *Haaretz,* 9 September 2007, in which he offers a critical reading of "A New Jewish Time: Jewish Culture in a Secular Age, An Encyclopedic Look" (Yirmiyahu Yovel, chief editor), noting among other things: "After all, the patterns of religiosity and secularism in Israel are not ethnically neutral, and a large Mizraḥi population does not submit to distinctions between 'secular' and 'religious.'" He points to the redefinition of the *masorti* Jewish category by Meir Buzaglo, Haviva Pedaya, and Yaacov Yadgar as a "nominal and assertive category in its own right." http://www.haaretz.com/hasen/spages/917177.html.

27. Yigal Ḥared quoted in Tobi, *"ha-Melekh"* (The King): *Research.*

28. A leaf used by Yemenites as a chewing tobacco.

29. A traditional fried Yemenite bread.

30. Yael Zerubavel, *Recovered Roots: Collective Memory and the Making of Israeli National Tradition* (Chicago: University of Chicago Press, 1997), 215.

31. The use in songs of non-Hebrew women's names was a way of exploring the moment of cultural contact. In the case of "Marlen," the lyrics were originally written in Spanish by Eddy Maroum, and they were translated into Hebrew by Uzi Ḥiṭman. The incorporation of the name Marlen into the song was Asher Reuveni's idea. Zohar Argov, "Marlen," *Kakh 'overim ḥayay* (So My Life Goes By) (1985), original tune composed by Enrico Macias, Reuveni Brothers.

32. Shlomi Namdar, interview by author, tape recording, Jerusalem, 11 October 1992.

33. Zerubavel, *Recovered Roots,* 214.

34. Yosef Trumpeldor was a Russian Jewish immigrant to Palestine who was killed in battle in 1920; legend has it that his final words were, "Never mind, it is good to die for our country."

35. Zerubavel, *Recovered Roots,* 214.

36. Asher Reuveni, quoted in Ben-David and Zunder, "Ekh 'avru ha-shanim," *Iton Tel Aviv,* 40.

37. Ohad, "Libi ba-Mizraḥ," *Haaretz* (Tel Aviv), 17.

Chapter 5

1. Rabbi Israel Abu-Ḥasira, known as Baba Sali (our praying father), was a learned Moroccan scholar of Torah and Kabbalah. He was known for his healing powers and his grave in southern Israel is a pilgrimage site for many Mizraḥim.

2. See Katharine Young's discussion of "narrative embodiments" in *Presence in the Flesh: The Body in Medicine* (Cambridge, Mass.: Harvard University Press, 1997), 32–45.

3. Daniela London, "Elinor, at yafah kemo malakh" (Elinor, You Are as Beautiful as an Angel), *Yedi'ot Aḥaronot* (Tel Aviv), 1994, 36–38.

4. Wayland Hand, ed., *American Folk Legend: A Symposium* (Berkeley: University of California Press, 1971); Yoram Bilu, "Veneration of Saints and Pilgrimage to Sacred Sites as a Universal Phenomenon," in *To the Tombs of the Righteous: Pilgrimage in Contemporary Israel* (Jerusalem: Israel Museum, 1998), 11–26.

5. Linda Degh and Andrew Vazsonyi, "Legend and Belief," *Genre* 4, no. 3 (1971): 296–97.

6. Yael Zerubavel, *Recovered Roots: Collective Memory and the Making of Israeli National Tradition* (Chicago: University of Chicago Press, 1997).

7. Pierre Maranda, ed., *Mythology* (Middlesex: Penguin Books, 1972), 214.

8. See chapter 7 for Argov's complete quote. Michael Ohad, "Libi ba-Mizraḥ" (My Heart Is in the East), *Haaretz* (Tel Aviv), 25 September 1981.

9. Shemuel Hasfari, playwright and director, *ha-Melekh* (The King) (n.p., 1992), script.

10. Jean-Pierre Vernant and Pierre Vidal-Naquet, *Myth and Tragedy in Ancient Greece,* trans. Janet Lloyd (New York: Zone Books, 1990), 242.

11. Zerubavel, *Recovered Roots.*

12. Amir Ben-David and Michal Zunder, "Ekh 'avru ha-shanim" (How the Years Have Passed), *Iton Tel Aviv,* 2 November 1990, 46.

13. *Zohar ha-melekh* (Zohar the King), film directed by Lina Chaplin, produced by Dafi Kaplansky (Jerusalem: Israel Television, 10 May 1994).

14. Hasfari, *ha-Melekh.*

15. Ibid., 1.

16. Interviews with family, friends, and co-workers carried out during the research process for the play contradict the notion of a death wish and his sense of guilt over his father's death.

17. Yehudit Yeḥezḳeli and Ḥavatselet Damari, "Zohar amar she-hu rotseh lamut" (Zohar Said He Wanted to Die), *Yedi'ot Aḥaronot* (Tel Aviv), 8 November 1987, 28–29.

18. Hasfari, *ha-Melekh,* 8.

19. Ibid., 32.

20. Ibid., 41.

21. Ibid., 27–28.

22. Hasfari, quoted in Calev Ben-David, "Return of the King," *Jerusalem Report,* 17 December 1992, 42.

23. "Small head" is army slang for someone who doesn't want to deal with big issues.

24. Zohar Argov, quoted in Kobi Bruk, "Yam shel Dema'ot" (A Sea of Tears), *Yedi'ot Aḥaronot* (Tel Aviv), *Musaf Shiv'ah Yamim,* 21 March 1986, 12.

25. This is a slang phrase literally meaning "just a person," but implying worthlessness.

26. Argov, quoted in Bruk, "Yam shel Dema'ot," 12.

27. Hasfari, *ha-Melekh,* 36–37.

28. Adrian Poole, *Tragedy: Shakespeare and the Greek Example* (Oxford: Basil Blackwell, 1987), 2.

29. Dorthea Krook, *Elements of Tragedy* (New Haven, Conn.: Yale University Press, 1969), 16–17.

30. Malka Orkabi, quoted in Tobi, "*ha-Melekh*" (The King): *Research.*

31. Hasfari, *ha-Melekh,* 10.

32. Ibid., 24.

33. Aristotle, *On the Art of Poetry,* trans. T. S. Dorsch (London: Classical Literary Criticism, 1967), 12.

34. Avihu Medina, quoted in Tobi, "*ha-Melekh* (The King)*: Research.*

35. Clifford Leech, *Tragedy* (Norfolk: Methuen, 1969), 46.

36. Avihu Medina, quoted in Amran, *Aliyato u-nefilato shel elil ha-zemer ha-Mizraḥi Zohar Argov,* 21.

37. Teḥiyah Adar, "Zohar Argov ḥai ṿe-shar" (Zohar Argov Is Alive and Singing), *Yedi'ot Aḥaronot* (Tel Aviv), 2 December 1987, 11. "Glamour" is a play on words since the name Zohar means "glamour."

38. Not all such changes in status are positive. According to Schuman, Schwartz, and D'Arcy, "There are certainly other examples of radical change in the reputations of celebrated individuals and events. Charles Lindbergh was treated to hero worship after his solo flight to Paris in 1927, but by the beginning of the 1940s his celebrity status had almost completely vanished. . . . Warren G. Harding was highly regarded while he was president, but after his death his prestige fell as his supporters disappeared and others condemned him for scandals that occurred under his watch. . . . Recent Israeli scholarship has transformed the mass suicide at Masada, once regarded by Israelis as an event worthy of solemn commemoration, into an object of indifference at best." Howard Schuman, Barry Schwartz, and Hannah D'Arcy, "Elite Revisionists and Popular Beliefs: Christopher Columbus, Hero or Villain?" *Public Opinion Quarterly* 69, no. 1 (2005): 2–29.

39. Gila Golan, quoted in Tobi, *"ha-Melekh"* (The King)*: Research.*

40. Yossi Blich, quoted in ibid.

41. Yehezkel Adiram, "Hit'abed ma'arits shel Zohar Argov" (A Zohar Argov Fan Commits Suicide), *Yedi'ot Aḥaronot* (Tel Aviv), 2 December 1987, 16.

42. Shimon Alkabetz, "ha-Ḳaseṭot nigmeru tokh sha'ot" (The Cassettes Were Finished within Hours), *Ḥadashot* (Tel Aviv), 8 November 1987, 7.

43. Avihu Medina, quoted in Amran, *Aliyato u-nefilato shel elil ha-zemer ha-mizraḥi Zohar Argov,* 13.

44. Malka Orkabi, quoted in Tobi, *"ha-Melekh"* (The King): *Research.*

45. *Mezuzah,* literally "doorpost" in Hebrew, here refers to a scroll of a portion of the Torah that is placed on the doorposts of Jewish homes. Some Jews practice a custom of touching the *mezuzah* and then kissing their fingers as a sign of devotion to the Torah when passing through doorways.

46. Tova [no last name given], quoted in Tobi, *"ha-Melekh"* (The King)*: Research. Kapparah* is Hebrew for "[vicarious] atonement." There are numerous interpretations that derive from biblical sources and relate to sacrificial practices. In contemporary Israel some Mizraḥim still practice *kapparah,* especially around Yom Kippur, the Day of Atonement. In this case the egg serves as a combination of vicarious atonement and protection.

47. David Hume, "On Tragedy," in *Essays: Moral, Political, and Literary*, ed. T. H. Green and T. H. Grose (1757; London, 1875), 18.

48. Amy Shuman, *Other People's Stories: Entitlement Claims and the Critique of Empathy* (Urbana: University of Illinois Press, 2005).

49. Dani Sanderson is an Ashkenazi Israeli popular musician who co-founded the band Kaveret. He wrote and performed a popular satire on Mizraḥi music, *Mah ha-dawin shelakh* (What's Your Shtick), that some Mizraḥi musicians considered a co-optation.

50. Argov, quoted in Bruk, "Yam shel dema'ot," *Yedi'ot Aḥaronot* (Tel Aviv), 12.

51. Hasfari, quoted in Ben-David, "Return of the King," 43.

Chapter 6

1. The singer's name is romanized variously as Umm Kulthum, Um Kulthum, Om Kalsoum, Umm Kulthoum, Om Kalthoum, Umm Kalsum, and Oum Kalthum.

2. Meretz is a left-leaning Israeli political party. Likud is the largest of the right-leaning Israeli political parties.

3. Yehudit Ravitz, interview by author, tape recording, Tel Aviv, 20 December 1986.

4. Zehava Ben, *Ṭipat mazal* (A Drop of Luck) (1992), Eli Banai Productions, Ultratone Studios.

5. Lea Inbal, "Zehava," *Yedi'ot Aḥaronot* (Tel Aviv), *Musaf Shiv'ah Yamim* (Seven-Day Supplementary), 1 April 1991, 32–33.

6. Yonatan Gefen, "ha-'Etsev hu Ashkenazi" (Sadness Is Ashkenazi), *Ma'ariv* (Tel Aviv), 15 May 1992, 3.

7. Disputed territory refers to both a geographically situated regional struggle in which Israel occupies Palestinian land as well as a metaphorical way of describing dissonant spaces such as exist between Jewish Israeli ethnic groups.

8. See discussion of Mediterranean categories in Edwin Seroussi, "Yam Tikhoniyut: Transformations of the Mediterranean in Israeli Music," in *Mediterranean Mosaic: Popular Music and Global Sounds*, ed. Goffredo Plastino (New York: Routledge, 2003).

9. Rino Tsror, "The Neighborhood Abandoned Hebrew," *Ma'ariv* (Tel Aviv), June 1991.

10. The original Turkish tune is called "Dil Yarisi," composed by Orshan Gencebay.

11. Ben, *Ṭipat mazal.*

12. *Ṭipat mazal* (film), directed by Ze'ev Revach (Tel Aviv: Noah Films, 1992).

13. Yehuda Poliker, *These Eyes of Mine* (1985), audiocassette, NMC Music 26445–2.

14. Etti Anrky and David D'or, *Live Show* (1998), Hed Arzi 64026; Alabina, "Eshebo (Chebba)," composed by Safy Boutella, *Alabina* (1997), Astor Place.

15. The *santur* is the "Dulcimer of the Middle East, south-eastern Europe and South and East Asia. It is used in Iran, Iraq, India, Kashmir, Turkey, Greece, Armenia, China and Tibet. The prototype instrument may be seen in a harp carried horizontally and struck with two sticks." Jean During, Scheherazade Qassim Hassan, and Alastair Dick, "Santur [sadouri, santūr, sant'ur, santuri, sintir, tsintsila]," in Macy, *Grove Music Online.*

16. See Mary Douglas's *Purity and Danger: An Analysis of Concepts of Pollution and Taboo* (London: Routledge and Kegan Paul, 1966), in which she argues that cultural anxiety is reduced by keeping categories intact. Interestingly, in one part of her work ("The violations of Leviticus"), she discusses the Jewish system of *kashrut*, or dietary laws.

17. Zehava Ben, *Zehava Ben sharah 'Aravit* (Zehava Ben Sings Arabic) (1995), Eli Banai Productions.

18. *Zehava Ben: Solitary Star,* written and directed by Erez Laufer, produced by Dalia Migdal (Tel Aviv: Idan Productions, 1997). This eighty-four-minute documentary is in Hebrew, with English subtitles.

19. Zehava Ben, *Zehava Ben sharah 'Aravit: Enta Omri* (Zehava Ben Sings Arabic: You Are My Life) (1995), Helicon.

20. Kirin Narayan, "Songs Lodged in Some Hearts: Displacements of Women's Knowledge in Kangra," in *Displacement, Diaspora and Geographies of Identity,* ed. Smadar Lavie and Ted Swedenburg (Durham, N.C.: Duke University Press, 1996), 187. "As ethnomusicologists have observed, gender and other planes of social differentiation are mapped onto musical spheres," Narayan writes, citing Ellen Koskoff, "An Introduction to Women, Music, and Culture," in *Women and Music in Cross-Cultural Perspective* (Urbana: University of Illinois Press, 1989), 1–24. Deborah A. Kapchan, *Gender on the Market: Moroccan Women and the Revoicing of Tradition* (Philadelphia: University of Pennsylvania Press, 1996).

21. Gila Svirsky, "The Peace Process Needs Women," *Israel Insider,* 30 October 2002, http://web.israelinsider.com/Views/1578.htm.

22. Hannah Naveh, "Nine Eleven: An Ethics of Proximity," *Signs: Journal of Women in Culture and Society* 28 (2002): 452.

23. Zehava Ben, interview by author and Esther Namdar, telephone, 1 September 2002.

24. Ibid.

25. *Jerusalem Post,* "Zehava Ben to Appear on al-Jazeera," 12 November 2003, http://209.157.64.200/focus/f-news/1020516/posts. It is important to note here that goods (in this case, the virtual Zehava in the form of television broadcast to the Arab world) move when people cannot. See Robert Barsky's work on border controls of immigrants and goods, *Arguing and Justifying: Assessing the Convention Refugees' Choice of Moment, Motive and Host Country* (Aldershot: Ashgate, 2000).

26. Mikhail Bakhtin, *Rabelais and His World,* trans. Helene Iswolsky (Cambridge, Mass.: MIT Press, 1968).

27. Amy Horowitz, "Dueling Nativities: Zehava Ben Sings Umm Kulthum," in *Palestine, Israel, and the Politics of Popular Culture,* ed. Rebecca L. Stein and Ted Swedenburg (Durham, N.C.: Duke University Press, 2005).

28. Amy Horowitz, "*Musika Yam Tikhonit Yisraelit* (Israeli Mediterranean Music): Cultural Boundaries and Disputed Territories," Ph.D. diss., University of Pennsylvania, 1994.

29. Judith Cohen, "Romancing the Romance: Perceptions (and Boundaries) of the Judeo-Spanish Ballad," in *Ballads and Boundaries: Narrative Singing in an Intercultural Context,* ed. James Porter (Los Angeles: UCLA Press, 1995), 209–17. In Cohen's article she discusses the romanticization of the Spanish-Jewish music genre "Romances." Gene Knudsen Hoffman, *Compassionate Listening and Other Writings by Gene Knudsen Hoffman* (Torrence, Calif.: Friends Bulletin, 1999).

30. Horowitz, "Dueling Nativities."

31. Peter Seitel, *The Powers of Genre: Interpreting Haya Oral Literature* (New York: Oxford University Press, 1999).

32. Amy Shuman, *Other People's Stories: Entitlement Claims and the Critique of Empathy* (Urbana: University of Illinois Press, 2005). Amy Shuman, *Storytelling Rights: The Use of Oral and Written Texts by Urban Adolescents* (Cambridge: Cambridge University Press, 1986).

33. For an example of a critique Ben received, see Khalid Amayreh, "PA Spreads Moral Decadence in the Territories," *Palestine Times* 87, no. 10 (1998), 4–6.

34. Suheir Hammad, "Composites," *Signs: Journal of Women in Culture and Society* 28, no. 1 (2002), 471.

Chapter 7

1. Amnon Shiloah, "Eastern Sources in Israeli Music," *Ariel* 88 (1992): 4.

2. It is possible that Imber drew *U-lefa'ate* (turn) *mizraḥ* (east) *ḳadimah* (forward) from the Hebrew Bible (Exodus 27:13 and 38:13 and Numbers 2:3), in which the pairing *ḳedmah Mizraḥah* and the phrase *le-f'at ḳedmah Mizraḥ* (Hebrew words built from the same roots as the words in Imber's ballad) appear in relation to the placement (front-east) of the encampment of the tribe of Judah and the direction (front-east) for the building of the Tabernacle (the sanctuary the Israelites built during their first year in the Sinai wilderness following the Exodus and carried with them into Canaan).

3. Shiloah, "Eastern Sources in Israeli Music," 4.

4. Ibid. Imber's source for the melody of "ha-Tiḳv.ah" is a controversial topic in itself. Claims include a Moldovian or Romanian folksong and a theme from a tone poem by Czech composer Bedrich Smetana, likely derived from folk melodies familiar to the artist. Other possibilities include a Sephardi liturgical tune. It is most likely that the melody of "ha-Tiḳv.ah" was a European import like much of the *ha-Shir ha-Erets Yisre'eli* repertoire composed at around the same time. See the YIVO Institute for Jewish Research web site for a discussion of this debate, http://epyc.yivo.org/content/13_6.php.

5. Michael Ohad, "Libi ba-Mizraḥ" (My Heart Is in the East), *Haaretz* (Tel Aviv), 25 September 1981.

6. Barbara Kirshenblatt-Gimblett, "Spaces of Dispersal," *Cultural Anthropology* 9, no. 3 (1994): 340. In her terms, my study, like those of "Gilroy, Mercer, and the Boyarins[,] transvalue[s] diaspora from a negative state of displacement to a positive condition of multiple location, temporality, and identification—while not forgetting the often violent conditions that produced it" (339–40). She problematizes anthropological concepts that set up "a situation where some peoples create a 'common' or 'distinctive' or 'homogeneous' culture, while others borrow from them" (340). She uses the term "ghetto" to mean difference, and it is assumed that "if detached conceptually from race, such differences would disappear when the social isolation that produced them was removed" (341).

7. Adelaide Reyes Schramm, "Ethnic Music, the Urban Area and Ethnomusicology," *Sociologus* 29, no. 1 (1979): 7.

8. Frederik Barth, "Introduction," *Ethnic Groups and Boundaries: The Social Organization of Cultural Difference,* ed. Frederik Barth (Boston: Little, Brown, 1969), 10. See also Donald Horowitz, "Ethnic Identity," *Ethnicity, Theory, and Experience,* ed. Nathan Glazer, Daniel P. Moynihan, and Corinne Sposs Schelling (Cambridge, Mass.: Harvard University Press, 1975), 111–40.

9. Zali Gurevitch and Gidon Aran, "*Al ha-makom: Antropologyah Yisre'elit*" (On the Locality: Israeli Anthropology), *Alpayim* 4 (1991): 10–12.

10. Gershon Shaked, *The Shadows Within: Essays on Modern Jewish Writers* (Philadelphia: Jewish Publication Society, 1987), 103; Itamar Even-Zohar, "The Emergence of a Native Hebrew Culture in Palestine: 1882–1948," *Studies in Zionism* 4 (1981): 171–73.

11. Peter Manuel, *Popular Musics of the Non-Western World: An Introductory Survey* (Oxford: Oxford University Press, 1988), 21–22.

12. Richard Middleton, quoted in ibid., 21–22.

13. Haim Moshe and Meir and Asher Reuveni, interview by author, Tel Aviv, 5 August 1984.

14. Eviatar Zerubavel, *The Fine Line: Making Distinctions in Everyday Life* (Chicago: University of Chicago Press, 1993), 62.

15. Ibid., 70.

16. Nancy Fraser, "Rethinking the Public Sphere: A Contribution to the Critique of Actually Existing Democracy," in *Justice Interruptus: Critical Reflections on the "Postsocialist" Condition* (New York: Routledge, 1997), 69–98.

17. Zerubavel, *The Fine Line,* 67.

18. Ibid., 70.

19. Ibid.

20. Rebecca Solnit, *Hope in the Dark* (Edinburgh: Canongate Books, 2004), 31. Charter 77 was a social movement in Czechoslovakia that took its name from a document drafted in 1977 that criticized the Czech government for violating the human rights provisions of laws it had passed and agreements it had signed. Vaclav Havel was one of the leaders of the movement. See also http://www.furious.com/perfect/pulnoc.html for a history of The Plastic People of the Universe.

21. Bernice Johnson Reagon, "'Nobody Knows the Trouble I See,' or 'By and By I'm Gonna Lay Down My Heavy Load,'" *Journal of American History* 78, no. 1 (1991): 17–19.

22. Ivan Karp and Steven Lavine, eds., *Exhibiting Cultures: Poetics and Politics of Museum Display* (Washington, D.C.: Smithsonian Institution Press, 1991); Joan Alway, *Critical Theory and Political Possibilities* (Westport, Conn.: Greenwood Press, 1995).

23. See Suzanna Walters, *All the Rage: The Story of Gay Visibility in America* (Chicago: University of Chicago Press, 2001); John Hutnyk, *Critique of Exotica: Music, Politics and the Culture Industry* (London: Pluto Press, 2000), 119. Hutnyk asks, "Does sanctioned visibility in the centre occlude secret agendas and invisibility for the rest? Can high profile be traded for redress?"

24. The *Saharana* also originated as a Kurdish Passover festival.

25. For further discussion see Harvey Goldberg, "The *Mimouna* and the Minority Status of the Moroccan Jews," *Ethnology* 17, no. 1 (1978): 75–87; Shlomo Deshen and Moshe Shokeid, *The Predicament of Homecoming: Cultural and Social Life of North African Immigrants in Israel* (Ithaca: Cornell University Press, 1974).

26. Guy Haskell, "The Development of Israeli Anthropological Approaches to Immigration and Ethnicity: 1948–1980," *Jewish Folklore and Ethnology Review* 11, nos. 1–2 (1989): 23–24.

27. Cited in Thomas Friedman, "Using Songs, Israelis Touch Arab Feelings," *New York Times,* 3 May 1987, 1:1.

28. Samir Shukry, *Rona Shely* (My Rona) (n.d.), Kolifone: Sigma (Azoulay Brothers); Shefi Gabay, "Kahir mishtaga'at al Samir Shukry" (Cairo Goes Mad about Samir Shukry), *Ma'ariv* (Tel Aviv), 26 May 1991, *Ha-Yom,* 8. See http://uri.webpoint.co.il/shukri2/biography.html.

29. Moshe and Reuveni, interview.

30. Friedman, "Using Songs, Israelis Touch Arab Feelings," *New York Times,* 3 May 1987, 1:1.

31. Alan Sipress, "The Pop Culture of Israel Embraces Its Arabic Heritage," *Philadelphia Inquirer,* 28 June 1994, E1.

32. *Nigen* is Yiddish for a melody or a song.

33. Klezmorim are musicians who play music in the Klezmer style. Klezmer first referred to the instruments used in the music, then came to refer to the musicians, and later referred to the style of music. Klezmer music is also sometimes known as Yiddish music as it comes out of an Ashkenazi tradition from Eastern Europe.

34. Yael Zerubavel, *Recovered Roots: Collective Memory and the Making of Israeli National Tradition* (Chicago: University of Chicago Press, 1997).

35. Gilles Deleuze and Felix Guattari, *A Thousand Plateaus: Capitalism and Schizophrenia* (Minneapolis: University of Minnesota Press, 1987). The kind of "complex appropriations" discussed here fit within Deleuze and Guattari's concept of the rhizome that I describe in chapter 1.

"Ezo medinah" (What a Country)

Words and music by Eli Luzon and Yoni Ro'eh

Ezo medinah (3x), meyuḥedet be-minah
Memshalah loḥetset, medinah nilḥetset
Ezo medinah, ezo medinah

Anashim bokhim, meḥirim 'olim
Le-shalem misim ve-gam ḳupat ḥolim.
En kevar 'avodah, ha-ḳupah reḳah
En mi-mah liḥyot, sagru et ha-lishkah.
Ba-knesset hem yoshvim, 'aleynu hem 'ovdim,
Lakḥu ha-ḥeskhonot, halkhu ha-pitsuyim
Lanu kevar nim'as, dafḳu lanu 'od ḳnas
Gam 'al he-ḥalav hosifu et ha-mas.

Ezo medinah (3x), meyuḥedet be-minah
Memshala doreshet, kesef mevaḳeshet
Ezo medinah, ezo medinah.

Yesh lanu sarim, raḳ kise rotsim.
Lo 'osim davar ve-raḳ mavtiḥim
Efo ha-shivyon, efo he-ḥazon.
Efo ha-musar, ezeh bizayon.
Ma ashir lakhem, umah asaper.
Yesh devarim rabim 'alehem nevater.
Lamrot Habalagan veha-hesronot
Et medinatenu le-dore dorot

Ezo medinah (3x), meyuḥedet be-minah
Memshalah loḥetset, medinah nilḥetset
Ezo medinah, ezo medinah

English translation:
What a country (3x), one of a kind
The government squeezes us tight
The country is uptight
What a country, what a country

People, they cry, prices always rise
The health plan to pay and taxes are high
Work—there is none, the cash box money is gone
There's nothing to live from, and the employment office closed down.

They sit in the Knesset, don't mean what they say
They took all the savings, and the severance pay
We're fed up this time, they've stiffed us with one more fine,
Even a tax on the milk has been assigned

What a country! (3x), one-of-a-kind
The country makes demands, takes the money from our hands
What a country, what a country

We have ministers, they care only for their seats
They don't do a thing, just their promises repeat
Where's equality? What vision do they see?
What a shame—where's morality?

What will I sing to you, and what can I relate?
There are many things on which we won't capitulate
Despite the mess
and the disadvantages
Our country, for generations lives

What a country (3x), one of a kind
The government squeezes us tight
The country is uptight
What a country, what a country

Luzon, Eli. "Ezo medinah" (What a Country) (1987). Ben-Mosh Productions.

One of the first topical songs in the Mediterranean Israeli music genre, "Ezo medina" by Eli Luzon and Yoni Ro'eh, juxtaposes an upbeat dance melody with a text that lightly addresses social problems in Israeli society. The opening *muwwal* begins with violins, adds other instruments, then brings in the voice. The vocal and instrumental lines follow the Eastern musical approach of unison without harmony. This is especially true of the string section, which provides the response to the melodic call. In pursuit of this blending, Luzon combines the violins with the synthesized sound of a *santur,* and renowned *darabukka* player Ikky Levy's live drumming with sampled drum sounds. These juxtapositions insist on the hybridity of Mediterranean Israeli music. In the lyrics, the definite article *ha* is dropped, as in *memshalah* (government) rather than *ha-memshalah* (the government).

The song is one of a genre Tamar Katriel calls "complaint songs," part of the verbal ritual of griping in Israeli culture. In contrast to American protest music, the protester here is within the system by choice so that his protest exhibits exasperated affection rather than a call for radical change.

"Mal'u asamenu bar" (Our Silos Are Filled with Grain)

Words by Pinḥas Lender; music by David Zehavi

Mal'u asamenu bar, ve-yḳaveynu yayin
Batenu homim, homim me-tinoḳot
U-vehemtenu porah
Mah 'od tevaḳshi me-itanu mekhorah
V-en v-en 'adayin
Mah 'od tevaḳshi me-itanu mekhorah
V-en v-en 'adayin

English translation:
Our silos are full of grain, our winery flows through,
Our houses resound with the voices of the young
And our cattle are fertile
What more can you ask of us, land of our birth
That we have not fulfilled for you?

"Malu asamenu bar" was written by composer David Zehavi, born in 1910 in Palestine to Romanian parents. Zehavi grew up in Tiberias but later moved to Kibbutz Na'an, where he conducted a choir and other musical events for which he began composing. His dozens of compositions comprise a substantial part of the Zionist canon, including songs of the Palmach, and some are set to words by Israeli poets such as Leah Goldberg and Hannah Senesh. According to critic Ariel Hirschfeld, in contrast to Zehavi's original songs that describe an experience in a lyrical first-person style, "Mal'u asamenu bar" belongs to the genre of songs that describe the collective experience of pioneering. Zehavi's songs, part of the *ha-Shir-ha-Erets-Yisre'eli* genre, have also been rearranged and performed by Mizraḥi singers. Avihu Medina noted the influence of this song on some of his compositions.

"Ḥanaleh hitbalbelah" (Little Hannah Got Confused)

Words by Natan Alterman; traditional music

Me-Afulah henah yaḥad banu
Be-rakevet yom shishi
yesh li dag maluaḥ
betsalaḥat ve-tisroḳet le-roshi
ve-ʿalai simlat Shabat
ʿim arnaḳ shel ʿor
ba-yad ho ima,
kamah zeh neḥmad,
Yehudah hivtiaḥ lah she-yishmor lah emunah
kemo lifne ha-ḥatunah.
Yareaḥ devash lifne ha-ḥatunah
zefet aḥare hadevash
ha-ḥatan rotseh li-heyot le-aba
ben me-Ḥanaleh darash
Ḥanaleh amra lo ben
zeh le-gamre lo yafeh
lo oveh ve-lo ertseh
im tirtseh ben o bat
lekh ʿaseh lekha levad
ki ḥofesh peʿulah uferat

Yom Shishi Tartza"t parshat Va-yomer
berit milah heyetah ba-ir
seʿudah nitnah ke-yad ha-melekh
u-mazal tov la-gevir
Ḥanaleh hitbalbelah
mah pitʿom berit milah
ve-hi ʿodena betulah
gam ha-baʿal lo zakhar
ketsad ba lo ben zakhar
Ve-lismoaḥ me'uhar
Et ha-ben hevi'u el ha-rabi

Vayomru lo rabi kaḥ
hi omeret zeh lo sheli
Ve-hu omer zeh ken shel lakh
az ha-rabi hit'anyen
shenehem makḥhishim ba-ben
ve-zeh davar lo yitakhen
Neḥakeh 'ad she-yigdal
az oto mi-piv nish'al
Me'ayin bata menuval

Hevi'ani el bet hayayin (3x)
Ve-daglu 'alai ahavah (3x)
samekhuni ba-ashishot,
rapeduni ba-tapuḥim (3x)
ki ḥolat, ki ḥolat ahavah ani (2x)

English translation:
We went together from Afula
On the Friday train
I have a herring in a plate
My hairdo all arranged.
I'm wearing a Sabbath dress
With a leather purse in hand
Oh mama—how grand!
Yehuda promised her
That he will be loyal to her
Like before the wedding ceremony
Honeymoon before the wedding
Then, tar that follows honey.
The bridegroom wanted to be a father
And he demanded it from Ḥani
Ḥanaleh told him "nay"
It's not such a nice thing to say
In short, "no way"
I shall not obey.
If you want a little girl
Or a son
Go make one on your own!
The individual's freedom is known
Friday 1939, "Vayomer" is the weekly reading

And in town, a bris, congratulations to the fine man
And a splendid meal set forth, all are eating
Ḥanaleh's confused—why a circumcision
And yet here she is, still a virgin
But her husband cannot recall
How was born to him this son
And it's too late to regale

They brought the son to the rebbe, and said to him, "Rabbi, for you"
She says he's not mine, and he says "he is, too"
The rabbi began to question
They both deny a connection
It's outrageous beyond perception
We'll wait until he grows
Then we'll ask the scoundrel if he knows
From whence he arose
"He brought me to the banquet room
And his banner of love was over me
Sustain me with raisin cakes
Refresh me with apples
For I am faint with love
And his banner of love was over me"

According to Edwin Seroussi, this klezmer tune was recorded by Naftule Brandwein in the 1920s. Natan Alterman, one of the most renowned poets of the *ha-Shir ha-Erets Yisre'eli* period, used this theme for a Hebrew song, "He and She," composed for a Purim party in Tel Aviv in the 1930s. He later composed a parodic version that became popular among youth movements and was rearranged as an early Mediterranean Israeli favorite performed by Daḳlon, Tselile ha-Kerem, Tselile ha-'ūd, and other groups. In this topsy-turvy poem, Alterman writes about a wedding between an Ashkenazi boy and a Mizraḥi girl. The text mirrors the cultural gap between the two communities.

In a more traditional klezmer song, clarinet, contrabass, bass drums, and possibly violin would be used; in order to accommodate the clarinet, the key would probably be F major (with B flat). In the rearranged Mizraḥi version, both Tselile ha-Kerem and Daḳlon try to maintain the central Eastern European vocal style by not employing much melisma or microtonality. The bass, instead of being "square" (like a 4/4 *hora* dance), uses an augmented second in two places. Though the vocal line and the minor melody retain a klezmer feeling, the accompaniment employs a Greek rhythm and an Eastern *darabukka*. They change the traditional klezmer "pattern of eights" by conflating every two bars into one, with ornamentation filling the spaces. The band deepens the Eastern feeling of the percussion section by introducing a live *darabukka* player, who is situated close to the simple and often monotonous drum machine line (played in half time), to keep the instrumental section lively. Both the guitar and bass play in the Greek popular style. The guitarists bend notes in the style of 1960s rhythm and blues, creating a sense of microtonality. This tune has become an anthem for the Jerusalem soccer team, composed primarily of Mizraḥi athletes and fans.

"Shabeḥi Yerushalayim" (Praise, Jerusalem)

Words from Psalms 147:12–13; music by Avihu Medina

Shabeḥi Yerushalayim et adonai
Haleli elohayikh Tsiyon
Ki ḥizaḳ brikhe she'arayikh
Berakh banayikh be-ḳirbekh
Haleli, haleli elohayikh Tsiyon

English translation:
Praise, Jerusalem,
Praise your God, O Zion!
For he strengthened the bars of your gates,
And blessed your children within you

The Holy Scriptures: The New JPS Translation, According to the Traditional Hebrew Text. Philadelphia: Jewish Publication Society, 1988.

This is one of Medina's most widely sung and cherished songs, both in Israel and abroad. It appears in corners as diverse as a comprehensive web site on Mizraḥi liturgical poetry and in the repertoire of Greek singers Glykeria and Haris Alexiou, and is also frequently sung in Jerusalem Day celebrations in Israel, usually in May.

"'Et Dodim Kalah" (The Time of Love, O Bride)

Words from liturgical text by R. Ḥayyim ben Sahel, incorporating excerpts from Song of Songs; traditional Yemenite music

'Et dodim kalah
Bo'i le-gani
'Et dodim kalah
Wallak, bo'i le-gani
Parḥah ha-gefen
Henetsu rimonim

Ḥalaf ha-geshem
Ha-stav ʿavar
Wallak ḥalaf ha-geshem
Ha-stav ʿavar
Ḳumi raʿayati
Ha-ḥesheḳ gavar
Yaradnu . . .
Lirot ba-ganim
Sham be-vet dodai
ʿEnayikh yonim

Mah yafit
U-mah naʿamt
Ka-sheleg shinayikh
Wallak, ma yafit
Ve- naʿamt
Ka-sheleg shinayikh
Devash ve-ḥalav
Taḥat leshonekh

English translation:
It's the time for love, o bride
Come to my garden
It's the time for love, o bride
Wallak, come to my garden (2x)
The grapevine has blossomed
The pomegranates bud forth (2x)

The rain has passed
Fall is gone
Arise my beloved
Passion has won (2x)

We have gone down
To pasture in the gardens
There in the house of my love
Your eyes are like doves

How beautiful you are
And how pleasant

Like snow, your tooth
Wallak, how beautiful you are,
And how pleasant
Like snow is your tooth
Milk and honey under your tongue (2x)

The text "'Et Dodim Kala" is sung in some Mizraḥi communities as part of the early morning *baḳashot* services held during the Sukkot season and on other occasions. In Jewish mystical tradition, Kabbalists created passionate poetic texts to express their longing and devotion to the Sabbath. This prayer is part of that tradition. Zohar Argov renders the desire for the Sabbath as love for a woman. He employs vernacular pronunciation and syllabic emphasis (*ha-ḥesheḳ gavar*—the desire grew bigger) on certain biblical words. Traditionally, the Sabbath is intended as a day of rest and pleasure. Argov emphasizes this by inviting the woman into his garden (*bo'i el gani*), and by drawing out the *ḥ* in *ḥesheḳ* (desire), he adds a phonetic punch. This creates a very personal and direct communication, the effect of which he intensifies by interspersing liturgical words with street language and Arabic slang (*wallak*).

The song begins with a long guitar *muwwal* to which Argov responds vocally. The *muwwal* and response appear in the place of the standard verse and refrain as a verse and "interlude." Aesthetically, the voice signifies Eastern style by diverging from the melodic line that defines Western style. By contrast, the instruments, especially the guitar, imitate in the Western style, rather than improvise off it in the Eastern style. This cautious approach may be due to the limited skill of the guitarist, whose many mistakes are noticeable. The vagaries of the guitar playing contrast with the automaticity of the drum machine.

"Ha-Peraḥ be-gani" (The Flower in My Garden)

Words and music by Avihu Medina

Yom aviv bahir ve-tsaḥ
Otakh ani zokher
U-kevar me-az heṭev yad'ati she-lo avater
Ki li hayyit bevat 'eini
Be-khol yom ve-kol lel
Hayyit li ke-malakh ha-El mi-tokh ha-arafel

Ratsiti levaḳesh yadekh
Ratsiti lakh lomar
Sod ahavah shebi-levavi shemor mi-kol mishmar
Ratsiti lakh lomar ahavti, ahavti ve-nigmar
Akh lo he'azti gam keshe-hayah kevar meuḥar

At ʿolami ʿim shaḥar
At li kol ha-yom
At ʿolami ba-lailah
At he-ḥalom
At be-dami, be-ruḥi uvi-levavi
At ha-niḥoaḥ ha-matoḳ, ha-peraḥ be-gani

ʿAz halakht
Yomi ḳoder, arokh u-meshaʿmem
Lashav rotseh ani lishkoaḥ, ulehitʿalem
Ḥizri maher ki bilʿadayikh ʿolami shomem
Nadamu metare ḳoli ve-khinori domem

At ʿolami . . .

English translation:
A bright and clear spring day
I remember you just so
And already then I knew well that I wouldn't let you go
Because you were the apple of my eye
Every day and every night
You were for me God's angel, from in the mist, a light

I wanted to ask your hand
To you I wished to say
The secret love within my heart, safeguard in every way
I wanted to say to you, I loved—and then my love did abate
But no, I did not dare, even when it was late

You are my world at daybreak
You're mine the livelong day
You are my world at nighttime
You are the dream away
You're in my blood, in my spirit, and in my heart—
You are the sweetest scent, the flower in my garden

Then you left
My day is dark, long and a bore
In vain I only want to forget, and to ignore
Come back soon, because without you my world's a barren hill
My vocal chords have gone silent, and my violin is still

Although written by Avihu Medina and arranged by Nancy Brandes for Shimi Tavori, it is for Zohar Argov that "ha-Peraḥ be-gani" played the most important role. His performance of it won him first place in the Mizraḥi Music Festival of 1982. The subsequent album that included "ha-Peraḥ be-gani" may have sold as many as 250,000 copies. Argov performs the song in a mixed style that has both Eastern and Western elements. The instrumental introduction and accompaniment features a brass section but is also interspersed with interludes by a Middle Eastern string section. Lest the listener be misled by the opening trumpeting, a brief *muwwal* and occasional vocal embellishments throughout root the song well within the Mediterranean Israeli music genre.

"Marlen"

Lyrics translated into Hebrew by Uzi Ḥiṭman;
original lyrics by Eddy Maroum; music by Enrico Macias

Af pa'am be-ḥayai 'od lo hirgashti kemo 'akhshav
Ze goral shel ish me'ohav
Mar li ve-'atsuv, ratsiti she-tashuv
Ve-hi halkhah ve-lo amrah le-an
Hishḳeti ve-ṭipalti bah kol reg'a me-ḥayai
Nasati et Marlen sheli be-shete kapot yadai

Marlen sheli, Marlen
Im raḳ tagidi ken
Marlen sheli, Marlen
Et kol ḥayai eten

'Amadti leylot ve-'od yamim mul ḥalonah
Ve-sharti serenadah 'atsuvah
Shalaḥti lah peraḥim, ve-elef ḥiyuḥim
Katavti lah milim shel ahavah
Hishḳeti ve-ṭipalti bah, gadlah—kevar lo yaldah
Amrah shalom ve-histalḳah, le-an ish lo yed'a

Marlen sheli . . .

Ba-lailah ḳar ve-gam raṭuv, 'amadti mul betah
Ra'iti ish 'oleh ba-madregot
Pitom kava ha-or, ra'adeti mi-ḳor
Gam le-ish gadol mutar livkot

Amru li ḥaverim, 'azov, Marlen lo bi-shevilkha
Ve-kama she-tirdof hi tamid tivraḥ lekha

English translation:
Marlen
I feel now in my life as I've never felt to date
A man in love, this is his fate
I'm bitter and sad,
I wanted her to come back
And she took off—and did not say to where
Every moment of my life I cared, invested—understand
I bore my Marlen alone on my own two hands

Marlen, Marlen o mine
If you would just say "fine"
Marlen, Marlen o mine
Our lives I would entwine

Across from her window I stood nights and days
And to her I sang a sad serenade
I sent her flowers in piles
And a thousand smiles
For her I wrote down many words of love
I invested and I cared for her—she grew—a girl no more
She said 'good-bye'—gone where? Who knows—she walked right out that door

Marlen, Marlen o mine . . .

At night it's cold and wet; I stood across from her house
I saw a man going up the stair
Suddenly the light went out; I trembled from the cold
A grown man is allowed to shed a tear
Friends told me: 'Just forget it—she's not your cup of tea'
And as much as you chase after her, she'll bolt and then break free

The music for "Marlen" was taken from "Le violin de mon pere," a song released in 1988 by the Jewish French singer Enrico Macias, born in Algeria in 1938, and is an example of the cross-influences in Mediterranean Israeli music. The Hebrew words were written by Uzi Ḥiṭman, among whose prolific works are a number of songs written for Zohar Argov. Ḥiṭman counts Macias as one of the artists he heard in his childhood home, along with the Rolling Stones, the Beatles, and various exponents of Jewish liturgical music, among others. Macias, incidentally, was a source of inspiration for the mainstream (mixed Mizraḥi-Ashkenazi) band Tipex, which even mentions him in one of their songs.

"Baladah le-Ḥaver" (Ballad for a Friend)

Words and music by Avihu Medina

Neshamah ṭovah me'unah
Besorat nidonim 'agunah
Uve-shirat Elohim ḥanunah
veha-neshamah, el-'al ta'uf
Akh ḳolkha le-olam nofet tsuf.
Sham ba-shamayim be-ỵadai
Ben malakhim u-mul Shadai
Shuv lo tashir Elohai
Ad matai, Elohai, hayah li dai

Neshamah tovah me'unah
Ekh 'alekha ruḥi homiyah
Ve-atsuvah nafshi bokhiyah
Ben, kol shirekha nishma'im
Beli neshamah u-veli ḥayim
Ki nadam zamir, ḳol ha-meshorerim
'Atah eli shemor na 'alav
Raḥem oved bi-demi yamaỵ
Ki zeh ha-peraḥ mi-gani
Elohai hayah lo dai

English translation:
Good, tortured soul
Chained in prison row;
But in God's song for you—the blessings flow
And the soul to the heights ascend
Your voice, nectar flowing with no end
There, in heaven, it's assured
Among the angels, in the presence of the Lord

You shall not sing again, heaven hear my woes
Until when, oh God, he had enough, God only knows

Good, tortured soul
How my spirit to you does call
And in my sorrow deep, my soul does weep
Son, your songs resounding far
Without soul, no living heart
Because the nightingale is silent—The voice of the every bard
God, please protect him in all ways
Have mercy on the one who died in the prime of his days
This is the flower that in my garden grows
He had enough—God only knows.

"Ballad for a Friend," not to be confused with a song of the same name by Boaz Sharabi, was composed by Avihu Medina as a tribute to the memory of Zohar Argov. The song evokes the traditional melody of the prayer for the ascension of souls, *El Male Raḥamim.* Except for a few contained guitar riffs echoing the melody, the keyboards play bass chords in liturgical style. The arrangement is dominated by solo vocals that repeat the words "until when, my God" (*Ad matay, elohai*). The words are also the title of a song written for Argov by Uzi Ḥitman after returning from a visit to Argov's once majestic house, which he found in shambles, its contents sold for drug money. Argov is viewed by many Mizraḥi singers as a spiritual precursor and model, the inspiration for entire albums by such singers as Noam Sherif, Zehava Ben, and Eyal Golan.

"Avraham Avinu" (Abraham, Our Father)

Words and music by Avihu Medina

Avraham Avinu sham le-ma'lah
Mabit le-maṭa ve-ro'eh
Ki Ya'aḳov ḥazar ha-baitah
Ve-hu bari todah la-El
Ki Ya'aḳov ḥazar ha-baitah
Ve-hu bari todah la-El

Ha-mishpaḥah ka-et be-yaḥad
Samaḥ saba akh sho'el
'Al mah ha-riv she-yesh 'adayin
Ben Yisrael ve-Yishma'el

ʿAl mah ha-riv she-yesh ʿadayin
Ben Yisrael ve-Yishmaʿel

Lamah ha-banim zorḳim sham avanim
Ve-lo medaberim
Lamah lo bi-meḳom lilḥom vela-halom
Le-daber shalom

Avraham Avinu sham le-maʿlah
Ḳore elav et ha-avot
U-makhrizim bi-yeshivah shel maʿlah
Ki ha-matsav mevish me'od

Ben ha-shekhenim hare yaduʿa
Avraham ohev ve-rodef shalom
Akh ba-sholshelet lo raguʿa
Lo mistadrim sham ʿad ha-yom

Lama ha-banim . . .

English translation:
Our father Abraham, up there
Looks down and sees
That Jacob has come home
May he stay healthy, God please

The family is now together
Grandpa's happy but wants to know
Over what do they still argue?
Israel and Ishmael are having a row

Why do the boys throw rocks
Rather than having talks?
Why fight, strike and tease
When they could have peace?

Our Father Abraham called and all the Patriarchs came
And they declared in the Heavenly Court
That the situation brings them shame

It's well known among the neighbors
Abraham loves peace and peace pursues
But in the restless dynasty
To get along they still refuse

Why do the boys . . .

Avihu Medina released this song on his 1991 album *Ma yihyeh* (What Will Be). Like Eli Luzon and Yoni Ro'eh's "Ezo medina" (What a Country) and Avner Gadassi's "Aḥim bokhim ba-layla" (Brothers Cry in the Night), this is one of the rare songs in the genre of Mediterranean Israeli music that takes a critical view of current events. The lyrics rely on the position of Abraham the patriarch, "sa'idna Ibrahīm" (in Arabic), as "grandfather" of the fighting nations. The song does not take sides, but rather posits the shared patriarch as pursuer of peace (an association attributed in Judaism to Aaron the priest) and the "boys" as both unruly and culpable for failing to get along.

"Ṭipat mazal" (A Drop of Luck)

Hebrew words by Dani Shoshan; music and words by Orhan Gencebay

Elohim
Ten li raḳ ṭipat mazal
Ten ahavah bi-levavi
Mar gorali
Veha-'olam akhzar
Ten neḥamah be-tokhi

Eni rotsa armonot shel zahav
Dai li
Be-pinah ḥamah
Ten li baḥur
She-oti raḳ ohev
Eten lo et ha-neshamah

Elohim, Elohim
Hoi Elohai, 'ad matai
Shema ḳoli
Tefilati
'Ayafti dai
Be-ḥayai

Ḥayai ko aforim
Ve-lelotai ḳarim
Ko atsuva u-vodedah
Raḳ ḥalomot nisharim
Ten li simḥah
Ve-ten li ḳetsat or
Ko afelim hem yamai
Raḳ ten li shevil
Laḥazor
Raḳ ten ḳetsat
Or le ʿenai

English translation:
God
Give me only a drop of luck
Put love within my heart
Bitter is my fate
And the world is cruel
Place comfort within me

I do not want golden palaces
I am content with
A warm corner
Give me a lad
Who will love only me
I will give him my soul

God, God
Oh my God, till when?
Listen to my voice,
My prayer.
Enough have I tired
In my life.

My life is so gray
And cold are my nights
Ever so lonely and sad
Only dreams remain
Give me happiness
And give me some light

For dark are my days
Just give me a path
To return
And give a little
Light to my eyes

Dani Shoshan wrote lyrics to a Turkish folk tune called "Dil Yarasi," composed by Orhan Gencebay (who is considered the father of the Arabesque style). This song is *Ṭipat mazal,* also the title of a cassette and feature movie of the same name in which Zehava Ben appeared as the co-star. The film presents a fictionalized account of Ben's father's life. A musician in Morocco, he immigrated to Israel in the early 1950s. During the production of this film, Ben traveled to Morocco to research her father's roots. In the film, the Hebrew lyrics to Gencebay's song have been rewritten by Yoni Ro'eh and the song is entitled *Akh mistovov ḥagal.* Ben's rendition of this Turkish tune demonstrates her fluency in Eastern singing.

The recording suffers from the overuse of sequencing and meter changes. The arrangement is minutely quantized. The fluidity of the sequencing technology allows for a hybrid musical product that combines Eastern and Western forms. A new generation of computer music technicians developed an aesthetic based on this approach, but anyone who could learn to operate a midi, computer, and module could arrange music. The results were mixed.

"Keturna masala" (When Luck Returns)

Words and music by Ze'ev Neḥama and Tamir Ḳlisḳi

Avi lah even
Me-admot beti
Keturna masala
Ve-gam peri me-'ets ha-te'enim
Keturna masala
Avi lah ḳetoret
Mi-pirḥe ha-yasmin
Keturna masala
U-manginah me-erets reḥoḳah

Mah lo natati lah
Ve-hi shalḥah bi esh
Esh lo heveti
Mah okhal levaḳesh

Ahavah

Keturna masala
Avi la ḥol mi-meḳomot ḳedoshim
Keturna masala
Ve-gam besamim, mine besamim
Keturna masala
Avi lah nezem
Ve-shisha tsemidim
Keturna masala
U-manginah me-erets reḥoḳah

English translation:
I will bring her a stone
From the lands of my home
When luck returns
And a fruit from the fig tree
When luck returns
I'll bring her incense
Made out of jasmine flowers
When luck returns
A tune from a distant land

What did I deny her?
Yet she sent me fire
I did not bring fire
What can I ask for?
Love

When luck returns
I'll bring her sand from holy places
When luck returns
And also a variety of perfume
When luck returns
I'll bring her a nose ring
And six bracelets
When luck returns
And a tune from a distant land

While Etnix incorporates some Eastern motifs within their rock sound, their music is basically European pop/disco. The song "Keturna Masala" shifts more to the East than most of their repertoire. The main meeting point of the Eastern and Western styles occurs in the context of the refrain in the dual vocal line, which is presented as a call and response between Nehḥama and Ben. Neḥama sings the verses in a standard rock vocal style, though he inserts some slow and simple trills that are reminiscent of his Bulgarian heritage. Ben sings the refrain in an Arabic vocal style, which demonstrates her mastery of Eastern forms, including proper use of microtones. Their vocals create a stylistic contrast. The feeling is that she explodes the Western boundary and he brings the song back. However, her vocal lines are all the same. Rhythmically, Ben's vocal line starts early (syncopation) on the word *ahava* (love).

"Inta 'umrī" (You Are My Life)

Words by Aḥmad Shafiq Kāmil; music by Muḥammad 'Abd al-Wahāb

Raja'ūnī 'aynayik la-ayāmī illī rāḥu
'Allamūnī 'andum 'ala al-māḍī wa-jarāḥuh
Illī shuftuh qabli ma tashūfak 'anayh
'Umrī ḍāyi' yaḥ'sibūh izāy 'allaya?

Inta 'umrī illi ibtada binūraka ṣabāḥuh

Qadh ayh min 'umri qablak rāḥ wa-'adda
Ya ḥabībī qadh ayh min 'umri rāḥ
Wa-lā shāf al-qalb qablak farḥah wāḥdah
Wa-la dāq fī al-dunya ghayir ṭa'm al-jiraḥ
Ibtadit bil-waqti bas aḥibb 'umri
Ibtadit bil-waqti akhāf la al-'umri yajri
Kulli farḥah ishtāqahā min qablak khiyāli
Al-taqāhā fi nūr 'aynak qalbi wa-fikri
Ya ḥayāt qalbī, ya āghla min ḥayāti
Lih mā qābilni hawāk, ya ḥabībī badrī
Illi shuftuh qabli ma tashufak 'anayh
'Umrī ḍā yi' yaḥ'sibūh izāy`'allaya?

Inta 'umrī illi ibtada binūraka ṣabāḥuh

Al-Layāli al-ḥilwah wa-al-shawq wa-al-maḥabbah
Min zamān wa-al-qalbi shāyilhūm 'ashanak
Dūq ma'āyā al-ḥūbb, dūq ḥabbah bi-ḥabbah min
Ḥannan al-qalbī illi ṭal shawqahu li-ḥanānak

Hāt 'anayk tisraḥ fi dunyathum 'anayyah
Hāt īdayk tarayyāḥ lil-mus'tahm īdayah
Ya ḥabibi, ta'āli wa-kafāyah illi fātna
Huwwa ili fātna ya ḥabībī al-ruḥ shuwayh
Illī shuftuh qabli ma tashūfak 'anayh
'Umrī ḍāyi' yaḥ'sibūh izāy 'allaya?

Inta 'umrī illi ibtada binūraka ṣabāḥuh

Ya āghli min ayyāmī
Ya āḥla min aḥlāmī
Khudnī li-ḥananak khudnī
Min al-wūjūd wa-ba'idnī
Ba'īd, ba'īd, ānā wa-inta
Ba'īd, ba'īd, waḥdīna
'A al-hūbb tis'ḥa ayyāmna
'A al-shawq tinnām layyālīna
Ṣaliḥtu bīk ayyāmī
Samiḥtu bīk al-zaman
Nasitni bīk alāmī
Wanasīt ma'āk al-shajan

Raja'ūnī 'aynayik la-ayyāmī illī rāḥu
'Allamūnī 'andum 'ala al-māḍi wa-jarāḥuh
Illī shuftuh qabli ma tashūfak 'anayh
'Umrī ḍāyi' yaḥ'sibūh izāy 'allaya?
Inta 'umrī illi ibtada binūraka ṣabāḥuh

In Egyptian dialect, the Jīm is pronounced as a hard "g," i.e., Gamal Nasser, not Jamal. The LOC transliteration system assumes Standard Modern Arabic (*fusḥa*) and transliterates it as a soft "g," i.e., Raja'ūnī, not Raga'ūnī, which would be Umm Kulthum's original pronunciation.

English translation:
Your eyes took me back to days that are gone
They taught me to regret the past and its wounds
Whatever I saw before my eyes beheld you was a wasted life
How could they consider that part of my life?
With your light, the dawn of my life started
How much of my life before you was lost?

It's a wasted past, my love
My heart never saw happiness before you
My heart never saw anything in life other than the taste of pain and suffering
Only now did I start to love my life
And began to worry that my life would run away from me
Every happiness that I longed for before you,
My dreams found it in the light of your eyes
Oh my heart's life, you are more precious than my life
Why did I not meet your love long ago
Whatever I saw before my eyes beheld you, was a wasted life
How could they consider that part of my life?
You are my life, whose dawn begins with your light
The beautiful nights, the yearning, the great love
For so long, my heart has been holding them for you
Taste the love with me, morsel by morsel
From the kindness of my heart, that is longing for the kindness of yours
Bring your eyes close, so that my eyes can get lost in the life of your eyes.
Bring your hands so that mine will rest on them
My love, come, and enough
What we missed is not trivial, o love of my soul
Whatever I saw before my eyes beheld you, was a wasted life
How could they consider that part of my life?
You are my life, whose dawn begins with your light
You are more precious than my days
You are more beautiful than my dreams
Take me to your sweetness
Take me away from the universe
Far, far away, you and me
Far, far away, alone
With love, our days will awaken
We spend the nights longing for each other
I reconciled with days for you
I forgave time because of you
Through you I forgot my pains
With you I forgot my misery
Your eyes took me back to days that are gone
They taught me to regret the past and its wounds
Whatever I saw before my eyes beheld you, was a wasted life

This classic of Umm Kulthum was released in a 1995 recording by Zehava Ben. She comes to Umm Kulthum's repertoire from her background as a Jew from an Arab country, daughter of immigrant parents from a struggling family. For Ben, Umm Kulthum was intertwined with reclaiming her Jewish-Arab identity. Her music has been well received in the Arab world. Al-Jazeera even invited her in 2003 to take part in a centennial celebration of Umm Kulthum's birth. Ben performs shortened versions, in contrast to Umm Kulthum's performances, which were sometimes several hours long, in which she would enter a trance-like state, repeat lyrics, and alter elements of the song, drawing the audience with her into a subtly modulated emotional and sensual experience.

Works Cited

Periodicals

Al-Ahram (Cairo)
Haaretz (Tel Aviv)
Ḥadashot (Tel Aviv)
Iton Tel Aviv
Jerusalem Post
Kol ha-ʿIr (Jerusalem)
Maʿariv (Tel Aviv)
New York Times
Philadelphia Inquirer
Yediʿot Aḥaronot (Tel Aviv)
Yediʿot America (New York)

Books and Essays

Abu-Lughod, Lila. "Bedouins, Cassettes and Technologies of Public Culture." *Middle East Report,* no. 159 (1989): 7–47.

Adler, I., N. Lewin-Epstein, and Y. Shavitm. "Ethnic Stratification and Place of Residence in Israel: A Truism Revisited." *Research in Social Stratification and Mobility* 23 (2004): 155–90.

Ahiassaf, Oded, Ra'anan Ahiassaf, and Radad Goni, eds. *Leḳsiḳon ha-sleng ha-ʿIvri ṿeha-tsevaʾi* (The Lexicon of Hebrew and Army Slang). Tel Aviv: Prolog Printers, 1993.

Alcalay, Ammiel. *After Jews and Arabs: Remaking Levantine Culture.* Minneapolis: University of Minnesota Press, 1993.

———. "Israel and the Levant: 'Wounded Kinship's Last Resort.'" *Middle East Report* (July/August 1989): 18–25.

———, ed. *Keys to the Garden: New Israeli Writing.* San Francisco: City Lights, 1996.

Almog, Oz. *The Sabra: The Creation of the New Jew.* Berkeley: University of California Press, 2000.

Alway, Joan. *Critical Theory and Political Possibilities.* Westport, Conn.: Greenwood Press, 1995.

Amran, Liat. *Aliyato u-nefilato shel elil ha-zemer ha-Mizraḥi Zohar Argov* (The Rise and Fall of the Mizraḥi Song Idol Zohar Argov). Unpublished research paper, archive in the Edwin Serrousi collection at Bar Ilan University, 1991.

Amry, Suad. *Sharon and My Mother-in-Law: Ramallah Diaries.* New York: Random House, 2003.

Amzallag, Avraham Eilam. "*Musiḳat ha-ḳaseṭot-lo musiḳah Mizraḥit*" (Cassette Music—Not Eastern Music). *Musika* (Music) 9 (1987): 34–35.

Aristotle. *On the Art of Poetry.* Trans. T. S. Dorsch. London: Classical Literary Criticism, 1967.

Ayalon, H., and A. Gamoran. "Stratification in Academic Secondary Programs and Educational Inequality in Israel and the United States." *Comparative Education Review* 44 (2000): 54–80.

Bailey, John. "Cross-Cultural Perspectives in Popular Music: The Case of Afghanistan." *Popular Music* 1 (1981): 105–122.

Baker, Houston A., Jr. *Black Studies, Rap, and the Academy.* Chicago: University of Chicago Press, 1993.

Bakhtin, Mikhail. *The Dialogic Imagination: Four Essays by M. M. Bakhtin.* Ed. Michael E. Holquist. Trans. Caryl Emerson and Michael E. Holquist. Austin: University of Texas Press, 1981.

———. *Rabelais and His World.* Trans. Helene Iswolsky. Cambridge, Mass.: MIT Press, 1968.

Baron, Robert, and Ana C. Cara. "Introduction: Creolization and Folklore—Cultural Creativity in Process." *Journal of American Folklore* 116, no. 459 (2003): 4–8.

Barsky, Robert F. *Arguing and Justifying: Assessing the Convention Refugees' Choice of Moment, Motive and Host Country.* Aldershot: Ashgate, 2000.

Barth, Frederik. "Introduction." In *Ethnic Groups and Boundaries: The Social Organization of Cultural Difference,* ed. Frederik Barth. Boston: Little, Brown, 1969.

Bein, Alex. *Theodore Herzl: A Biography.* 1941. Reprint, Philadelphia: Jewish Publication Society, 1962.

Ben-Amos, Dan. "Analytical Categories and Ethnic Genres." In *Folklore Genres,* ed. Dan Ben-Amos. Austin: University of Texas Press, 1976.

Ben-David, Calev. "Return of the King." *Jerusalem Report,* 17 December 1992.

Ben-Gurion, David. "The Call of the Spirit of Israel." In *Rebirth and Destiny of Israel,* ed. David Ben-Gurion. New York: Philosophical Library, 1954.

Bilu, Yoram. "Veneration of Saints and Pilgrimage to Sacred Sites as a Universal Phenomenon." In *To the Tombs of the Righteous: Pilgrimage in Contemporary Israel,* 11–26. Jerusalem: Israel Museum, 1998.

Bourdieu, Pierre. "The Field of Cultural Production, or: The Economic World Reversed." *Poetics* 12 (1983): 311–56.

Buchanan, Mark. *Nexus: Small Worlds and the Groundbreaking Theory of Networks.* New York: W. W. Norton, 2003.

Caspi, Dan. *Media Decentralization: The Case of Israel's Local Newspapers.* New Brunswick, N.J.: Transaction Books, 1986.

Caspi, Dan, and Yehiel Limor. *The In/Outsiders: The Mass Media in Israel.* Cresskill, N.J.: Hampton Press, 1999.

Castelo-Branco, Salwa El-Shawan. "Some Aspects of the Cassette Industry in Egypt." *World of Music* 29 (1987): 39–40.

Chetrit, Sami Shalom. "'Either the Cake Will Be Shared or There Will Be No Cake.' 30 Years to the Black Panthers in Israel." *Kedma–Middle Eastern Gate to Israel,* n.d., http://www.kedma.co.il/Panterim/PanterimTheMovie/EnglishArticles.htm.

———. "Mizraḥi Politics in Israel: Between Integration and Alternative." *Journal of Palestine Studies* 29, no. 4 (2000): 51–65.

Chow, Rey. *Ethnics after Idealism.* Bloomington: Indiana University Press, 1998.

Cieri, Marie. "Irresolvable Geographies." Ph.D. diss., Rutgers University, 2004.

Clifford, James. "Introduction: Partial Truths." In *Writing Culture: The Poetics and Politics of Ethnography,* ed. James Clifford and George E. Marcus. Berkeley: University of California Press, 1986.

Cohen, Erik. "The Black Panthers and Israeli Society." *Jewish Journal of Sociology* 14 (1972): 93–109.

Cohen, Erik, and Amnon Shiloah. "Major Trends of Change in Jewish Oriental Ethnic Music in Israel." *Popular Music* 5 (1985): 199–223.

Cohen, Judith. "Romancing the Romance: Perceptions (and Boundaries) of the Judeo-Spanish Ballad." In *Ballads and Boundaries: Narrative Singing in an Intercultural Context,* ed. James Porter. Los Angeles: UCLA Press, 1995.

Dahan-Kalev, Henrietta. "Breaking Their Silence: Mizrahi Women and the Israeli Feminist Movement." In *Studies in Contemporary Jewry: Sephardic Jewry and Mizrahi Jews,* ed. Peter Meding, 193–209. Oxford: Oxford University Press, 2007.

———. "Tensions in Israeli Feminism: The Mizraḥi Ashkenazi Rift." *Women's Studies International Forum* 24 (2001): 1–16.

Degh, Linda, and Andrew Vazsonyi. "Legend and Belief." *Genre* 4, no. 3 (1971): 281–304.

Deleuze, Gilles, and Felix Guattari. *A Thousand Plateaus: Capitalism and Schizophrenia.* Minneapolis: University of Minnesota Press, 1987.

Deshen, Shlomo, and Moshe Shokeid. *The Predicament of Homecoming: Cultural and Social Life of North African Immigrants in Israel.* Ithaca: Cornell University Press, 1974.

Douglas, Mary. *Purity and Danger: An Analysis of Concepts of Pollution and Taboo.* London: Routledge and Kegan Paul, 1966.

Druyan, Nitza. *Without a Magic Carpet: Yemenite Settlement in Eretz Israel (1881–1914)* [in Hebrew]. Jerusalem: Ben Zvi Institute, 1981.

Even-Zohar, Itamar. "The Emergence of a Native Hebrew Culture in Palestine: 1882–1948." *Studies in Zionism* 4 (1981): 167–84.

———. "The Emergence of a Native Hebrew Culture in Palestine: 1882–1948." *Poetics Today* 11, no. 1 (1990): 175–91.

Fabbri, Franco. "Nowhereland: The Construction of a 'Mediterranean' Identity in Italian Popular Music." *Journal of Musical Anthropology of the Mediterranean* 6 (2001), http://research.umbc.edu/eol/ma/index/number6/fabbri/fab_0.htm.

Fahim, Hussein M., ed. *Indigenous Anthropology in Non-Western Countries: Proceedings of a Burg Wartenstein Symposium.* Durham, N.C.: Carolina Academic Press, 1982.

Fraser, Nancy. "Rethinking the Public Sphere: A Contribution to the Critique of Actually Existing Democracy." In *Justice Interruptus: Critical Reflections on the "Postsocialist" Condition.* New York: Routledge, 1997.

Gershon-Kiwi, Edith. "Musicology in Israel." *Acta Musicologica,* vol. 30, Fasc. 1/2 (1958): 17–26.

Goldberg, Harvey. "The *Mimouna* and the Minority Status of the Moroccan Jews." *Ethnology* 17, no. 1 (1978): 75–87.

Goldscheider, Calvin. "The Demography of Asian and African Jews In Israel." In *Ethnicity, Identity and History Essays in Memory of Werner J. Cahnman,* ed. Joseph B. Maier and Chaim I. Waxman. New Brunswick, N.J.: Transaction Books, 1983.

Gordon, Deborah, ed. *Feminism and the Critique of Colonial Discourse.* Special edition of *Inscriptions* 3–4 (1988): 1–154.

Gurevitch, Zali, and Gidon Aran. "*Al ha-Makom: Antropologya Yisre'elit*" (On the Locality: Israeli Anthropology). *Alpayim* 4 (1991): 10–12.

Halevi, Ilan. *A History of the Jews.* London: A. M. Berrett, 1987.

Hall, Stuart. "Cultural Identity and Diaspora." In *Diaspora and Visual Culture: Representing Africans and Jews,* ed. Nicholas Mirzoeff. New York: Routledge, 2000.

Halper, Jeffrey. "The Absorption of Ethiopian Immigrants: A Return to the Fifties." *Israel Social Science Research* 3, nos. 1–2 (1985): 112–39.

Halper, Jeffrey, Edwin Seroussi, and Pamela Kidron. "*Musica mizrakhit:* Ethnicity and Class Culture in Israel." *Popular Music* 8, no. 2 (1989): 131–41.

Hammad, Suheir. "Composites." *Signs: Journal of Women in Culture and Society* 28, no. 1 (2002): 470–71.

Hand, Wayland, ed. *American Folk Legend: A Symposium.* Berkeley: University of California Press, 1971.

Hasan-Rokem, Galit. "Dialogue as Ethical Conduct: The Folk Festival That Was Not." In *Research Ethics in Studies of Culture and Social Life,* ed. Bente G. Alver, Tove I. Fjell, and Ørjar Øyen. Helsinki: Suomalainen Tiedeakatemia, 2007.

———. "Not the Mother of All Cities: A Feminist Perspective of Jerusalem." *Palestine-Israel Journal of Politics, Economics and Culture* 2, no. 3 (1995). http://www.pij.org/details.php?id=627.

Hasfari, Shemuel. *Ha-Melekh* (The King) (script). N.p., 1992.

Haskell, Guy. "The Development of Israeli Anthropological Approaches to Immigration and Ethnicity: 1948–1980." *Jewish Folklore and Ethnology Review* 11, nos. 1–2 (1989): 19–26.

Herzfeld, Michael. *Cultural Intimacy: Social Poetics in the Nation State.* New York: Routledge, 1997.

Hever, Hannan, Yehouda Shenhav, and Pnina Motzafi-Haller, eds. *Mizrahim in Israel: A Critical Observation into Israel's Ethnicity* (Hebrew). Jerusalem: Van Leer Institute/Hakibbutz Hameuchad, 2002.

Hoffman, Gene Knudsen. *Compassionate Listening and Other Writings by Gene Knudsen Hoffman.* Torrence, Calif.: Friends Bulletin, 1999.

Horesh, T. "Music Therapy, Regression and Symbolic Distance in Substance Abusers and Their Preferred Music." *Music Therapy Today* 8, no. 3 (2007).

Horowitz, Amy. "Dueling Nativities: Zehava Ben Sings Umm Kulthum." In *Palestine, Israel, and the Politics of Popular Culture,* ed. Rebecca L. Stein and Ted Swedenburg. Durham, N.C.: Duke University Press, 2005.

———. "*Musika Yam Tikhonit Yisraelit* (Israeli Mediterranean Music): Cultural Boundaries and Disputed Territories." Ph.D. diss., University of Pennsylvania, 1994.

———. "Rerouting Roots: Zehava Ben's Journey from Shuk to Suk." In *The Art of Being Jewish in Modern Times,* ed. Barbara Kirshenblatt-Gimblett and Jonathan Karp. Philadelphia: University of Pennsylvania Press, 2007.

———. "Resetting Ethnic Margins, Sephardic Renaissance through Film." *Jusur* 5 (1989): 91–104.

———. *Side by Side: Creators on Restless Soil* (radio series). Ed. Ziv Yonatan. Washington, D.C.: private collection, 1986 (audio cassette).

Horowitz, Donald. "Ethnic Identity." In *Ethnicity, Theory, and Experience,* ed. Nathan

Glazer, Daniel P. Moynihan, and Corinne Sposs Schelling. Cambridge, Mass.: Harvard University Press, 1975.

Hume, David. "On Tragedy." In *Essays: Moral, Political, and Literary,* ed. T. H. Green and T. H. Grose. 1757. London: 1875.

Hutnyk, John. *Critique of Exotica: Music, Politics and the Culture Industry.* London: Pluto Press, 2000.

Imanu'el, Mosheh Yitsḥaḳ. *Ha-Pa'ar* (The Gap). Holon, Israel: Ami, 1968.

Kallus, Rachel, and Hubert Law Yone. "National Home/Personal Home: Public Housing and the Shaping of National Space in Israel." *European Planning Studies* 10, no. 6 (2002): 765–79.

Kalmar, Ivan Davidson. "Research." 30 June 2004. http://www.chass.utoronto.ca/~ikalmar/research/research.html.

Kapchan, Deborah A. *Gender on the Market: Moroccan Women and the Revoicing of Tradition.* Philadelphia: University of Pennsylvania Press, 1996.

Kapchan, Deborah A., and Pauline Turner Strong, eds. "Theorizing Hybridity." *Journal of American Folklore* 112, no. 445 (1999).

Karp, Ivan, and Steven Lavine, eds. *Exhibiting Cultures: Poetics and Politics of Museum Display.* Washington, D.C.: Smithsonian Institution Press, 1991.

Katriel, Tamar. *Communal Webs: Communication and Culture in Contemporary Israel.* Albany: State University of New York Press, 1991.

Keren, Michael. *Ben-Gurion and the Intellectuals: Power, Knowledge and Charisma.* Dekalb, Ill.: Northern Illinois University Press, 1983.

Kirshenblatt-Gimblett, Barbara. *Destination Culture: Tourism, Museums, and Heritage.* Berkeley: University of California Press, 1998.

———. "Spaces of Dispersal." *Cultural Anthropology* 9, no. 3 (1994): 339–44.

Kligman, Mark L. *Maqām and Liturgy: Ritual, Music, and Aesthetics of Syrian Jews in Brooklyn.* Detroit: Wayne State University Press, 2008.

Koskoff, Ellen. "An Introduction to Women, Music, and Culture." In *Women and Music in Cross-Cultural Perspective,* ed. Ellen Koskoff. Urbana: University of Illinois Press, 1989.

Krook, Dorthea. *Elements of Tragedy.* New Haven, Conn.: Yale University Press, 1969.

Kuhn, Thomas. *The Structure of Scientific Revolutions.* 2nd ed. Chicago: University of Chicago Press, 1970.

Lather, Patti. "Fertile Obsession: Validity after Poststructuralism." *Sociological Quarterly* 34, no. 4 (2005): 673–93.

Leech, Clifford. *Tragedy.* Norfolk: Methuen, 1969.

Macy, L., ed. *Grove Music Online.* http://www.grovemusic.com.

Maier, Joseph B., and Chaim I. Waxman, eds. *Ethnicity, Identity and History: Essays in Memory of Werner J. Cahnman.* New Brunswick, N.J.: Transaction Books, 1983.

Manuel, Peter. *Cassette Culture: Popular Music and Technology in North India.* Chicago: University of Chicago Press, 1993.

———. *Popular Musics of the Non-Western World: An Introductory Survey.* Oxford: Oxford University Press, 1988.

Maranda, Pierre, ed. *Mythology.* Middlesex: Penguin Books, 1972.

McCarthy, Justin. "Palestine's Population during the Ottoman and the British Mandate Periods." 8 September 2001. http://www.palestineremembered.com/Acre/Palestine-Remembered/Story559.html.

Mendlezweig, R., and N. Magor. *Aliyah u-kelitah, hitpatḥut u-megamot* (Immigration and Absorption, Development and Trends). Jerusalem: Government Press Office, 1984.

Morris, Benny. *The Birth of the Palestinian Refugee Problem, 1947–1949.* Cambridge, UK: Cambridge University Press, 1988.

Narayan, Kirin. "Songs Lodged in Some Hearts: Displacements of Women's Knowledge in Kangra." In *Displacement, Diaspora and Geographies of Identity,* ed. Smadar Lavie and Ted Swedenburg. Durham, N.C.: Duke University Press, 1996.

Naveh, Hannah. "Nine Eleven: An Ethics of Proximity." *Signs: Journal of Women in Culture and Society* 28, no. 1 (2002): 450–52.

Ohnuki-Tierney, Emiko. "'Native' Anthropologists." *American Ethnologist* 11, no. 3 (1984): 584–86.

Pappé, Ilan. *The Making of the Arab–Israeli Conflict, 1947–1951.* London: I. B. Taurus, 1992.

Pareles, Jon. "Cassette Culture: Home Recording or Original Music on Cassettes." *Whole Earth Review* 5 (Winter 1988): 110–11.

Patai, Raphael. *Israel between East and West.* Westport, Conn.: Greenwood, 1970.

Peled, Y. "Towards a Redefinition of Jewish Nationalism in Israel: The Enigma of Shas." *Ethnic and Racial Studies* 21, no. 4 (1998): 703–27.

Perelson, Inbal. *A Great Joy Tonight: Arab-Jewish Music and Mizraḥi Identity* (Hebrew). Tel Aviv: Resling Publishing, 2006.

———. "Power Relations in the Israeli Popular Music System." *Popular Music* 17, no. 1 (1998): 113–28.

Piterberg, Gabriel. "Domestic Orientalism: The Representation of Oriental Jews in Zionist/Israeli Historiography." *British Journal of Middle Eastern Studies* 23, no. 2 (1996): 125–45.

Poole, Adrian. *Tragedy: Shakespeare and the Greek Example.* Oxford: Basil Blackwell, 1987.

Portelli, Alessandro. *The Battle of Valle Giulia: Oral History and the Art of Dialogue.* Madison: University of Wisconsin Press, 1997.

Ram, Uri. "Postnationalist Pasts: The Case of Israel." *Social Science History* 22, no. 4 (1998): 513–45.

Raz-Krakotzkin, Amnon. "Diaspora within Sovereignty: Critique of 'Negation of the Diaspora' in Israeli Culture." *Te'oryah u-viḳoret* (Theory and Critique) 4 (1993): 23–55.

Reagon, Bernice Johnson. "'Nobody Knows the Trouble I See,' or 'By and By I'm Gonna Lay Down My Heavy Load.'" *Journal of American History* 78, no. 1 (1991): 111–19.

Rebhun, Uzi, and Chaim Isaac Waxman, eds. *Jews in Israel: Contemporary Social and Cultural Patterns.* Hanover, N.H.: Brandeis University Press, 2003.

Regev, Mordechai. "The Coming of Rock: Meaning, Contest and Structure in the Field of Popular Music in Israel." Ph.D. diss., Tel Aviv University, 1990.

Regev, Motti, and Edwin Seroussi. *Popular Music and National Culture in Israel.* Berkeley: University of California Press, 2004.

Roumani, Maurice M. "The Military, Ethnicity, and Integration in Israel Revisited." In *Ethnicity, Integration, and the Military,* ed. Henry Dietz, Jerrold Elkin, and Maurice Roumani. Boulder, Colo.: Westview, 1991.

Saada-Ophir, Galit. "Borderland Pop: Arab Jewish Musicians and the Politics of Performance." *Cultural Anthropology* 21, no. 2 (2006): 205–33.

Sachar, Howard M. *A History of Israel: From the Rise of Zionism to Our Time.* New York: Knopf, 1976.

Said, Edward. *Orientalism.* New York: Random House, 1978.

Schramm, Adelaide Reyes. "Ethnic Music, the Urban Area and Ethnomusicology." *Sociologus* 29, no. 1 (1979): 1–21.

Schuman, Howard, Barry Schwartz, and Hannah D'Arcy. "Elite Revisionists and Popular Beliefs: Christopher Columbus, Hero or Villain?" *Public Opinion Quarterly* 69, no. 1 (2005): 2–29.

Segev, Tom. *1949: The First Israelis.* Trans. Arlen Neal Weinstein. New York: Free Press, 1986.

Seitel, Peter. *The Powers of Genre: Interpreting Haya Oral Literature.* New York: Oxford University Press, 1999.

Selzer, Michael. *The Outcasts of Israel: Communal Tensions in the Jewish State.* Jerusalem: Council of the Sephardi Community, 1965.

Seroussi, Edwin. "Ḥanalah Hitbalbelah (Hanale Was Rattled)." In *Fifty to Forty Eight: Critical Moments in the History of the State of Israel,* ed. Adi Ophir. Special issue of *Te'oryah u-viḳoret* 12–13 (1999): 269–78.

———. "Yam Tikhoniyut: Transformations of the Mediterranean in Israeli Music." In *Mediterranean Mosaic: Popular Music and Global Sounds,* ed. Goffredo Plastino. New York: Routledge, 2003.

Shahar, Natan. "The Eretz-Yisraeli Song 1920–1950: Sociomusical and Musical Aspects" [in Hebrew]. Ph.D. diss., Hebrew University, 1989.

Shaked, Gershon. *The Shadows Within: Essays on Modern Jewish Writers.* Philadelphia: Jewish Publication Society, 1987.

Shelemay, Kay Kaufman. *Let Jasmine Rain Down: Song and Remembrance among Syrian Jews.* Chicago: University of Chicago Press, 1998.

———. *Soundscapes: Exploring Music in a Changing World.* New York: W. W. Norton, 2001.

Shenhav, Yehouda. *The Arab Jews: A Postcolonial Reading of Nationalism, Religion, and Ethnicity.* Stanford: Stanford University Press, 2006.

———. "Ethnicity and National Memory: The World Organization of Jews from Arab Countries (WOJAC) in the Context of the Palestinian National Struggle." *British Journal of Middle Eastern Studies* 29, no. 1 (2002): 27–56.

———. "No Room for 'Misfits.'" http://www.haaretz.com/hasen/spages/917177.html.

Shiloah, Amnon. "Eastern Sources in Israeli Music." *Ariel* 88 (1992): 4–19.

Shohat, Ella. "The Invention of the Mizraḥim." *Journal of Palestine Studies* 29, no. 1 (1999): 5–20.

———. *Israeli Cinema East/West and the Politics of Representation.* Austin: University of Texas Press, 1989.

———. "Sephardim in Israel: Zionism from the Standpoint of Its Jewish Victims." *Social Text* 19/20 (Autumn 1988): 1–35.

———. *Taboo Memories, Diasporic Voices.* Durham, N.C.: Duke University Press, 2006.

Shokeid, Moshe. *The Dual Heritage: Immigrants from the Atlas Mountains in an Israeli Village.* Manchester: Manchester University Press, 1971.

Shuman, Amy. "Dismantling Local Culture." *Western Folklore* 52 (1993): 345–64.

———. *Other People's Stories: Entitlement Claims and the Critique of Empathy.* Urbana: University of Illinois Press, 2005.

———. *Storytelling Rights: The Use of Oral and Written Texts by Urban Adolescents.* Cambridge: Cambridge University Press, 1986.

———. "Strategic Romanticism." Paper presented at the Feminist Rhetoric Conference, Corvallis, Ore., 1997.

Simon, Rachel. "Reference Sources for Sephardic Studies." 1994. http://www.princeton.edu/~rsimon/jl.html.

Slobin, Mark. "Rethinking 'Revival' of American Ethnic Music." *New York Folklore* 9, nos. 3–4 (1983): 37–44.

Slyomovics, Susan. *The Object of Memory: Arab and Jew Narrate the Palestinian Village.* Philadelphia: University of Pennsylvania Press, 1998.

Smooha, Sammy. "Israel and Its Third World Jews: Black Panthers—The Ethnic Dilemma." *Society* 9, no. 7 (1972): 31–36.

———. *Israel: Pluralism and Conflict.* London: Routledge and Kegan Paul, 1978.

———. "The Mass Immigrations to Israel: A Comparison of the Failure of the Mizraḥi Immigrants of the 1950s with the Success of the Russian Immigrants of the 1990s." *Journal of Israeli History* 27, no. 1 (2008): 1–27.

Solnit, Rebecca. *Hope in the Dark: The Untold Story of People Power.* Edinburgh: Canongate Books, 2004.

Sutton, R. Anderson. "Commercial Cassette Recordings of Traditional Music in Java: Implications for Performers and Scholars." *World of Music* 27, no. 3 (1985): 23–45.

Svirsky, Gila. "The Peace Process Needs Women." *Israel Insider,* 30 October 2002, http://web.israelinsider.com/Views/1578.htm.

Szwed, John F. "Metaphors of Incommensurability." *Journal of American Folklore* 116, no. 459 (2003): 9–18.

Tamari, Salim. *Mountains against the Sea: Essays on Palestinian Society and Culture.* Berkeley: University of California Press, 2009.

Tobi, Merit, compiler. *"Ha-Melekh"* (The King)*: Research.* Background Research for the Script. N.p., 1992.

Tsoffar, Ruth. "A Land That Devours Its People: Mizraḥi Writing from the Gut." *Body & Society* 12, no. 2 (2006): 25–55.

Tzfadia, Erez. "Public Housing as Control: Spatial Policy of Settling Immigrants in Israeli Development Towns." *Housing Studies* 21, no. 4 (2006): 523–37.

Vernant, Jean-Pierre, and Pierre Vidal-Naquet. *Myth and Tragedy in Ancient Greece.* Trans. Janet Lloyd. New York: Zone Books, 1990.

Virginia Tech Multimedia Music Dictionary. 1996–2007. http://www.music.vt.edu/musicdictionary.

Wallis, Roger, and Krister Malm. *Big Sounds from Small Peoples: The Music Industry in Small Countries.* London: Constable, 1984.

Walters, Suzanna. *All the Rage: The Story of Gay Visibility in America.* Chicago: University of Chicago Press, 2001.

Wittgenstein, Ludwig. *Philosophical Investigations.* 50th Anniversary Commemorative Edition. Trans. G. E. M. Anscombe. Malden, Mass.: Blackwell, 2001.

Yiftachel, Oren. "Social Control, Urban Planning and Ethno-class Relations: Mizraḥi Jews in Israel's 'Development Towns.'" *International Journal of Urban and Regional Research* 24, no. 2 (2000): 418–38.

Yosha, Nissim. "The Heritage of Oriental Jewry in Israeli Education and Culture." In *Encyclopedia Judaica 1983–85 Yearbook,* ed. Geoffrey Wigoder. Jerusalem: Keter, 1983.

Young, Katharine. *Presence in the Flesh: The Body in Medicine.* Cambridge, Mass.: Harvard University Press, 1997.

Zerubavel, Eviatar. *The Fine Line: Making Distinctions in Everyday Life.* Chicago: University of Chicago Press, 1993.

Zerubavel, Yael. *Recovered Roots: Collective Memory and the Making of Israeli National Tradition.* Chicago: University of Chicago Press, 1997.

Select Discography

Anrki, Eti, and David D'or. "Eshebo." Composed by Safy Boutella. *Live Show* (1998). Hed Arzi 64026.

Argov, Zohar. "Elinor." *Elinor* (1980). Reuveni Brothers 43/1.

———. "'Et dodim Kalah" (The Time of Love, O Bride). *Elinor* (1980). Reuveni Brothers 43/1.

———. *Ḥafla ve-shire matsav ruaḥ, hofa'ah ḥayah be-Tsarfat* (Party and Good Humor Songs; live performance, France) (1985). Tal Productions.

———. "Ha-Peraḥ be-gani" (The Flower in My Garden). Composed by Avihu Medina. *Nakhon le-hayom* (Up to Date) (1982). Reuveni Brothers 220/4.

———. *Hayu zemanim* (There Was a Time) (1982). Reuveni Brothers.

———. "Kol yom she-'over" (Every Day That Passes). Composed by Moshe Nagar. *Demo Tape* (1977). Kolifone Studio.

———. "Levad" (Alone). Composed by Avinu Medina. *Nakhon le-hayom* (Up to Date) (1982). Reuveni Brothers 220/4.

———. "Levad yoshev" (Sit Alone). Composed by Uzi Ḥiṭman. *Lihiyot adam* (To Be Human) (1985). Ben-Mosh Productions. Kessar.

———. *Lihiyot adam* (To Be Human) (1985). Tal Productions.

———. "Marlen." Hebrew lyrics by Uzi Ḥiṭman. *Kakh 'overim ḥayay* (So My Life Goes By) (1984). Reuveni Brothers.

———. "Yaldah, ḥikiti shanim" (Girl, I Have Waited Years). Composed by Moshe Nagar. *Demo Tape* (1977). Kolifone Studio.

———. *Yam shel dema'ot* (Sea of Tears) (1985). Ben-Mosh Productions: Kessar.

Ben, Zehava. "Etnix" (Ethnics). *Keturna masala* (When Luck Returns) (1991). Composed by Ze'ev Neḥama and Amir Ḳlisḳi. Masala. Helicon.

———. *Ṭipat mazal* (A Drop of luck) (1992). Eli Banai Productions: Ultratone Studios.

———. *Zehava Ben sharah 'Aravit* (Zehava Ben Sings Arabic) (1995). Eli Banai Productions.

———. *Zehava Ben sharah 'Aravit: Enta omri* (Zehava Ben Sings Arabic: You Are My Life) (1995). Helicon.

Daḳlon. *Ḥafla 'im Daḳlon: Ahuvat levavi* (Party with Daḳlon: My Beloved) (1988). Reuveni Brothers: Kessar Studios AC 305.

———. *Ḥafla 'im Daḳlon le-khol ha-ḥaverim* (Party with Daḳlon for All the Friends) (1978). Reuveni Brothers BC 130/8.

———. *Ḳol ḳore li ba-midbar* (A Voice Calls Me in the Desert) (1990). Reuveni Brothers.

———. *Mesibah 'im Daḳlon le-khol ha-ḥaverim* (Party with Daḳlon for All the Friends) (1980). Reuveni Brothers: Levitan Studios CR 306.

———. *Zemer bi-mish'ole ha-arets* (Song in the Land's Paths) (1991). Reuveni Brothers.

Gadassi, Avner. *Menagen ve-shar* (Play and Sing) (1978). Reuveni Brothers 92/5.

Gi'at, Moshe. *Hashkini yayin* (Let Me Drink Wine) (1982). Reuveni Brothers 8/367.
Golan, Zion. *Ayumah be-har ha-mor* (Awesome at the Mount of Myrrh) (n.d.). Reuveni Brothers 222–3.
———. *Bi-lehiṭe zahav* (In Golden Hits) (n.d.). Reuveni Brothers. 131/7.
———. *'Et ratson, ya jama'a* (Good Times, Gang) (1988). Reuveni Brothers R.C. 240.
———. *Lehiṭe Teman #1* (Hits of Yemen #1) (n.d.). Reuveni Brothers 1048/74.
———. *Lehiṭe Teman #2* (Hits of Yemen #2) (n.d.). Reuveni Brothers 1048/75.
Ḥavarut Shiru Shir, Hadasah Sigalov (solo). "Mal'u asamenu bar" (Our Silos are Filled with Grain). Composed by David Zehavi. Lyrics by Pinḥas Lender. 2008. NMC.
Levy, Ofer. *Eheyeh lakh le-melekh* (I'll Be Your King) (1992). Lin Productions, Michaeli 92.
Luzon, Eli. *Ezo medinah* (What a Country) (1987). Ben-Mosh Productions.
Medina, Avihu. "Al tira, Yisrael" (Don't Fear, Israel). *Pirḥe gani* (The Flowers in My Garden) (1988). AM Productions 001–02.
———. "Avraham avinu" (Abraham Our Father). *Mah yihyeh* (What Will Be) (1992). AM Productions 004.
———. "Baladah le-ḥaver" (Ballad to a Friend). *Asher ahavti* (That I Loved) (1990). AM Productions 003.
———. "Lamah, El" (Why, God). *Mah yihyeh* (What Will Be) (1992). AM Productions 004.
———. "Shabeḥi Yerushalayim" (Praise, Jerusalem). *Pirḥe gani* (The Flowers in My Garden) (1988). AM Productions 001–02.
Moshe, Haim. "Linda, Linda." Composed by Samir al-Tawil. *Ahavat ḥayai* (Love of My Life) (1982). Reuveni Brothers.
———. *Ha-ḳolot shel Pireus* (The Voices of Pireus) (n.d.). Reuveni Brothers RV 272.
———. *Tsa'ad Temani* (Yemenite Step) (n.d.). Reuveni Brothers RC 8/399.
Oranim Zabar. *Shalom!* (1958). Elektra Records.
Ozeri, Ahuva. "Heikhan he-ḥayal" (Where Is the Soldier?). Composed by Ahuva Ozeri (1975). *Bonboniera Yam Tikhonit* (1997). Reuveni Brothers.
Poliker, Yehuda. *These Eyes of Mine* (1985). NMC Music 26445–2.
Ray, Adam. *Adam Ray* (1994). Gilyos International Enterprises.
Saroussi, Nissim. "Yerushalayim." *Yerushalayim* (1979). Ness Productions.
Shukry, Samir. *"Linda, Linda": Etmol, ha-Yom, u-maḥar* (Yesterday, Today, and Tomorrow). New York: Samir Shukry.
———. "Mi-Mosheh ve-'ad Muhamad" (From Moses to Muhammed). Lyrics by Yoram Teharlev. Music by Nurit Hirsch. 1982.
———. *Rona Shely* (My Rona) (n.d.). Kolifone: Sigma (Azoulay Brothers).
Tsan'ani, Margalit. *Menta* (Mint) (1988). Reuveni Brothers: Sigma.
———. *Pegishah* (A Date). (1991). Reuveni Brothers: Galkol.
Tselile ha-Kerem. *Dakmosh #2* (1974). Yasu Reuveni Brothers.
———. "Ḥanaleh hitbalbelah" (Little Hannah Got Confused). 1974.
———. "Shabeḥi Yerushalayim" (Praise, Jerusalem). Composed by Avihu Medina. *Ḥafla shel shirim she-ahavnu* (Party of Songs That We Loved) (1986). Reuveni Brothers RC 161/62.
———. *Shoshanat Teman* (Rose of Yemen) (n.d.). Yasu Reuveni Brothers.
"Yalla" (Let's Go) (1990). Hitlist Egypt. Compiled by David Lodge. Island Records.
Zemer Yam Tikhoni (Mediterranean Singer). Ed. Arieh Tsuberi. Tel Aviv: Modin, 1987.

Videography

The Black Panthers (in Israel) Speak. Written and directed by Eli Hamo and Sami Shalom Chetrit. Israel, 2003. Videotape. 53 Minutes.

Forget Baghdad. Written and directed by Samir. Switzerland, 2003.

Mi-Meni, Meni (From Me, Meni). Meni Peer, interview with Zohar Argov. Jerusalem: Israel Broadcasting Authority, 1987.

Od lahiṭ (Another Hit). Hosted by Regi Bitlin and Kobi Rekht. "Performances by Margalit Tsan'ani, Eti Ankri, Zohar Argov, Aster Shamir, Shlomo Arẓi, Ofer Akerling." Jerusalem: Israel Television, 1 September 1983.

Pa'ame ha-Mizraḥ (Footsteps of the East). "Mits'ad ha-pizmonim ha-mizraḥi be-Ḳiryat Gat" (The Eastern Hit Parade in Kiryat Gat). Produced by Yosef Ben Israel. Jerusalem: Israel Television, 12 October 1983.

Sha'ah ṭova (Good Hour). Daniel Peer, interview with Zohar Argov. Jerusalem: Israel Television, 7 January 1983.

Ṭipat mazal (A Drop of Luck). Directed by Ze'ev Revach. Tel Aviv: Noah Films, 1992.

Yoman ha-shavu'a (Weekly Journal). Yoel Esteron, interview with Zohar Argov. Jerusalem: Israel Television, 1981.

Zehava Ben: Solitary Star. Written and directed by Erez Laufer. Tel Aviv: Idan Productions, 1997.

Zohar ha-melekh (Zohar the King). Directed by Lina Chaplin. Jerusalem: Israel Television, 10 May 1994.

Index

absorption, 150, 155, 182n. 11; policy of, 36–39, 43–45, 51–54 (*see also* assimilation)
ACUM (Composers, Authors and Publishers Society of Israel), 18, 22
aesthetics, 21, 22–23, 27, 30–32, 35, 45, 50–51, 55–56, 59, 61–62, 65–67, 72, 74, 78, 81, 98–100, 103–4, 109, 123, 125, 126, 138, 140, 141, 147, 150–52, 157, 162–65, 167; and politics, 7, 147, 150–52, 154, 161–65, 169, 172–75, 187n. 32, 205, 214 ; "politics of the aesthetic," vii, 30, 36, 99, 150–54, 162–70
Alcalay, Ammiel, 10, 46
alien, 7, 27, 150; alienation, 71, 109, 119, 163. *See also* foreign
aliya, 38, 87
al-Jazeera, 147, 222
alternative Israeli music, 1, 2, 9, 15, 29, 165
'amami. See folk
Amar, Jo, 75
ambiguity, paradox, contradiction, 4, 7, 12, 34–35, 46, 63, 66–67, 79, 83, 86, 123, 125, 130, 147, 164, 178n. 16
Amzallag, Avraham, 54, 97–98
Ankry, Etti, 140–41
appropriation, vii, viii, ix, 3, 30–32, 56, 69, 77, 79, 126–27, 130, 132, 142, 153, 162, 166, 172–73, 196n. 35; "appropriate appropriation," viii, 30, 150, 152–53
Arab Jews, 11, 18, 39, 55, 144, 147
Argov, Zohar, vii, viii, 2, 15, 17, 20, 22, 29, 50, 69, 72–73, 75, 79, 85–104, 105–27, 129, 132, 134–35, 138, 140, 153, 159, 172, 188n. 3, 205, 207, 209, 210
Ashkenazi. *See* identity
asli. See authenticity
assemblage, 165
assimilation, 20, 52, 109, 110; Israelization, 6. *See also* identity
auditory. *See* audibility
audibility, 7, 44, 63, 69, 91, 104, 150, 161, 165
auditory, 3, 171
aural, 23, 159; memory (*see* memory)
authenticity, 6, 29, 67–68, 76–78, 86, 95–98, 100, 102, 121, 143, 147, 160–62, 178n. 11, 186n. 1; politics of, 96
asli, asli mekorit, 60, 62–63, 65, 69, 71, 73, 186n. 1
avant garde, viii, 17, 111, 127
"Avraham Avinu," 79, 210–12
AZIT (*Amutat Zemer Yam Tikhoni*), 29, 56

Bakhtin, Mikhail, 147
"Baladah le-Ḥaver," 78, 209–10
Banai, Eli, 5, 143
Bar, Shlomo, x, 47
bar/bat mitzvah, 8, 17, 72, 89, 134
barrier. *See* border
Barth, Frederik, 161
bazouki, 1, 161
Beit Lessin Theater, 17, 127
Ben, Zehava, ix, 5, 20, 22, 129–54, 171, 172, 210, 214, 219
Ben-Amos, Dan, 62, 186n. 10
Ben-David, Amir, 110–11
Ben-Israel, Yosef, 87
Ben-Mosh, Avigdor, 94
Ben-Mosh, Moshe, 49, 65, 98, 99
binary, 7, 30–32, 130, 152, 155–56, 189n. 26
Black: culture, 11, 47, 54, 116, 119, 136, 160; Jews, 159, 164; music, 2 (see also *Musikah*); Panthers, 11, 47, 54; *Sheḥorim* (blacks), 159
blending of the exiles. *See* exiles
border (boundaries, barriers, frontier), 4, 9, 27, 32, 75, 130, 138, 144, 147, 153–54, 160, 163–64, 167, 169, 171–73,

border (boundaries, barriers, frontier) (*cont.*) 181–82n. 2, 193n. 25; barrier, 10, 171; crossing, ix, 130, 144, 154, 171; frontier, 34
Bourdieu, Pierre, 6, 173
Brandeis, Nancy, 86, 96, 97, 207
brit milah, 88
Broman, Eva, xii, 93

canon, 3, 22, 27, 66, 110, 129, 138, 159, 199; canonization, 127. *See also* sound track
cassette: cover, 1, 20, 62, 63, 66, 67, 88, 143; producers (*see* product, production). *See also* network
category, 6, 10, 11, 27, 64, 132, 163, 165, 189n. 26; analytical, 108; typology, 60
catharsis, 109, 117, 121–23, 126
celebrity, 82, 114, 121–23, 191n. 38
class, 4, 6, 42, 46, 66, 71, 78, 88, 126, 132, 135, 177n. 6
classical tradition, 8, 27, 67, 75, 99, 117, 132, 139, 144, 173, 219
classification, 3, 5, 22, 27, 56, 60, 62, 86, 96, 105, 162–64. *See also* typology, category
Clifford, James, 14
Club: Ariana, 90; Halleluya, 92; ha-Barvaz (The Duck), 90
Cohen, Erik, 5
Cohen, Yehuda, x, 56
colonialism, 78, 166
common ground, 74, 129, 148
cultural commonality, 35, 50
community, x–xi, 13–14, 18–20, 23, 27–29, 53, 62–63, 70, 74, 99, 103, 111, 118, 122, 124, 130–31, 160, 166–67; Ashkenazi, 34, 122; Mizraḥi, vii–viii, 34–35, 51, 67, 111, 116, 122, 126–27, 159, 161, 166, 172; musical, 6, 23, 67, 81, 161; musicians, 8, 25, 86
"community of communities," viii, 34–35. *See* also pan-ethnic
conservatism, 130, 164, 166
consumers, 6, 18, 23, 29, 63, 143, 165
context, ix, 3, 6, 10–12, 27–32, 53, 56–57, 60–63, 67, 72, 74, 81, 83, 86, 99, 102, 135, 143, 144, 148, 153, 163, 166, 168, 169, 178n.11, 178n.17, 184n. 45, 186n. 1, 186n. 10, 189n. 26, 194n. 8; musical, 74, 165, 169, 173, 215; political, vii, x, 155, 162, 167; religious, 63, 97–98
contradiction. *See* ambiguity
copyright, 22
creolization, 27, 142. *See also* hybridity
crime, 106, 113–14, 117
critics, viii, 5–7, 10, 56, 66, 67, 69, 74, 81–82, 127, 140, 199
criticism, critique, 9, 35, 44, 49, 54–56, 60, 72, 96, 121, 147, 153, 154, 177n. 6, 212
crying songs (*Shire bekhi*), 139, 143, 150
cultural formations, 3, 27, 29, 36, 47, 55, 126, 152–53, 159, 160, 177n. 6; multicultural, 9, 109; transcultural, 28, 30

Daḳlon, 20, 49, 63–68, 69, 70, 72, 73, 134, 202
darabukka, 4, 157, 177n. 5, 199, 202–3
Degh, Linda, 106
deterritorialization. *See* territory
development towns, 2, 40–44, 72–73
dialogism, dialogue, dialogical, xii, 3, 6, 7, 10, 12, 14, 28, 31, 56, 66, 111, 115, 116, 129, 152, 153–54, 156, 172. *See also* binary
diaspora, 3, 4, 38–39, 41, 45, 156, 159, 160, 173, 194n. 6
difference, 30
discourse, 7, 27, 35, 44, 52, 55, 56, 99, 123, 124, 127, 159, 163, 175, 177n. 6
discrimination, 17, 36, 40, 54–55, 78, 81, 108, 115, 165; *haflayah,* 55; *kipuaḥ* (deprivation), 159
disenfranchisement, vii, viii, 11, 28, 35–36, 56–57, 76, 78, 81, 101, 164, 170, 172; reenfranchisement, 56, 104
dislocation. *See* location
"dueling nativities." *See* native
disorientation, 3, 7
diwan, 61, 65

East for Peace (*Mizraḥ la-shalom*), 47
economics, 12, 28, 36, 40, 43, 47, 50, 55, 66, 100, 101, 140, 156, 159
Egyptian. *See* ethnicity
Elias, Tayseer, x, 130
"*Elinor,*" 22, 73, 90, 99, 106, 180n. 35
elite, 6, 116, 127, 178n. 11. *See also* class
emigration. *See* immigration
emotion, xii, 3, 46, 66, 67, 79, 87, 99, 103, 117, 123, 125, 135, 144, 150, 152, 162, 217, 222

empathy, 7, 109, 120, 121
engagement, terms of, 5–6
ethnic, ethnicity, vii, viii, ix, xv, 2, 4–7, 9–12, 13, 14, 17, 23, 27, 30, 32, 33–57, 63, 65–67, 71–73, 77, 80, 88, 96, 98–100, 104, 106, 108–10, 123, 125–27, 129–30, 132, 135, 140–41, 153, 157, 159–61, 163–64, 166–70, 172–74, 186n. 10, 188n. 3, 189n. 26, 192n. 7; pan-ethnicity, vii–viii, 4, 5, 10–11, 30–32, 34–36, 40, 42, 44–47, 51–52, 56–57, 65, 81, 97, 99–101, 126–27, 143, 157, 159–60, 166, 172, 184n. 44. *See also* discrimination; identity; markers
ethnicities: Egyptian, ix, 2, 18, 23, 25, 55, 62, 129, 131, 143, 154, 167, 171, 217; Greek, xii, 1, 3, 15, 18, 20, 22, 31, 32, 50, 61, 67, 73–77, 79, 82, 85, 96, 98–99, 109, 110, 119, 123, 126, 132, 134, 138–40, 157, 172, 184n. 45, 187n. 32, 202, 203; Iranian,10–12, 14, 102, 173; Iraqi, viii, 2, 33, 42, 83, 132, 154, 171; Jordanian, 55, 130, 171; Kurdish, viii, 2, 11, 14, 15, 25, 32, 33–36, 50, 57, 61, 66, 68, 83, 132, 157, 160, 162–163, 166–67, 171, 173, 1195n. 24; Libyan, 35; Moroccan, ix, 2, 22, 35, 40, 47, 54, 66, 75, 79, 87, 96, 97, 129, 131–32, 134, 139, 144, 147–48, 154, 166–67, 173, 190n. 1; Palestinian, x–xi, 1, 4–5, 10–11, 14–15, 18, 29, 31–32, 35–37, 39, 41, 45, 54–56, 69, 129, 130, 138, 142, 144, 153, 167, 170–71, 181–82n. 2, 183n. 15, 192n. 7; Syrian, x, 5, 35, 54–55, 83, 154, 169, 217; Turkish, xii, 15, 22, 31, 32, 50, 61, 73–74, 76–77, 98, 134–35, 139–40, 154, 157, 187n. 32, 214; Yemeni, Yemenite viii, ix, 1–3, 5, 11, 14, 15, 17–18, 22, 31, 35, 42, 46, 49–50, 56, 61–63, 65–73, 75–76, 78–79, 82–83, 85–89, 96–98, 100–101, 104, 108, 110–11, 116, 118, 121, 126, 132, 152–53, 157, 161, 164, 167, 172, 189n. 28
Ethnix, 141–42, 215–16
ethnography, ethnographer, vii, 1, 6, 9, 12, 14, 20, 22, 27, 177n. 4, 179n. 21, 179n. 23
ethnomusicology, 5, 6, 53, 54, 56, 161
entitlement, 153–54
exclusion, 3, 12, 25, 27, 57, 78, 81, 83, 101, 132, 160, 165. *See also* rejection; inclusion
exile, 41, 101, 104; blending of the exiles, 157, 159; "ingathering of the exiles" (*Ḳibuts galuyot*), 32, 35, 99, 159; *Mizug galuyot* (melting pot), 38. *See also* Law of Return
exoticism, 67, 132, 156, 161
"Ezo medinah," 22, 197–99

familiarity, 7, 12, 25, 34, 35, 39, 66, 67, 153, 163, 172, 179n. 23, 194n. 4; unfamiliarity, 12, 67, 130
festivals, 17, 42, 48, 77, 132, 160, 166–67, 184n. 44, 207; Abu Ghosh, 132; Arad, 17, 106; *ha-zemer ha-mizraḥi* (Festival of Eastern Song), 86–87, 92, 97, 109; Israel, 77; Eilat, 17; *Saharana,* 166–67, 195n. 24; Teymaniada, 17
folk (*'amami*), 22, 42, 62, 181n. 64
folklore, vii, 5, 8, 9, 22, 38, 42, 53, 56, 61, 67, 69, 142, 166, 179n. 23, 180n. 49, 181n. 64, 186n. 10
folk music. *See* music
foreign, 3, 6, 12, 22, 25, 29, 79, 148, 150, 157, 161–63. *See also* alien
Fraser, Nancy, 163
frontier. *See* border

Gabrielov, Miki, 18
Gadassi, Avner, 72–75
Gefen, Yonatan, 135, 139
gender and sexuality, 9, 13, 14, 89, 144, 177n. 5
genre, vii–viii, ix, 3, 5–6, 9, 12, 15, 17, 22, 25, 27–28, 30–32, 36, 50, 56–57, 62, 66–68, 73, 81, 88, 95–96, 98, 102, 108, 125, 127, 132, 143, 150, 153, 161, 163–66, 169, 186n. 10, 193n. 29, 198, 199, 207, 212
geography, 7, 25, 27, 29–30, 34, 38, 41, 101, 152, 153, 159, 181n. 65, 192n. 7
ghetto (*ha-geto*), 23, 41, 77–78, 95, 100, 132, 154, 158, 159–60, 172–73, 194n. 6. *See also* neighborhood
Gi'at, Moshe, 20, 62–64, 67, 94
Giz'anut. See racism
glamour, 90–92, 121, 191n. 37
global, globalization, viii, 14, 25, 30, 55, 83, 157, 175, 177–78n. 6
Golan, Tsiyon, 20, 62–64, 67

Haaretz, 44
ḥafla (party), 49, 55
Halper, Jeff, 6, 14

Hammad, Suheir, 154
"Ḥanaleh hitbalbelah," 50, 172, 200–203
Hasan-Rokem, Galit, 182n. 6
Hasfari, Shemuel, 111, 114, 117, 121, 127
"ha-Peraḥ be-gani" (The Flower in My Garden), 86, 96–97, 109, 122, 132, 134–35, 138, 205–7
"*ha-Tikv ah,*" 156
ha-Shir ha-Erets Yisre'eli. See music
ha-Melekh, 109, 111, 115, 120, 122, 127
ha-PIL (the Federation of Mediterranean Israeli Song), 29
henna, 48
hero, 86, 89, 100, 102–4, 110, 103, 105–11, 114, 117, 120–21, 123, 127, 191n. 38; tragic, viii, 89, 105, 109–10, 120, 126
hierarchy, 152, 160, 162
Ḥitman, Uzi, 17, 96, 208, 210
Hoffman, Gene Knudson, 148
Holocaust, 36, 38, 40, 49, 95, 140
homelands, viii, 4, 32, 34, 36, 46, 63, 153, 160, 173
hope, 3, 4, 44, 56, 109, 135, 147, 148
Houja (family), 20, 171, 189n. 26
Hume, David, 125
hybridity, 2–3, 5, 25, 27, 30, 59, 66–67, 79, 82, 96, 100, 121, 130, 132, 135, 143, 147, 157, 160, 164–67, 173, 177n. 6, 199, 214. *See also* straddling

ideal, idealism, idealization, 4, 29, 35, 46, 101, 104, 116, 126, 152, 167. *See also* romanticism
identity, vii, ix, xv, 4–6, 10–11, 22, 28, 30–31, 35–36, 38–39, 45–46, 51, 53, 56–57, 61–62, 65–66, 96, 100, 103–4, 126, 144, 147–48, 154, 155–57, 161, 166, 173, 181n. 68, 184n. 45, 194n. 8, 219; Arabness, 66, 154; Ashkenazi/Ashkenazim (definition), 10–11; Israeliness, 6, 7, 54, 57, 66, 73, 75, 79, 154, 178n. 11; *lehit-ashknez,* 69, 72, 139, 163; markers, xv, 11, 22, 61; Mizraḥi/*Mizraḥim* (definition), 5, 11; *Mizraḥiyut* (*Mizraḥ*-ness), 99, 108, 173; Sephardi/Sephardim (definition), 10; *Samekh Tet* (pure Sephardi), 10, 178n. 17; *Temaniyut* (Yemeniteness), 100. *See also* ethnicity
ideology, 4, 36, 41, 70, 75, 102, 127, 157, 163, 169

illegitimacy. *See* legitimacy
imaginary, 96, 152, 156, 166
Imber, Naftali Herz, 156–57, 194n. 2, 194n. 4
immigration, 8, 35–38, 44, 52–54, 72, 75, 131, 182n. 11, 214; emigration, 11; migration, vii, 10, 36, 52, 63, 101
inclusion, 11, 27, 32, 165, 171. *See also* exclusion
independence, 36
indigeneity, viii, 30, 144, 152, 154, 162, 172
ingathering. *See* exile
inheritance, vii–viii, ix, 7, 8, 30–32, 34–35, 42, 153–54, 155, 172–73, 175, 183n. 15; legacy, 7, 8, 17, 34, 109, 127, 140
innovation, 25, 28, 62–63, 74, 95, 153, 166, 173, 175; invention, vii, 23, 28, 85, 95, 104, 106, 126, 161–62, 173 (*see also* technology)
insider, 7, 10, 12–14, 18, 31, 49, 74, 148, 163, 179n. 23, 184n. 45. *See also* outsider
instability, 2, 6, 155, 165–66
invention. *See* innovation
Israeli Arab. *See* ethnicity
Israeli Hit Parade (*Mits'ad ha-pizmonim*), 77, 142
Israeliness. *See* identity
Israelization. *See* assimilation
IUPA (Israeli Union of Performing Artists), 18

Jerusalem Project, xi

Kala, Itzik, 167
Karp, Ivan, 166
Katriel, Tamar, 199
Keren, Michael, 44–45
Kessar, Yehuda, 17, 89–90, 92, 125
Kidron, Pamela, 6
kibbutz, 69, 75–76, 78
Ḳibuts galuyot. See exile
Kirshenblatt-Gimblett, Barbara, 160
Knesset (Israeli parliament), 17, 56, 167
Kuhn, Thomas, 23–24
Kulthum, Umm, 25, 129–54, 181, 192n. 1, 219
Kurdish. *See* ethnicity

Lahaḳot tseva'iyot (military band), 178n. 11
"Lamah, El," 79–80

Lavine, Steven, 166
Law of Return, 36, 40, 182n. 11. *See also* exile
language, 5, 7, 9, 10, 36, 38, 40, 56, 60–62, 106, 115, 132, 143–44, 157, 205; common, 13
leakage. *See* seepage
Leech, Clifford, 120
legacy. *See* inheritance
legend, viii, 89, 100, 105, 106–11, 129, 189n. 34
legitimacy, 79, 96, 114, 127, 140, 143, 152–53; illegitimacy, 5, 73, 141, 166–67, 173
Levy, Ofer, 154, 199
Levy, Yosef. *See* Daklon
Lidji, Marcel, 90, 92, 94
Likud, 47, 115, 130, 192n. 2
"Linda, Linda," 69–70, 172, 187n. 23
local, locality, localization, viii, 3, 5, 11, 13, 14, 17, 23, 25, 28–32, 35, 37–39, 42, 47, 59, 62, 82–83, 86, 87, 98, 100, 106, 109–11, 114, 131, 134, 150, 152–53, 163, 166, 169, 172; relocalization, 25, 83, 132, 153, 161, 161
location, 3, 27, 35, 38, 40–41, 69, 78, 83, 99, 163, 194n. 6; dislocation, 2, 29, 36, 148, 152–53; relocation, 2, 33–58, 149, 154
London, Yaron, 51–52
longing. *See* nostalgia
Luzon, Eli, 22, 197–99
lyrics. *See* song texts

ma'abarah. See transit camps
Manuel, Peter, 161
maqamat. See musical modes
Maranda, Pierre, 108
market, vii, 2, 7, 18, 23, 25, 28–29, 49, 60, 65, 70, 92, 139, 143, 167; marketplace, x, 4, 5, 17–19, 25, 27–28, 49, 65, 83, 90–91, 93, 132, 134, 147–49, 156, 173; *shuk* (market), 92, 132, 134, 147; *suk* (market), 147
margin, 41, 166, 171, 177n. 6; marginality, 6, 31, 66, 88, 104–5, 132, 144, 147, 160, 164. *See also* periphery
markers: aesthetic, 167; cultural, 39, 159; ethnic, 5, 39 (*see also* ethnic); identity, xv, 11, 22, 61 (*see also* identity)
"Marlen," 101, 189n. 31, 207–9
Masortiyut. See tradition
master narraative. *See* narrative
Medina, Avihu, vii, viii, ix, xv, 5, 18, 20, 59–66, 70–71, 75–83, 86, 94, 96–97, 103, 107–8, 111, 114, 119–20, 124, 158, 167, 203, 207, 210, 212
meḳ onenet (woman lamenter), 75
Middleton, Richard, 161
meaning, 11, 34, 66, 88, 110, 116, 124–26, 144, 147, 150, 163, 165, 173; musical, 6, 12, 22–23, 28, 150
Meḳ omonim, 17
melisma (*silsul*), 1, 3–4, 61, 69, 82, 86–87, 97–98, 100, 104, 106, 126, 134, 139, 157, 177n. 2, 202
memory, 34, 38, 66, 89, 100–101, 113, 135, 155, 157, 210; aural, 67; spaces, 4
Meretz, 130, 192n. 2
methods, vii, 12, 45
migration. *See* immigration
Mimouna, 47, 166–67, 184n. 44
Mizraḥi. *See* identity
Mizug galuyot. See exile
Moroccan. *See* ethnicity
Moshe, Haim ix, 14, 17–18, 20, 42, 67, 68–72, 94, 129, 148, 159, 161–62, 167, 169, 171, 172, 217
multiculturalism. *See* cultural
multivocality, multiple voices. *See* voice
music (see also *Musiḳah*): emergent music, 2, 29, 40, 56, 57, 59, 92, 97, 130, 143, 160, 166; ethnic, 44, 140, 173; folk, 3, 8, 31, 42, 61, 62, 67, 68, 76, 96, 131, 139, 173, 194n. 4, 214, 217; *ha-Shir ha-Erets Yisre'eli* (The Song of the Land of Israel), 22, 31–32, 42, 49, 61, 65–67, 72, 75, 82, 91, 99, 126, 130, 132, 142–43, 152–53, 194n. 4, 199, 202; industry, x, xv, 4, 6, 15, 23, 25, 27, 29, 50, 56, 82, 89, 131, 166, 173; liturgical, 3, 5, 21, 26, 62, 63, 69, 88, 98, 99, 131, 186n. 11, 194n. 4, 203, 205, 209, 210; modal music, 3; musical mode (*maqamat*), 86, 157, 180n. 49, 217; musical style, vii–ix, 2–3, 5, 10, 17–18, 20, 23, 25, 27–28, 30–32, 42, 47, 50, 53, 56, 59, 60–63, 65, 67, 69, 70, 72–78, 81–83, 90, 95–96, 98–100, 103, 114–15, 118, 121, 130–32, 134, 135, 139, 141–43, 150, 152–53, 157, 161–63, 165, 167, 171–73, 180n. 49, 187n. 32, 196n. 33, 202, 203, 205, 207, 210, 214, 217,

music: musical style (*cont.*)
215–16; neighborhood, 82, 131, 134, 172; pan-ethnic, 4, 35–36, 97, 157; popular, 3, 5, 6, 17, 23, 28, 50, 70–72, 74, 99, 109, 116, 131, 135, 138, 140, 143, 148, 178n. 11, 180n. 49, 192n. 49 (*see also* Israeli Hit Parade); traditional, 3, 61, 99; world, 143, 160, 166, 173
new musical forms/formations, vii, 3–6, 12, 14, 15, 22, 23, 27, 28, 31, 32, 40, 45, 57, 67, 73, 81–83, 97, 100, 135, 142, 144, 147–48, 150, 152, 155, 157, 162, 167, 172, 175, 180n. 49, 214, 216
Musiḳah (music): *Musiḳah asli meḳorit* (real roots, the real thing), 59, 60, 62–65, 69, 71, 73, 82, 186n. 1 (*see also* authenticity); *Musiḳah 'im gaṿan Yam Tikhoni,* 59, 61–62, 65, 67, 69–71, 73, 212; *Musiḳah 'im gaṿan Yam Tikhoni meḳori,* 59, 61, 65; *Musiḳah masortit im gaṿan Yam Tikhoni,* 60, 62; *Musiḳah Mizraḥit,* 6, 97; *Musiḳah sheḥorah* (Black music), 2; *Musiḳah shel tshaḥ tshaḥim* (cheap music), 2, 15; *Musiḳat ha-tah. anah ha-merkazit* (Central Bus Station music), 2, 15; *Musiḳat ḳaseṭot* (cassette music), 2, 6, 15, 92;
mutability, 2, 3, 60, 108, 164, 165, 175
muwwal, 25, 86–87, 97–98, 100, 134–35, 138, 147, 180n. 49, 148, 205, 207, 217
myth, 36, 104, 105–11, 116, 127, 155–56

Namdar, Reuven (Ruby), xii, 12–14, 179n. 23, 177n. 4
Namdar, Shlomi, 102, 105
narrative, 34, 50, 105, 108, 121, 123, 125, 155, 172, 190n. 2; master/dominant, 54, 103, 110
nationalism, vii, 3–4, 33, 61
native, nativity, 3, 6, 10, 12, 147, 161–62, 178n. 13; "dueling nativities," viii, 8, 30, 147, 153
Naveh, Hannah, 144
Near, Holly, 9
Nehamah, Ze'ev, 141
neighborhoods: Katamon Vav, 20, 33, 57, 171; Kerem ha-Temanim, 49, 63, 69, 89; Shekhunat ha-Tiḳvah, 15, 49, 122, 148; Shikun ha-Mizraḥ, 87–88, 95, 100, 111, 125. *See also* music; networks
networks, 6, 30, 66; cassette, viii, 15, 23–30, 166; music, vii, ix, x, 2, 8, 15, 69, 82, 166, 186n. 1; neighborhood, 4, 50, 82; newspaper,17; radio broadcasting, 42, 90; television, 147
1967 Six Day War, 45
1973 Yom Kippur War, 8, 45, 50, 130
nostalgia, longing, 7–8, 34–37, 46, 60, 66, 96, 98–99, 101, 117, 148, 173, 205

Orientalization, 6, 10, 32, 37, 97, 178n. 16
Oslo Accords, 129
outsider, 7, 10, 12–14, 27, 31, 49, 60, 96, 143, 148, 163. *See also* insider
Ozeri, Ahuva, 69, 187n. 21

pain, 12, 50, 104, 108, 109, 114, 116, 121–22, 124, 125–27
Palestine, xi, 3, 31, 37–38, 42, 70, 72, 87, 172, 189n. 34, 199
Palestinian. *See* ethnicity
pan-ethnicity. *See* ethnic; "community of communities"
Parnas, Shimon, 14,
peace, ix, 4–5, 20, 35, 47, 56, 129–31, 134, 138, 142–49, 169, 171–72, 175, 212
pe'ot (sidelocks or earlocks), 87, 100
periphery, 27, 40–42, 54, 56. *See also* border; margin
permeablility, 31, 130, 167
personal, viii, 14, 35, 51, 59, 103–4, 108, 117, 122, 124, 129, 143–44, 150, 205
perspective, vii-viii, 12, 14, 23, 27, 54, 74, 102
pirate, 7, 18, 25, 134
piyyuttim, 61, 66, 99, 118, 126
Poole, Adrian, 117
Poliker, Yehuda, 104, 140–41
"politics of the aesthetic." *See* aesthetic
popular music. *See* music
pre-state, 37, 38, 42, 54
product (musical), musical production, ix, 2, 17–18, 20, 22–23, 25, 28–30, 60, 65, 70, 78, 81, 90, 105, 140, 147, 169, 214
propinquity. *See* proximity
proximity, propinquity, 2–3 7, 11, 30, 35–36, 40, 46, 67, 99, 103, 144, 152, 157, 164

qānūn, 4, 177n. 5

race, 9, 11, 44, 116, 163–64, 177n. 6, 94n. 6; racism (*giz'anut*), 55, 89, 119
radio stations: *Gale Tsahal,* 135, 160

Ram, Uri, 55
Reagon, Bernice Johnson, 9, 59–60, 66, 81, 166
recontextualization. *See* context
recording technology. *See* invention, technology
reformation. *See* formation
Regev, Mordechai (Motti), 6
religion and music, 60–63, 66–67, 69, 73–74, 98, 144, 157, 164
rejection, viii, 3–4, 15, 20, 27, 29, 32, 34, 39, 50, 67, 72, 90, 104, 121, 131, 140, 143, 154, 160, 163, 165. *See also* exclusion
relocation. *See* location
repertoire, viii, xii, 3, 8, 15, 20, 22, 28, 42, 50, 57, 60, 62–63, 65–67, 69, 72–73, 75, 81–82, 98–99, 105–6, 129, 132, 140–41, 143–44, 153, 160, 161, 165, 194n. 4, 203, 215, 219
reterritorialization. *See* territory
Reuveni, Asher, 15, 17, 28, 48–51, 68–69, 90–94, 104, 118, 148
Reuveni, Meir, 17, 22, 48–51, 68–69, 90–94, 118, 148
Reuveni Brothers/brothers, 17, 29, 49, 50, 68, 90–92, 94, 148
revolution, 5, 23, 49; music, 9, 14, 23, 104, 130, 167
rhizome, 31–32, 82, 181n. 68, 186n. 2, 196n. 35; rhizomatic musical network, 6, 60, 152, 183
Rishon le-Tsiyon, 87, 89, 134. *See* also neighborhood
romanticism, 3–4, 7, 38, 78, 116, 148, 152, 162, 193n. 29. *See also* idealization
roots, 10, 12, 31, 32, 47, 152, 214; musical, 14, 31, 32, 62, 96, 100, 129, 130–50, 173, 207
routes, 32, 152; musical, 2–5, 25, 32

Said, Edward, 10, 55
Salmon, Shafik, 18, 169
Saharana. See festival
Samekh Tet. See identity
santur, 142, 192n. 15, 199
Saroussi, Nissim, 18, 51–52, 57
scandal, 106–7, 117, 121–22, 191n. 38
Schramm, Adelaide Reyes, 161
seepage, 6, 30, 130, 154, 169; leakage, 22
Seitel, Peter, 153
Shemer, Naomi, 66, 71, 130, 139
sentiment, 49, 96, 125–26, 150, 157, 162, 164. *See also* emotion
Sephardi. *See* identity
Seroussi, Edwin, 6, 54, 202
sex, sexism, sexualities, 14, 89, 144, 177n. 6; sexual abuse, assault, violence, 89, 108, 120, 122. *See also* gender
Shabazi, Rabbi Shalom, 61–62, 65–66, 74
Shelemay, Kay Kaufman, 72
Shiloah, Amnon, 5–6, 54, 156–57
Shiran, Haim, 47
Shire bekhi. See crying songs
Shohat, Ella, 46, 54, 55
Shoshan, Dani, 134, 139–40, 214
shuk. See market
Shukry, Samir, 69, 169, 187n. 23
Shuman, Amy, 78, 153, 181 64
Solnit, Rebecca, 30, 164
song texts, 5
sound track, 3, 14, 25, 28, 30–32, 96, 99, 132, 142, 154, 155, 172, 175. *See slso* canon
soundscape, 25, 28, 31, 66, 69, 72, 78, 98, 122, 132, 135, 140, 147–48, 150, 154, 156, 165, 172–73, 175; synthesized, 4, 140, 142, 161
stereotypes, 100, 126
straddling, 9, 59–60, 62–63, 66–67, 70, 72, 74, 81, 138. *See also* hybridity
style, musical. *See* musical style
subaltern voices. *See* voice
sūq. See market
Sukkot, 48, 205
synthesized sounds. *See* soundscape

Tavori, Shimi, 72–74, 207
te'amim, 98
technology, 23, 140, 214; recording, vii, 23, 25, 27–28, 130, 140
Temaniyut. See identity
territory, 34–35, 45–46, 68, 82, 132, 135, 147, 148, 181n. 68; disputed, 1–32, 135, 147, 155–75, 181n. 65, 192n. 7
texts. *See* song texts
"Ṭipat mazal," 212–14
Tobi, Merit, 111, 119, 122, 124–25
tradition, 13, 32, 153, 175, 186n. 10; cultural, vii, xi, 20, 36–37, 39, 42, 47, 48, 53, 56, 59, 70, 79, 103, 130, 161, 166, 173; religious, 63, 66, 67, 73, 87,

tradition: religious (*cont.*)
98–99, 144, 205; *masortiyut* (traditionality), 60, 61, 63, 98, 189n. 26; traditional clothing, 33, 126; traditional music (*see* music)
tragedy, 44, 79–80, 86, 105–6, 109–10, 114, 117, 119, 121–23, 125–26, 154, 210
tragic hero. *See* hero
transcultural. *See* global
transformation: aesthetic, 114, 115, 119, 121, 123, 124, 125; cultural, 37–38, 45, 47, 53–54, 56, 78, 108, 114, 127, 161, 191n. 38; musical, ix, 17, 30, 78, 86; personal, viii, 86, 105, 107–8; political, 30, 37–38, 156
transgression, 99, 129–54, 171–75
transmogrification, 106, 108
transit camps (*ma'abarah*), 2, 40–43, 71–75, 87, 100, 101, 126, 131
Tsan'ani, Margalit, 18, 68–73, 134, 159, 167
Tselile ha-Kerem, 50, 63–68, 72, 89, 132, 172, 202
Tselile ha-'ūd, 89, 172, 202
Tshaḥ tshaḥ im. See music
Tsror, Rino, 138–139
typology. *See* category

'ūd, x, 4, 89, 90, 131, 139, 157, 161, 172, 177n. 5, 217
univocality. *See* voice
unfamiliarity. *See* familiarity
unstable. *See* instability

variation, 28, 31, 82, 100, 217
Vazsonyi, Andrew, 106
Vernant, Jean-Pierre, 109
visibility: aesthetic; 54, 82, 96; commercial; 134; cultural; 39, 50, 54, 63, 195; ethnic; 44–45, 51, 56, 122, 156, 166; theoretical; 81
voice, vocal, vocalization, vii-ix, 1, 3–4, 14, 17, 20, 22, 25, 35, 42, 47, 50, 55, 56, 61, 63, 67, 69, 72–74, 76, 81, 85–87, 88, 90, 95–104, 106, 108–9, 111, 114, 118, 122, 124–26, 131–32, 134–35, 138, 141–44, 147, 157, 159, 162, 164, 172, 175, 179n. 21, 23, 199, 202, 205, 207, 210, 215–16; multivocality, multiple voices, vii-ix, 7, 22, 30, 103, 177n. 6; univocality, monovocal, single voice vii, 32, 144

Wadi Salib riots, 47
Walker, Alice, 172
war, 4, 8, 32, 36, 45–46, 48, 50, 79–81, 101, 103, 114, 129–30, 153, 156, 163, 175
weddings, 4, 6, 8, 17, 36, 47–50, 65, 71, 72, 90–91, 99, 122, 125, 130–32, 134, 172, 202
Wonder, Stevie, ix, 72

Yedi'ot Aḥaronot, 115, 121, 123, 135
Yemenite. *See* ethnicity
Yishuv, 104, 178n. 13
Young, Katharine, 105, 190n. 2

Zerubavel, Eviatar, 162–64
Zerubavel, Yael, x, 100, 103–4, 110, 173
Zion, Zionist, Zionism, 35, 37, 54–55, 87, 99–101, 199
Zunder, Michal, 110–11
zurna, 25, 180n. 49

CD Liner Notes

This volume includes a companion CD, illustrating the transformation of the soundscape in Israel from the mid-1970s to the mid-1990s, the period covered by the book. Of the CD's nineteen songs, thirteen are cited in the text (tracks 1, 2, 4, 6, 7, 8, 12, 13, 14, 15, 16, 17, 18), some of which are discussed at great length. In addition, eight of the songs are transliterated and translated in the song lyrics appendix (tracks 2, 4, 6, 12, 13, 15, 16, 18). In mastering the songs for reproduction on the CD, the mastering engineer has endeavored to retain the aesthetic texture of the cassettes on which they originally appeared in the marketplace.

Performances of many of the songs included on this CD, as well as hundreds of other songs from this period, can be found under title or performer searches on YouTube. Hebrew lyrics can be accessed at www.shiron.net and translations and transliterations at www.hebrewsongs.com.

Track 1 (Medley)

Passover Kiddush (Blessing: Fruit of the Vine)

Rabbi Shalom Tsadok, (Yemenite), Rabbi Shmuel Toledano, (Moroccan) and Cantor Ezra Barnea (Sephardi-Jerusalemite)

Music and lyrics: Traditional.

Source: The Yemenite, Moroccan, and Sephardi-Jerusalemite Passover Tradition CDs. The Institute for Jewish Music, *Renanot.*

"Inta 'umrī" (You Are My Life)

Umm Kulthum

Music: Muhammad Abdel-Wahab. Lyrics: Ahmad Shafiq Kamel.

Source: *The Diva of Arab Music Oum Kolthoum.* Sidi Records, Jeddah, Saudi Arabia

"My Yiddishe Mama"

Salim Halali

Music and lyrics: Jack Yellin and Lou Pollack.

Source: *Salim Halali Le plus grand chanteur oriental.* Ascot Music

Hours of listening to Afghani, Libyan, Turkish, Greek and many other liturgical recordings at *Renanot* (Jubilations) opened my ear to the dialogue I present on this CD between Middle Eastern and North African musics in Israel. The CD's opening *muwwal* is a medley of three sonic memories. The Yemenite and Moroccan Passover Kiddush excerpts make audible the nuances of pronunciation and melody that are coalescing into the Sephardi-Jerusalem style heard on the third example. A fleeting excerpt from Umm Kulthum's iconic fifty-nine minute performance of "Inta 'umrī" honors her status as a beloved singer for Jews, Muslims, and Christians throughout the region. The medley closes with an Arabic-Yiddish version of "My Yiddishe Mama," by Salim Halali, a prolific Algerian-Jewish singer to whose recordings and career his niece, Etty Lassman, introduced me in 2000.

Track 2

"Mal'u asamenu bar" (Our Silos are Filled with Grain)
Ḥavurat shiru shir (The sing-along group)
Music: Pinchas Lander. Lyrics: David Zehavi. Conductor/arranger: Meir Harnik.
Source: *Ḥavurat shiru shir.* NMC Records.

This is an example of *ha-Shir-ha-Erets Yisre'eli* (The Song of the Land of Israel), the Euro-Israeli genre that emerged in the 1880s and dominated the public soundscape through the 1970s and beyond. Many American Jews who came of age during this period considered songs like these, replete with grain-filled silos, as *the* Israeli music. This vast music genre contains Russian, French, Spanish, and Yemenite elements, whose complexities I began to hear under Natan Shahar's tutelage. Avihu Medina provided me this version, featuring Hadasah Sigalov's Yemenite vocal solo, which Medina noted influenced his composition of such songs as "Al Tira" (Do Not Fear) and "Na'aleh" (featured as track 3).

Track 3

"Na'aleh" (We Will Ascend to Israel)
Shimi Tavori
Music and lyrics: Avihu Medina.
Source: *Pirḥey gani,* 1971–1987. AM productions.

Shortly after the 1982 Lebanon War, Avihu Medina wrote "Na'aleh" in the spirit of his earlier composition, "Al Tira" (Do Not Fear) and the *ha-Shir-ha-Erets Yisre'eli* song "Mal'u asamenu bar" (track 2). The song retains the romantic nationalistic spirit of the *ha-Shir-ha-Erets Yisre'eli* repertoire. In contrast to the previous track in which Sigalov's vocal line occupies a brief portion of the composition, here Shimi Tavori's solo is the song's signature line. Tavori's Yemenite vocal centers the song's march-like quality. It was a rendition of this song by Zion Golan that made me realize that musicians are constantly confounding the categories and boundaries their work defines. Consultations with Medina helped me sort out these complexities to fashion the repertoire continuum discussed in chapter 3. To demonstrate the uncontainability and emergent quality of Mediterranean Israeli music, my compilation features Golan's traditional ("authentic" or *asli*) Yemenite performance of "Ya Mehija" as well as this Eastern European–inspired counterpoint.

Track 4

"Ḥanaleh hitbalbelah" (Little Hannah Got Confused)
Daḳlon
Music: Adaptation of traditional Klezmer music. Lyrics: Natan Alterman.
Source: *Tslile ha-kerem-Dakmosh #2.* Reuveni Brothers.

Natan Alterman composed an earlier version of "Ḥanaleh Hitbalbelah" for a Tel Aviv Purim party in the carnivalesque spirit of the holiday. The song describes the topsy-turvy marriage between an Ashkenazi woman and a Mizraḥi man, who celebrate their honeymoon before their marriage but cannot figure out how their son came into being. Here the original klezmer tune is adapted to a Mizraḥi style featuring Yemenite vocals, Greek guitar, and bass rhythms, and a live *darabukka* player accompanying the repetitive beats of a drum machine. The tune has become an anthem for the primarily Mizraḥi athletes and fans of the Jerusalem Beitar soccer team. Renditions of the song were issued on cassette in 1975 by Tselile ha-ʻūd (Tunes of the *ʻūd*) and Tselile ha-kerem (Tunes of the vineyard). According to Meir Reuveni, this song, recorded at his brother Asher's wedding in 1974, was the catalyst for the formation of the Mizraḥi music distribution network.

Track 5

"Ḥomot ḥemar" (Walls of Clay)

Margalit Tsanʻani

MUSIC: Margalit Tsanʻani. Lyrics: Rachel Shapira.

SOURCE: *Ḥomot ḥemar.* Reuveni Brothers.

One evening, as we drove between her three back-to-back singing engagements, Margalit Tsanʻani demonstrated her proficiency in multi-ethnic vocal styles by singing a five-minute medley that included Ḥasidic, *ha-Shir ha-Erets Yisreʾeli,* Yemenite, Kurdish, Moroccan, Sephardi, Greek, Turkish, and African American gospel styles. Her fluidity in moving among music genres, languages, and pronunciations served her well as she performed at hundreds of diverse Mizraḥi and Ashkenazi weddings. The lyricist, Rachel Shapira, defines *walls of clay* as a metaphor for the confines of tradition in some ethnic societies. The woman in the song tries to break free from those "walls," but as her actions undermine the stability of her traditional society, community members try to stop her.

Track 6

"Ezo medinah" (What a Country)

Eli Luzon

MUSIC AND LYRICS: Eli Luzon and Yoni Ro'eh.

SOURCE: *Ezo Medinah.* Ben-Mosh productions.

There is a gentle, almost humorous quality to the lyrics of this topical song that initially obscured the social critique at the heart of the composition. It took me a long time to realize that cultural humor is not immediately understandable to outsiders. Eventually, I came to see this as an exasperated kvetch song that pokes fun at governmental shortcomings rather than a call for social transformation. Teasing remarks like "Where's the equality?" "What vision do they see?" "What a shame—where's morality?" are juxtaposed with idealistic claims like "Despite the mess and the disadvantages / Our country, for generations lives." Musically the juxtapositions put a synthesized *santur* in conversation with live violins, and a live *darabukka* player with a drum machine. The Eastern quality is underscored by an opening *muwwal* and by unison until the E minor chord at the finale.

Track 7
"Elinor"
Zohar Argov
Music: Pythagoras Papastamatiou. Hebrew lyrics: Jackie Makaytan.
Source: *Elinor.* Reuveni Brothers.

"Elinor," which I originally heard blasting from a booth in Tel Aviv's central bus station in the mid-1980s, utilizes the tune from "Iparho" (I Exist), originally composed by Papastamatiou for the beloved Greek singer Stelios Kazantzidis. As a Communist, Kazantzidis experienced political censorship but nonetheless refused to adapt his songs to acceptable conventions. The "Iparho" recording was his last until 1987, coincidentally the year that Zohar Argov died. This quote by Kazantzidis is reminiscent of Argov's statements about his music: "I sing for the poor, the immigrants and the suffering people . . . generally for the lower social classes. They can't go to the expensive nightclubs. They buy my discs and they regard them as their Gospels." Jackie Makaytan's Hebrew lyrics transformed "Iparho" into an unrequited love song for Elinor.

Track 8
"Hekhan he-ḥayal" (Where is the Soldier)
Ahuva Ozeri
Music and lyrics: Ahuva Ozeri.
Source: *Hekhan he-ḥayal.* Reuveni Brothers.

Ahuva Ozeri's lament is structured in a call and response tradition in which she voices both the leader's and the congregations' parts. As a child she served as *meḳonenet*, a professional woman lamenter, at traditional Yemenite funerals and loved to listen to Ladino ballads. Here her voice is suspended over an instrumental bed that moves between guitar riffs, percussive beats, and her virtuosic performance on the Bulbul Tarang, an instrument whose sources include Japanese, Indian, and Pakistani instruments as well as possibly the European hurdy-gurdy. Though this 1975 composition was immensely popular throughout Israel, it was pulled off the radio, possibly due to the traumas following the 1973 war. Shortly after this, Ozeri disappeared from the music scene. After struggling with throat cancer, she has returned in recent years to find a new voice as a performer, composer, and public advocate for those suffering with this disease.

Track 9
"Gevarim bokhim ba-lailah" (Men Cry at Night)
Avner Gedassi
Music: Meli Komemi and Meni Komemi. Lyrics: Alon Avidar.
Source: *Gevarim bokhim ba-lailah.* Reuveni Brothers.

The cover image for Avner Gedassi's 1978 cassette *Play and Sing* shows Gedassi sitting cross-legged beating on a *darabukka* amid layers of visual hybridities: guitar, *Ḥamsa,* and hookah juxtaposed with Indian tapestries, a harbinger of world music complexities of the future. The graphic subversions cued me to the sonic transgressions of Gedassi's music. I encountered the visual image before I heard this song, "Gevarim bokhim ba-lailah"

(Men Cry At Night), in which blues, Mediterranean, and rock elements frame Gedassi's Yemenite vocal center in his take on the taboo subject of male vulnerability.

Track 10
"Ya mehija" (The Way)
Zion Golan
MUSIC AND LYRICS: Traditional.
SOURCE: *La-hite Teman* (Hits of Yemen). Reuveni Brothers.

Zion Golan's contemporary rendition of this traditional song from the Yemenite *diwan* (a collection of seventeenth-century liturgical poetry attributed to the renowned Yemenite Rabbi and Talmudist, Shalom Shabazi) is accented by a solitary percussive beat reminiscent of the petrol cans and tin trays that served as the main instruments for Jews in Yemen and continue as part of the Yemenite Israeli soundscape. A synthesizer simulates sounds of the *qanun,* flute, and keyboard, and a drum machine fills out the percussion section. Songs such as this from the Yemenite *diwan* that begin with "Ya mehija" often describe the wedding engagement of the biblical figures Rebecca and Isaac. These songs belong to the *Zafa* genre, sung as the bride is brought to the groom, or as the groom is brought to the *Ḥupah* (Jewish marriage canopy). In this version, Abraham's servant Eliezer has returned with a bride for Isaac.

Track 11
"Barkhenu" (Bless Us)
Shimi Tavori
MUSIC: Avihu Medina. Lyrics: Adapted from the liturgy.
SOURCE: *Shevu'at olam* (Eternal Oath). Reuveni Brothers.

Medina drew his inspiration and text for *Barkhenu* from the prayer for a year of peace and prosperity, found in the *Shemonah 'Esreh* and recited daily. In the song, he combined Ashkenazi, Yemenite, and Sephardi elements and he considers it to be a musical mixture of all the motifs in Israel. Medina gave Shimi Tavori the song to perform at Israel's Ḥasidic Festival in 1980, at which Tavori won second place.. Medina points to this as a landmark event, because up to then Mizraḥi singers had been relegated to the "Oriental" Festival during this period. Although Tavori's victory did not result in a recording contract until three years later, the song spread by word of mouth throughout the country.

Track 12
"Ha-Peraḥ be-gani" (The Flower in My Garden)
Zohar Argov
MUSIC AND LYRICS: Avihu Medina. Arrangers: Medina and Nancy Brandes.
SOURCE: *Nakhon le-hayom* (To Date). Reuveni Brothers.

Songs take on lives and afterlives. Avihu Medina was inspired to compose this song by his first love affair at sixteen. Zohar Argov won first place with it at the Festival of Mizraḥi Song in 1982. The Reuveni Brothers cassette on which it originally appeared the same year is estimated to have sold 250,000 copies, an impressive figure for a small country.

In the composition, Medina, working with arranger Nancy Brandes, combines an Arabic string section, a brass band, and rock elements with Argov's melismatic vocals and abbreviated opening *muwwal.* The composition underscores Medina's claim that there is no such thing as *musiḳah mizraḥit,* and that his music has always combined Eastern and Western elements.

Track 13
"Baladah le-ḥaver" (Song to a Friend)
Avihu Medina
MUSIC AND LYRICS: Avihu Medina.
SOURCE: *Asher ahavti* (That I Loved). AM Productions.

Avihu Medina wrote "Baladah le-ḥaver" in memory of Zohar Argov. The mood evokes the traditional prayer for the ascension of souls, *El male raḥamim,* and may also draw upon memories of his aunt's voice as she performed lamentations at Yemenite funerals. Medina's quiet and intimate vocals dominate the composition whose liturgical feeling is accented by the bass chords on the keyboard and sparse guitar riffs that echo the melody line. Medina ends the first verse with the phrases "Until when, my God?" (*'Ad matai Elohai?*), and "he had enough," a reference to Argov's drug addiction and suicide in prison.

Track 14
"Linda, Linda"
Haim Moshe
MUSIC AND LYRICS: Traditional.
SOURCE: *Ahavat ḥayai* (Love of my Life). Reuveni Brothers.

Haim Moshe's version of "Linda, Linda" was the first song to cross over into Ashkenazi communities from the Arab repertoire performed by Mizraḥi singers in the 1980s. This may be due to the performance at the Karmiel Festival in 1984 of an Israeli folkdance that had been choreographed to the song. Earlier versions of "Linda, Linda" had been sung at weddings, clubs, and summer camps in Syria, Lebanon, and Egypt in the 1970s. It may originally have been composed by Samir el-Tawil. Moshe's repertoire includes Arab songs like "Linda, Linda," Greek melodies like "Todah" (Thank You), and Western tunes like "Nishbah" (I Swear). He thinks of his music as akin to country music in the United States—the music that most of the population loves—but also compares his vocal melisma to that of Stevie Wonder, whom he affectionately describes as Yemenite.

Track 15
"Keturna masala" (When Luck Returns)
Ethnix (Ethnics)
MUSIC AND LYRICS: Ze'ev Neḥama and Tamir Ḳalisḳi.
SOURCE: *Masala.* Helicon Records.

This groundbreaking collaboration between Ethnix and Zehava Ben in 1992–93 can be seen as a catalyst for the duets between mainstream Western and Mizraḥi singers that began to appear in the 1990s. In the 1980s, when Mizraḥi singer Jackie Makayton invited Ashkenazi singer Naomi Shemer to sing a duet with him, she responded that she felt this would be a bit contrived because they had nothing in common. Later Mizraḥi–Ashkenazi collaborations, such as the duet between Ofer Levy and Lea Lupatin on Shemer's song "Ha-Kol patuaḥ" (Everything is Possible), and more recently Ahuva Ozeri's joint creation with the band ha-Dag ha-Naḥash's (The Snake Fish), "Shirat ha-stickerim" (The Bumper Sticker Song), became common.

Track 16
"Ṭipat mazal" (A Drop of Luck)
Zehava Ben
MUSIC: Orhan Gencebey. Hebrew lyrics: Dani Shoshan.
SOURCE: Play Records.

"Ṭipat mazal" (A Drop of luck) was one of the Turkified songs that inspired Yonatan Gefen's statement that the Ottomans had conquered Tel Aviv in the early 1990s. Zehava Ben's rendition was pejoratively labeled a "crying song," about which one of Israel's most famous comedy troupes, *ha-Gashash ha-ḥiver,* made a skit entitled "Festival of Depressing Songs" on their 1992 CD. The song's tune was taken from *Dil Yarasi,* a composition by the prolific Turkish musician, composer, and film star Orhan Gencebay and set to Hebrew lyrics by Dani Shoshan. Because there were no formal intellectual property agreements between Turkey and Israel at that time, such tunes tended to be regarded in Israel as public domain. Gencebay's style fuses Turkish with Western classical, jazz, rock, country, and progressive music, as well as Indian, Arabic, Spanish, and Greek style. Like his Mediterranean Israeli musician counterparts, who took issue with limiting designations for their musical style, Gencebay resisted subsuming the new music genre he helped create under such generic labels as Arabesque.

Track 17
"Mi-Mosheh ve-'ad Muḥamad" (From Moses to Muhammed)
Samir Shukry
MUSIC: Nurit Hirsch. Lyrics: Yoram Teharlev.
SOURCE: Samir Shukry Productions.

The voice of Samir Shukry's signature electric violin provides the opening for "Mi-Mosheh ve-'ad Muḥamad" in which he invokes Moses and Muhammed to help their children in an elusive yet essential search for peace. Shukry's rendering of the Hebrew lyrics, punctuated by occasional Arabic vocal trills, vocalizes his complex identity as an Israeli Arab. The introspective opening gives way to a percussive beat invoking Moses's and Mohammad's ascent to the holy land. Speaking about the song, Shukry commented, "When I participated in the Children's FestiGal in 1989, I was the first Arab-Israeli singer to perform at such an event. A song like this, so full of emotion and that creates a bridge between the two peoples, was very appropriate for me to sing. And the song was nominated for first place at the FestiGal. Through my music and songs, wherever I am in the world, I will always be an ambassador and bridge for peace between the two nations."

Track 18

"Inta 'umrī" (You Are My Life)

Zehava Ben

Music, Moḥammed 'Abd al-Wahāb. Lyrics: Aḥmad Shafiq Kāmil.

Source: *Zehava Ben Inta 'umrī.* Helicon Records.

Zehava Ben's rendition of iconic Egyptian singer Umm Kulthum's anthem "Inta 'umrī" (You Are My Life) epitomizes the crossbreeding of music in Israel. Ben is herself a transcultural personality who oscillates between formal performances of Umm Kulthum's repertoire with Haifa's Arabic orchestra in Nablus, Jericho, southern France, and Italy, and renditions of Naomi Shemer and Aviv Gefen songs at such mainstream events as the official memorial ceremonies for Prime Minister Yitzhak Rabin. She spontaneously offers her renditions of Umm Kulthum on the streets of Cairo and Alexandria to the receptive Egyptian listeners who applaud her. She saw no contradiction in performing for a left-wing *Meretz* campaign advertisement and a rival Likud campaign barbecue in *Ḳiryat Shemonah* after a bomb explosion shook the community. Ben regards her performances of Umm Kulthum and other Arabic music as her inheritance and as contributions to peace in the region.

Track 19

"Tefila shel aba" (Father's Prayer)

Avihu Medina

Music and lyrics: Avihu Medina.

Source: Avihu Medina *Mi-meṭav ha-shirim ha-sheḳeṭim* (The Mellow Song Collection). AM Productions.

This CD begins with the prayer of a Yemenite cantor, part of the inheritance that Middle Eastern and North African Jews carried with them to Israel, and closes with the prayer of another Yemenite cantor, Avihu Medina's father. Medina's sonic memory of his father leading *Seliḥot* prayers at his synagogue is audible toward the end of the song, in which Medina embeds an archival recording of his father's call and the worshippers' response. Between these counterpoints, Medina weaves his own contemporary vocal line into his father's prayer.

Credits:

Audio CD produced by Amy Horowitz. Mastered by Mike Monseur, Airshow Mastering. Production assistance by Avihu Medina, AM Productions, Steve Rathe, Murray Street Productions, and Jessica Bonn

Special thanks:

Alison de Grassi

Meir Reuveni (Reuveni Brothers, www.ahim-reuveni.co.il)

Samir Shukry (sshukry@optonline.net)

Eli Azarzar

Moshe Ben-Mosh

Ron Cole (Helicon Records, www.helicon.co.il)

Dror Kalisky and Ethnix (www.ethnix.co.il)

Cantor Ezra Barnea and Renanot (www.renanot.co.il)
Avihu Medina (www.avihu-medina.co.il)
Etty Lassman
P.I.L. The Israeli Federation of Independent Record Producers (www.pil.org.il)
Paul Kotheimer (OSU-HIS)
Yossi Ohana *Kehilot Sharot* (www.piyut.org)
Yaron Elhanani
Alex Ben-Arieh (www.Historama.com)
Charles Ibgui, Ascot Music (www.ascotmusic.fr)
Sylvia Onder
Henri Barkey
Katharine Young
Amy Shuman
Reuven (Ruby) Namdar
Yossi Galron-Goldschlaeger
Ann Blonston and Charlie Pilzer (www.airshowmastering.com)
Patrick E. Visel